Personalized Learning in Vocational and Continuing Education

Efthymia Petridou

Personalized Learning in Vocational and Continuing Education

Investigating Key Factors Influencing Learning Outcomes in Artificial Intelligence Within Adaptive Learning Environments

Springer VS

Efthymia Petridou
Psychologie und Pädagogik
Ludwig-Maximilians-Universität
München
München, Germany

This work was submitted as a doctoral dissertation to the Faculty of Psychology and Education at the Ludwig Maximilian University of Munich in 2025.

ISBN 978-3-658-51516-4 ISBN 978-3-658-51517-1 (eBook)
https://doi.org/10.1007/978-3-658-51517-1

This Springer VS imprint is published by the registered company Springer Fachmedien Wiesbaden GmbH, part of Springer Nature.
The registered company address is: Abraham-Lincoln-Str. 46, 65189 Wiesbaden, Germany

Foreword

The use of digital technologies in teaching and learning contexts has been studied and researched for over half a century. Initially, this was mainly in higher education contexts, then in companies, and finally in the context of teaching at general education schools. Vocational schools and continuing education institutions have tended to receive less attention in this regard—perhaps due to the diversity of vocational and continuing training courses and the heterogeneous backgrounds of learners in this educational sector. Adaptive learning environments—i.e., learning environments that adapt to the individual learning levels and different progress of learners—offer new opportunities, especially for such a pluralistic learning environment as vocational and continuing education institutions are. However, for a long time, the development of adaptive learning environments was extremely time-consuming and costly, and therefore only an option in a few fields of application. This has changed with the availability of a wide range of AI applications. In her study, Efthymia Petridou shows the possibilities that adaptive learning environments offer in vocational and continuing education and training and how they are experienced by the learners themselves. In doing so, she makes an important and significant contribution at the interface of empirical educational research, media education research, and research on vocational and continuing education and training.

Efthymia Petridou uses a quantitative cross-sectional and time-sequenced data collection design to examine the significance of the adaptability of the learning environment and the learning styles of participants on learning success in an extracurricular qualification program for trainees in technical and commercial professions. The learning theory-based and technologically well-informed work focuses, among other things, on the possibilities of AI for designing personalized learning environments and, against this background, asks which learners benefit from this adaptivity in a specific context. This context is a semi-virtual additional qualification within dual training programs, in which trainees from technical and commercial professions participate. This brings the field of vocational and continuing training, which is often neglected by empirical educational research but is particularly important in Germany, into focus and raises the question of what technology-supported adaptivity means in this environment and what it can achieve. In a rigorous and consistent research process, Efthymia Petridou tests theoretically grounded hypotheses in a quasi-experimental study using a sample that is considerable for this context. The findings confirm some of the assumptions, and recommendations for the design of appropriate learning environments are formulated on this basis. Finally, a detailed analysis of methodological limitations in the study serves as the basis for the formulation of research desiderata and a description of alternative research designs.

This study is rigorous and has been conducted with great methodological care. The scope of the review of learning theory approaches and, above all, learning style research is particularly noteworthy, as is the precise examination of the state of research, which is also reflected in the large number of sources consulted. The questions examined are highly relevant and at the same time specific, enabling a differentiated investigation. Above all, the evaluation of the data meets all the standards of sound empirical social research in an exemplary manner and demonstrates the author's very strong research methodology skills.

This study, which is well worth reading and equally relevant for educational research and educational practice, makes a significant contribution to the understanding of the perception and acceptance of personalized learning environments. It can be highly recommended to all researchers and practitioners in this field.

Munich
February 24th 2026

Bernhard Schmidt-Hertha

Acknowledgements

While completing a dissertation necessitates resilience and a high degree of self-regulation, its accomplishment would not be feasible without the contribution of several individuals, to whom I owe my sincere acknowledgements.

First and foremost, I wish to express my warmest thanks to my dearest parents and brother for their loving care and wholehearted support throughout this journey. I am deeply grateful for the values and strength they instilled in me and their role in shaping who I am today. Without them, I would not have taken the lead to engage in this effort. I am equally thankful to my beloved partner, not only for his invaluable support during decisive phases but also for sharing much-needed moments of rejuvenation and reflection. His work ethic has been an inspiration, and his enduring encouragement made this journey achievable and meaningful.

My profound gratitude is hereby conveyed to the supervisors of this dissertation, whose guidance made this challenging path more manageable. The unwavering commitment of my primary supervisor, Prof. Dr. Bernhard Schmidt-Hertha, throughout every phase of this dissertation significantly shaped my academic and personal growth. His attentive approach, enriching feedback, and pragmatic, solution-oriented stance inspired an ethos of critical inquiry and scientific rigor in my research. At the same time, the guidance from my second supervisor, Prof. Dr. Moritz Heene, was instrumental in improving the quality and soundness of this work with his enlightening and robust methodological advice. His readily available contribution was vital in navigating complex statistical issues and pivotal for advancing my research.

I would further like to express my gratitude to my colleagues and fellow doctoral researchers at the chair of General Pedagogy and Educational

Research, as well as at the Doctoral Training Program in the Learning Sciences at Ludwig Maximilian University of Munich. I am especially grateful for the fruitful research environment in the doctoral colloquia and research retreats, which resulted in productive discussions and moments of mutual encouragement. Acknowledgement is further due to the staff of the Statistical Consulting Laboratory in the Institute of Statistics, Faculty of Mathematics, Informatics, and Statistics at the Ludwig-Maximilian University of Munich for their insightful methodological assistance.

My warm appreciation also extends to my international friends and valued individuals in Munich and abroad for their understanding and for sustaining my motivation throughout this ever-challenging and rewarding marathon. Their presence during difficult times and shared moments of joy assumed a crucial role in helping me maintain perspective and perseverance along the way.

To everyone who accompanied me on this path, whether academically or personally, I extend my sincere thanks.

Abstract

In light of the growing significance of artificial intelligence (AI) for the educational sector and its societal and economic impact on the contemporary workforce, investigating how AI applications can be leveraged to enhance learning outcomes in the framework of vocational education and training (VET) as well as continuing vocational education and training (CVET) constitutes a promising but underexplored field of research. While obtaining knowledge and competences in AI has become essential to navigate an ever-increasing AI-based workplace, AI literacy among learners remains low. This thesis serves to close this research gap by evaluating the delivery of an AI additional qualification offered through an adaptive learning software supported by AI technologies designed to facilitate the acquisition of AI knowledge and skills among individuals with different characteristics in an authentic blended learning setting. At the core of the thesis is the investigation of key learner characteristics and learning system features capable of enhancing AI learning outcomes. A quasi-experimental research design incorporating elements of both cross-sectional and time-sequenced data collection was employed. Two data collection rounds were conducted over two consecutive school years from 2022 to 2024. Self-reported questionnaires were utilized in standardized online surveys to capture learners' perceptions at the beginning, midpoint, and end of the AI course. In total, 222 learners participated in the surveys. The statistical analysis was performed with the statistical computing and programming language R.

The study provides empirical support for the effectiveness of AI prior knowledge and the system's individualized and adaptive features in improving AI learning outcomes, while it reveals that experience with digital learning applications does not exert any influence. Accommodating learners' prior knowledge and leveraging system features of individualization and adaptivity that enable one-to-one personalized instruction at scale significantly contribute to shaping AI learning outcomes. Nevertheless, merely being familiar with digital learning tools does not necessarily translate into more effective learning. This might be attributed to other factors influencing this relationship or to the limitations of the applied measurement approach. Furthermore, while accommodating learning styles has been considered instrumental to improve learning outcomes within adaptive learning systems, the analysis of AI learning outcomes across learning style groups could not yield any conclusive insights regarding the influence of learning preferences on cognitive achievements. Whether learners with certain learning styles can attain significantly better learning outcomes within adaptive learning environments remains an open question for future research.

Critical insights for educators and stakeholders in VET and CVET settings are drawn from the study findings, underscoring the importance of employing highly adaptive learning systems, providing comprehensive AI training, and utilizing blended learning approaches. The results further yield valuable implications for the instructional design of adaptive learning environments. Beyond incorporating adaptivity and individualization features that tailor the learning experience to individual needs, adaptive learning systems must also assess and adapt to learners' prior knowledge to enhance learning outcomes. Furthermore, the findings shed light on the necessity of ensuring seamless navigation, accommodating diverse learning preferences, and adhering to established pedagogical principles when designing adaptive learning environments. A pedagogical framework rooted primarily in fundamental principles of cognitivism and constructivism, further integrating core behavioral principles, is considered well-suited for effectively conveying AI-related content. By embedding foundational pedagogical principles into adaptive learning systems, it becomes feasible to bridge the gap between the technological affordances of AI-based learning tools and sound educational theory. This alignment ensures that adaptive learning systems do not solely deliver tailored content but actively support learners in building lasting knowledge and transferring acquired skills into real-world contexts. Further study limitations are underlined, and directions for future educational research and practice are highlighted, predominantly emphasizing the need for sophisticated and theory-grounded AI-based educational technologies to foster AI literacy and minimize the growing skills gap among learners with diverse backgrounds, needs, and competences, thereby laying the foundation for inclusive and sustainable educational opportunities.

Zusammenfassung

Seit der Etablierung der Künstlichen Intelligenz (KI) als eigenständiges Forschungsfeld im Jahr 1955 (McCarthy et al., 2006) hat die KI-Forschung ein erhebliches Wachstum erfahren, und eine Vielzahl von KI-Anwendungen wurde in unterschiedliche Bereiche integriert. Fortschritte in KI-Technologien, insbesondere in wissensbasierten Systemen und Expertensystemen, haben zu einer zunehmenden Zahl von KI-Anwendungen im Bildungsbereich geführt (Zhang & Aslan, 2021). Infolgedessen wurde im Jahr 1970 das Forschungsfeld ‚KI in der Bildung' offiziell gegründet (Brusilovsky & Peylo, 2003), wobei der Fokus darauf liegt, wie KI-Anwendungen genutzt werden können, um menschliches Lehren zu erforschen und menschliches Lernen zu unterstützen (Woolf, 1991). Insbesondere im Kontext der Berufsbildung (VET) sowie der beruflichen Weiterbildung (CVET) hat die zunehmende Umsetzung von KI-Lerntechnologien in verschiedenen Berufsfeldern den Erwerb von KI-bezogenen Kompetenzen zu einer Notwendigkeit gemacht (Pelletier et al., 2024; Le Borgne et al., 2023). Die gesellschaftlichen und wirtschaftlichen Auswirkungen von KI, insbesondere die damit einhergehenden Veränderungen von Arbeitsplätzen, verdeutlichen den dringenden Bedarf an Up- und Reskilling von erwachsenen Erwerbstätigen in europäischen Arbeitsmärkten (Cedefop, 2024). Um den sich wandelnden Anforderungen gerecht zu werden, sollte kontinuierliche Weiterbildung gefördert werden, damit sich Beschäftigte ständig an neue Herausforderungen und Veränderungen in ihrem Berufsalltag anpassen können (Twomey, 2018).

Nichtsdestotrotz erfolgt die Vermittlung von KI-Themen in Deutschland überwiegend an Hochschulen, während die Integration von KI-Inhalten in die Berufsbildung sowie die berufliche Weiterbildung erst in jüngerer Zeit begonnen hat (Rott et al., 2022). Weder Lernende noch Lehrende haben bislang umfassende KI-Kompetenzen erworben und verfügen derzeit meist nur über grundlegendes KI-Wissen (Lindner et al., 2019; Petridou & Lao, 2024; Stamenković et al., 2023). Infolgedessen bleiben KI-bezogene Themen und Anwendungen für Lernende und Lehrende bislang ein weitgehend unbekanntes Gebiet (Petridou & Lao, 2024). Die Herausforderung für die Berufsbildung und berufliche Weiterbildung besteht darin, KI-bezogenes Wissen und Kompetenzen effektiv in bestehende Curricula zu integrieren, geeignete Qualifizierungsangebote für Beschäftigte zu schaffen sowie zur Entwicklung neuer Berufsbilder im KI-Bereich beizutragen (Rott et al., 2022).

Diese Dissertation leistet einen Beitrag zur bestehenden Forschung, indem sie die Umsetzung einer KI-Zusatzqualifikation evaluiert, der mit Unterstützung einer KI-basierten adaptiven Lernsoftware durchgeführt wurde, die darauf ausgelegt war, den Erwerb von KI-Wissen und -Kompetenzen bei Personen mit unterschiedlichen Merkmalen in einem realen Bildungskontext zu fördern. Im Rahmen des Projekts ‚KI B^3 – Künstliche Intelligenz in die berufliche Bildung bringen', das ein vergleichsweise neues Bildungsangebot in Deutschland darstellt, wurde eine Zusatzqualifikation zu KI und Maschinellem Lernen für Lernende aus verschiedenen Berufsfeldern von Institutionen der Berufsbildung und der beruflichen Weiterbildung entwickelt. Das Projekt wurde von der Ludwig-Maximilians-Universität München (LMU) und fünf weiteren Partnern gemeinsam durchgeführt, wobei die LMU am Lehrstuhl für Allgemeine Pädagogik und Bildungsforschung für die wissenschaftliche Begleitung und Evaluation zuständig war. Der Kurs wurde für zwei aufeinanderfolgende Schuljahre im Blended-Learning-Format angeboten. Ein KI-gestütztes adaptives Lernsystem wurde in Moodle integriert, das interaktive, adaptive und Gamification-Elemente beinhaltet hat, um die heterogene Gruppe der teilnehmenden Lernenden zu unterstützen und ihnen damit eine personalisierte Lernerfahrung zu ermöglichen sowie ihren Lernerfolg zu verbessern.

Adaptive Lernsysteme zählen zu den bedeutendsten KI-Anwendungen im Bildungsbereich. Solche Systeme haben aufgrund ihrer Fähigkeit, individuell zugeschnittene Lernmaterialien bereitzustellen und sich an die Bedürfnisse der Lernenden anzupassen, zunehmend an Bedeutung gewonnen (Kabudi et al., 2021). Da individuelle Lernunterschiede eine entscheidende Rolle dafür spielen, wie Lernende sich in den Lernprozess einbringen und wie effektiv dieser verläuft, ist die Nutzung adaptiver Technologien, welche auf individuelle Unterschiede eingehen, von zentraler Bedeutung für den Lernerfolg. Traditionelle Präsenzlernformate, die auf einem One-to-Many-Lernansatz basieren, sind jedoch nicht in der Lage, diese individuellen Aspekte der Lernenden zu berücksichtigen (Popescu, 2010). In solchen Lernumgebungen erfolgt die Lernvermittlung typischerweise im gleichen Tempo, mit derselben Methode, auf demselben Lernpfad und in gleicher Weise für alle Lernenden, ohne die Heterogenität der Lernenden und ihre individuellen Bedürfnisse einzubeziehen. Im Vergleich zu traditionellen One-to-Many-Lernumgebungen hat sich gezeigt, dass One-to-One-Lernformen zu höherem Lernerfolg führen (Bloom, 1984). Daher bietet der Einsatz von KI-gestützten adaptiven Lerntechnologien, die personalisierte One-to-One-Lernlösungen in großem Umfang ermöglichen (Taylor et al., 2021), die Möglichkeit, die KI-Kompetenz angehender Fachkräften zu verbessern und ihre Lernergebnisse zu steigern, indem Lerninhalte an ihre persönlichen und beruflichen Interessen angepasst werden.

Um die Wirksamkeit adaptiver Lernsysteme zu optimieren, ist es von zentraler Bedeutung, deren Implementierung auf etablierten lerntheoretischen Konzepten zu fundieren. Trotz der zunehmenden Integration von KI-Anwendungen in Bildungskontexte lassen sich bislang keine präzisen didaktischen Leitlinien für die Entwicklung KI-basierter Lernumgebungen feststellen, die sich an bewährten theoretischen Rahmenwerken orientieren (Chen et al., 2020; Zawacki-Richter et al., 2019). Da KI-Unterstützung auf die individuellen Merkmale jedes Lernenden abgestimmt werden kann, können adaptive und individualisierte Funktionen dazu beitragen, bedeutungsvolle Interaktionen zwischen den Lernenden und dem adaptiven Lernsystem zu ermöglichen. Solche Interaktionen haben das Potenzial nach konstruktivistischen Ansätzen, individuelle Wissenskonstruktion zu fördern und dadurch personalisierte sowie kontextuell relevante Lernerfahrungen zu schaffen. Angesichts der hohen Heterogenität der Lernenden in der Berufsbildung sowie der beruflichen Weiterbildung, die sich hinsichtlich Alter, Bildungsbiografie und Berufserfahrung unterscheiden, kann die Einbettung adaptiver und individualisierter Funktionen in das adaptive Lernsystem dazu beitragen, individuelle Wissensaneignung zu fördern und sich gleichzeitig an diese unterschiedlichen Lernprofile anzupassen.

Eine grundlegende Rolle in adaptiven Lernumgebungen nimmt dabei die Anpassung an das Vorwissen der Lernenden ein. Vorwissen bezeichnet das vorhandene Wissen, die Fähigkeiten oder Kompetenzen, die Lernende in den Lernprozess einbringen (Jonassen & Grabowski, 1993). Nach kognitivistischen Prinzipien unterstützt Vorwissen den Aufbau und Erwerb neuen Wissens (Schunk, 2012). Somit bietet ein adaptives Lernsystem die Möglichkeit, den Lernerfolg zu fördern, indem sie die Lernerfahrungen an das Vorwissen der Lernenden anpasst. Dies ist besonders relevant im Kontext einer KI-Zusatzqualifikation, die in Einrichtungen der Berufsbildung sowie der beruflichen Weiterbildung umgesetzt wird. In diesem Lernkontext verfügen die Lernenden je nach Bildungshintergrund und den spezifischen Anforderungen ihrer Berufe über unterschiedliche Niveaus an KI-bezogenem Vorwissen. Durch die Berücksichtigung individueller Unterschiede im KI-Wissensstand sowie die Bereitstellung gezielter Unterstützungsangebote können adaptive Lernumgebungen Lernende dabei unterstützen, das noch relativ neue Thema KI effektiver in ihr bestehendes Wissen zu integrieren.

In diesem Zusammenhang wird die Durchführung eines KI-Trainingskurses in einem Blended-Learning-Format als vorteilhaft angesehen (Petridou & Lao, 2024; Rott et al., 2022). Dieses Lernformat ermöglicht es den Lernenden, Verantwortung für ihren eigenen Lernprozess zu übernehmen und bei Schwierigkeiten Unterstützung durch Lehrkräfte in Anspruch zu nehmen, indem selbstgesteuertes Online-Lernen mit regelmäßigen Präsenz- oder Online-Unterstützungs- und Beratungsangeboten kombiniert wird. Dadurch wird personalisiertes Lernen gefördert und die Motivation langfristig gestärkt. Da Blended-Learning jedoch auf technologiegestützter Vermittlung von Lerninhalten basiert, insbesondere wenn ein adaptives Lernsystem implementiert wird, stellt die digitale Kompetenz der Lernenden eine grundlegende Voraussetzung dar. Die Lernenden sollen in der Lage sein, die im Kurs integrierten digitalen Lernanwendungen effizient zu nutzen. Die Vertrautheit mit diesen Tools ermöglicht es den Lernenden, mit dem Lernsystem zu interagieren und hierdurch Wissen und Kompetenzen aufzubauen. Die bisherige Forschung hat gezeigt, dass Lernende mit umfangreicher Erfahrung im Umgang mit digitalen Lernanwendungen bessere Lernergebnisse erzielen (Brinkerhoff et al., 2001). Dies lässt sich ebenso in der Berufsbildung sowie der beruflichen Weiterbildung beobachten, wobei digitale Kompetenzen der Lernenden sich positiv auf ihren Lernerfolg auswirken (Pagani et al., 2016) und somit auch ihre beruflichen Perspektiven verbessern. Daher reicht es nicht aus, ausschließlich das Vorwissen der Lernenden zu berücksichtigen. Darüber hinaus stellt die bestehende Erfahrung der Lernenden mit digitalen Lernanwendungen einen entscheidenden Faktor für erfolgreiche Lernergebnisse in einem KI-Kurs dar, der im Rahmen einer adaptiven Lernumgebung der Berufsbildung und der beruflichen Weiterbildung umgesetzt wird.

Es lässt sich dennoch festhalten, dass trotz der vielversprechenden Befunde der aktuellen Forschung zum Potenzial adaptiver Lernsysteme zur Förderung von Wissens- und Kompetenzerwerb (Chrysafiadi et al., 2023; Gomede et al., 2021; Hwang, Sung, et al., 2020), bislang nur begrenzte empirische Unterstützung hinsichtlich ihrer Wirksamkeit zur Verbesserung von Lernergebnissen im Kontext der Berufsbildung und der beruflichen Weiterbildung vorliegt (Petridou & Lao, 2024; Rott et al., 2022). Vor diesem Hintergrund untersucht diese Arbeit, ob die in adaptiven Lernsystemen integrierten Merkmale der Adaptivität und Individualisierung sowie das Vorwissen und die Erfahrung mit digitalen Lernanwendungen einen Einfluss auf den Lernerfolg haben. Diese Faktoren werden als zentrale Einflussgrößen des Lernerfolgs im Kontext KI-basierten Lernens betrachtet und tragen dazu bei, bestehende Forschungslücken hinsichtlich der Wirkung personalisierter adaptiver Lernumgebungen auf Lernergebnisse zu schließen.

Ein weiterer wichtiger Fortschritt bei der Untersuchung der Verbesserung von Lernergebnissen liegt darin, dass Lernstile im Rahmen adaptiver Lernumgebungen berücksichtigt werden können. Lernstile umfassen individuelle Präferenzen hinsichtlich der Art und Weise, wie Lernende Informationen wahrnehmen und verarbeiten. Diese beeinflussen ihre Herangehensweise an Lernaufgaben und -inhalte. In der aktuellen Forschung wurde der Einbezug von Lernstilen in adaptive Lernumgebungen intensiv erforscht, wobei insbesondere ihr Zusammenhang mit dem Lernerfolg untersucht wurde. Dadurch konnte ihr Beitrag zur Optimierung von Lernergebnissen verdeutlicht werden (Alshammari & Qtaish, 2019; Bajraktarevic et al., 2003; Chang et al., 2016; El-Bishouty et al., 2019; Karagiannis & Satratzemi, 2018; Tseng et al., 2008). Vor diesem Hintergrund richtet diese Arbeit ein besonderes Augenmerk auf die Untersuchung des Einflusses unterschiedlicher Lernpräferenzen auf den Lernerfolg in adaptiven Lernumgebungen.

Um individuelle Lernstile zu berücksichtigen, wurden Lernpräferenzen in Lernstilmodellen abgebildet, die didaktische Ansätze mit den jeweiligen Lernstilen in Einklang bringen. Frühere Literatur Reviews sowie empirische Studien haben gezeigt, dass das Felder-Silverman Lernstilmodell (Felder & Silverman, 1988) das am häufigsten eingesetzte und bevorzugte Modell in adaptiven Lernumgebungen darstellt (Filippidis & Tsoukalas, 2009; Karagiannis & Satratzemi, 2018; Özyurt & Özyurt, 2015). Dieses Modell, das darauf basiert, wie Lernende Informationen bevorzugt aufnehmen und verarbeiten, unterscheidet zwischen aktiven und reflektiven, sensorischen und intuitiven, visuellen und verbalen sowie sequenziellen und globalen Lernenden. Die unterschiedlichen Lerntypen spiegeln differenzierte Lernansätze wider, die beeinflussen, wie Lernende mit Bildungsinhalten interagieren und diese verstehen. Obwohl weiterhin Forschungsbedarf besteht, um jene Lernstile zu bestimmen, die einen stärkeren Einfluss auf die akademische Leistung haben (Kinshuk, 2016), bleiben die Forschungsergebnisse hinsichtlich des Zusammenhangs zwischen bestimmten Lernstilen und Lernergebnissen uneindeutig. Insbesondere im Kontext der Berufsbildung und der beruflichen Weiterbildung ist bislang weitgehend unerforscht, inwieweit Lernende mit spezifischen Lernstilen bessere Lernergebnisse in adaptiven Lernumgebungen erzielen. Diese Arbeit adressiert diese Forschungslücke, indem sie untersucht, welche Lernstile mit verbesserten Lernergebnissen in einem KI-Qualifizierungskurs in Zusammenhang stehen.

Ein quasi-experimentelles Forschungsdesign, das Elemente sowohl der querschnittlichen als auch der zeitlich sequentiellen Datenerhebung integriert, wurde dabei eingesetzt, um die Merkmale der Lernenden sowie die Merkmale der adaptiven Lernumgebung zu untersuchen, die zu verbesserten KI-Lernergebnissen in der Berufsbildung und der beruflichen Weiterbildung beitragen. Die Datenerhebung erfolgte in zwei Erhebungswellen über zwei aufeinanderfolgende Schuljahre hinweg, von 2022 bis 2024. Mittels standardisierter Online-Fragebögen wurden die Selbsteinschätzungen der Lernenden zu drei Zeitpunkten – zu Beginn, in der Mitte sowie am Ende des KI-Kurses – erfasst. Insgesamt haben 222 Lernende an den Befragungen teilgenommen. Die statistischen Analysen wurden mit der Statistiksoftware R in der Version 4.3.1 (R Core Team, 2023) durchgeführt.

Empirische Befunde der vorliegenden Studie weisen darauf hin, dass sowohl das KI-Vorwissen der Lernenden als auch die von der Lernsoftware bereitgestellte adaptive und individualisierte Unterstützung einen positiven Einfluss auf die kognitive KI-Lernergebnisse hatten. Hingegen zeigte die Erfahrung der Lernenden mit digitalen Lernanwendungen keinen signifikanten Einfluss. Die Berücksichtigung des Vorwissens der Lernenden sowie der Einsatz von Individualisierungs- und Adaptivitätsfunktionen, die eine personalisierte Eins-zu-eins-Lernvermittlung in großem Umfang ermöglichen, tragen maßgeblich zur Förderung des KI-Lernerfolgs bei. Dies unterstreicht das umfassende Potenzial gut konzipierter, diagnostischer und anpassungsfähiger adaptiver Lernumgebungen, die Vorwissensdiagnostik mit Individualisierungs- und Adaptivitätsmechanismen kombinieren und sich somit als vielversprechende Ansätze für eine breit angelegte Umsetzung in modernen Lernsettings erweisen.

Aufgrund der nicht signifikanten Ergebnisse im Hinblick auf die Erfahrung mit digitalen Lernanwendungen wurde festgestellt, dass sich ein positiver Einfluss der Vertrautheit mit digitalen Lernwerkzeugen auf effektives Lernen hier nicht belegen lässt. Diese Ergebnisse widersprechen bisherigen Forschungsergebnissen, die einen positiven Zusammenhang zwischen digitaler Erfahrung und Lernerfolg belegen (Brinkerhoff et al., 2001; Hasan & Ali, 2004; Pagani et al., 2016). Das könnte daran liegen, dass weitere Einflussfaktoren eine Rolle spielen oder der eingesetzte Messansatz gewisse Einschränkungen aufweist. Dadurch wird deutlich, dass ein umfassenderer Ansatz erforderlich ist, der differenzierte Messinstrumente einsetzt und sowohl die Tiefe des Engagements mit digitalen Tools als auch die bereitgestellte Lernunterstützung berücksichtigt, um den Einfluss digitaler Erfahrung auf Lernergebnisse vollständig zu erfassen. Zudem konnten aus der Analyse der Lernergebnisse in Bezug auf verschiedene Lernstilgruppen keine eindeutigen Rückschlüsse auf die Rolle von Lernpräferenzen bei kognitivem Lernerfolg gezogen werden. Inwieweit Lernende mit bestimmten Lernstilen signifikant bessere Ergebnisse in adaptiven Lernumgebungen erzielen können, bleibt eine offene Frage für die zukünftige Forschung. Zukünftige Studien sollen hierfür eine angemessene Stichprobengröße anstreben sowie alternative, echtzeit-basierte Erhebungsinstrumente einsetzen, die eine Triangulation der Daten ermöglichen und somit die Objektivität der Studienergebnisse erhöhen.

Wesentliche Implikationen lassen sich aus den Ergebnissen der Studie für Lehrende und Entscheidungsträger in der Berufsbildung sowie der beruflichen Weiterbildung ableiten. Diese unterstreichen die Notwendigkeit, dynamisch adaptive Lernsysteme einzusetzen, umfassendes KI-Training anzubieten und Blended-Learning-Formate anzuwenden. Darüber hinaus liefern die Ergebnisse wertvolle Hinweise für die didaktische Gestaltung adaptiver Lernumgebungen. Um eine bedeutungsvolle Wissenskonstruktion zu fördern, sollten adaptive Lernsysteme mehrere Schlüsselelemente berücksichtigen. Neben Adaptivitäts- und Individualisierungsfunktionen, die das Lernerlebnis personalisieren, müssen diese Systeme das Vorwissen der Lernenden erfassen und angepasste Unterstützung bieten, um den Lernerfolg zu verbessern. Ferner verdeutlichen die Ergebnisse die Notwendigkeit, eine benutzerfreundliche Navigation zu gewährleisten, unterschiedliche Lernpräferenzen einzubeziehen und bei der Gestaltung adaptiver Lernumgebungen etablierte didaktische Prinzipien zu berücksichtigen. Ein pädagogisches Rahmenkonzept, das sich primär auf Kernprinzipien des Kognitivismus und Konstruktivismus stützt und zugleich zentrale behavioristische Elemente integriert, erweist sich als geeignet für die effektive Vermittlung KI-bezogener Inhalte. Durch die Einbindung grundlegender pädagogischer Prinzipien in adaptive Lernsysteme lässt sich die Lücke zwischen dem technologischen Potenzial KI-gestützter Lernanwendungen und einer fundierten bildungstheoretischen Grundlage überbrücken. Diese Abstimmung stellt sicher, dass adaptive Lernsysteme nicht lediglich angepasste Lerninhalte vermitteln, sondern Lernende aktiv dabei unterstützen, nachhaltiges Wissen aufzubauen und erworbene Kompetenzen in praxisnahe Anwendungskontexte zu übertragen.

Darüber hinaus werden die Limitationen der Studie hervorgehoben und Perspektiven für zukünftige Bildungsforschung und -praxis aufgezeigt. Mit dem weiteren Fortschritt des Forschungsfeldes der ‚KI in der Bildung' und der kontinuierlichen Entwicklung adaptiver Lerntechnologien stellt die Entwicklung anspruchsvoller und theoriegeleiteter Anpassungen von Lerninhalten zur Berücksichtigung der vielfältigen Bedürfnisse der Lernenden einen entscheidenden Schritt dar, um gerechte sowie nachhaltige Bildungsangebote zu schaffen.

Künftige Forschung sowie Akteure in der Berufsbildung sowie der beruflichen Weiterbildung sollten der Integration von KI-bezogenen Kursen in authentische, robuste adaptive Lernsysteme Priorität einräumen. Diese Systeme sollten nicht nur individuell auf die jeweiligen Lernbedarfe reagieren können, sondern auch auf fundierten didaktischen Konzepten basieren, um sicherzustellen, dass die unterschiedlichen Anforderungen der Lernenden adressiert und ihre Lernergebnisse maximiert werden. Eine solche Integration ist essenziell, um KI-Kompetenz zu fördern und damit der wachsenden Qualifikationslücke in der heutigen Arbeitswelt entgegenzuwirken. Durch die Förderung nachhaltigen lebenslangen Lernens bilden solche Lernansätze die Grundlage für inklusive und wirkungsvolle Upskilling- und Reskilling-Initiativen dar und stellen damit sicher, dass Lernende mit unterschiedlichen Hintergründen, Bedürfnissen und Kompetenzen die Möglichkeit erhalten, in einem sich rasch wandelnden technologischen Umfeld erfolgreich zu agieren.

Contents

Abbreviations

AI	artificial intelligence
AIEd	artificial intelligence in education
BMWi	Bundesministerium für Wirtschaft und Energie / Federal Ministry for Economic Affairs and Energy
CAI	computer-assisted instruction
CFA	confirmatory factor-analysis
ChatGPT	chat generative pre-trained transformer
CI	confidence interval
CLT	central limit theorem
CVET	continuing vocational education and training
DLA	digital learning applications
DQR	der Deutsche Qualifikationsrahmen für lebenslanges Lernen / the German qualifications framework for lifelong learning
EFA	exploratory factor analysis
EQF	European qualifications framework
FSLSM	Felder-Silverman learning style model
H	hypothesis
H5P	HTML5 package, a free and open-source content collaboration framework based on JavaScript
ILS	index of learning styles
InnoVET	Germany's federal innovation competition with the main goal of 'shaping the future—Innovations for excellent vocational education and training' ('Zukunft gestalten – Innovationen für eine exzellente berufliche Bildung')

IQR	interquartile range
IT	information technology
ITS	intelligent tutoring system
KIB^3	Künstliche Intelligenz in die berufliche Bildung bringen / Bringing Artificial Intelligence into Vocational Education (research project, in the framework of which this thesis was written)
KMO	Kaiser–Meyer–Olkin test of sampling adequacy
LMS	learning management system
LMU	Ludwig Maximilian University of Munich
LOESS	locally estimated scatterplot smoothing fit in regression
MBTI	Myers-Briggs type indicator
ML	machine learning
MLR	multiple linear regression
MOOCs	massive open online courses
Moodle	modular object-oriented dynamic learning environment
MSA	mean square of averages
OECD	Organisation for Economic Co-operation and Development
PCA	principal component analysis
PLS	publishers' licensing services
R	open-source programming language for statistical computing and data analysis named after its creators Ross Ihaka and Robert Gentleman
RMSEA	root mean square error of approximation index
RQ	research question
SAKI	self-adaptive keyboard trainer
SNCSC	Springer Nature and Copyright Clearance Center
TLI	Tucker Lewis index of factoring reliability
UNESCO	the United Nations educational, scientific and cultural organization
Unipark	an online survey provider specializing in survey and feedback solutions for scientific research and other purposes
VARK	visual, auditory, read, kinesthetic learning style inventory
VET	vocational education and training
VIF	variance inflation factor
ZPD	zone of proximal development

List of Figures

List of Tables

Introduction

1

1.1 Problem Statement

Despite the rapid growth of AI technologies in education and an ever-increasing demand for an AI-ready workforce, AI literacy among learners in vocational and continuing education remains low (Petridou & Lao, 2024; Rott et al., 2022). The far-reaching implementation of generative and other AI technologies across different fields has made the acquisition of AI-related skills a necessity (Pelletier et al., 2024; Le Borgne et al., 2023). The societal and economic impact of AI, especially the subsequent job transformations, has underscored the urgent need for upskilling and reskilling adult workers in European workplaces (Cedefop, 2024), as new competences and knowledge of AI have become essential for skilled workers (Rott et al., 2022). To navigate the changing landscape, continuous training in the workplace should be promoted to help workers readily adapt to new challenges and changes in their jobs (Twomey, 2018). However, both learners and educators have not yet become proficient in AI technologies and currently possess only basic AI knowledge (Lindner et al., 2019; Petridou & Lao, 2024; Stamenković et al., 2023). A recent survey revealed that only "one in seven adult workers in European labour markets usually work with digital tools or applications that can automatically do some of their tasks, using algorithms" (Cedefop, 2024, p. 2). AI content is predominantly offered in higher education institutions, with limited training opportunities available in VET and CVET institutions. This presents a substantial challenge for VET and CVET institutions in preparing skilled workers for the demands of AI (Rott et al., 2022). In response to the digital transformation driven by AI, learning with and about AI is increasingly recognized as essential for enhancing AI literacy and equipping individuals with the skills needed (Dignum, 2021; Rott et al., 2022; Stadelmann et al., 2021).

E. Petridou, *Personalized Learning in Vocational and Continuing Education*, https://doi.org/10.1007/978-3-658-51517-1_1

Learners engage in learning processes by initiating their individual characteristics, personal needs, and preferences. Traditional face-to-face learning approaches, in which one-to-many instruction is implemented, fail to take into account these individual aspects of learners (Popescu, 2010). In these learning environments, instruction is typically provided at the same pace, with the same approach, on the same path, and in the same manner for all learners. Similarly, online learning environments, while offering flexibility in terms of learning time and place and thus enable ubiquitous learning (Brown, 2007), "dwell on a single method of delivering learning content to all users...[which is] based on the one-size-fits-all traditional approach of learning" (Akuma & Ndera, 2021, p. 228). Hence, they fail to consider the heterogeneous group of learners and their individual needs, leading to significant dropout rates (Akhuseyinoglu & Brusilovsky, 2021). Compared to traditional one-to-many learning environments, one-to-one instructional learning has been found to lead to greater learning gains (Bloom, 1984). To address these challenges, leveraging AI learning technologies, which utilize personalized one-to-one learning solutions at scale (Taylor et al., 2021), has the potential to improve AI literacy among young professionals and enhance their learning outcomes by tailoring learning content to their personal and professional interests. The concept of adaptive instruction has the potential to promote individualization, as it aims to provide personalized learning experiences by tailoring educational content to the unique needs of each learner (Lehmann, 2010).

In the realm of AI in education (AIEd), which involves the application of AI technologies in education and has evolved significantly over the past three decades (Zawacki-Richter et al., 2019), adaptive learning technologies, being among the most prominent applications of AI in educational settings (Kabudi et al., 2021), are increasingly deployed in both synchronous and asynchronous learning environments. These technologies adjust learning support to meet the unique requirements of learners. Learners' individual activity, knowledge levels, and interactions are collected and analyzed, and adaptive learning support is provided, such as customized learning paths, contents, and scaffolds to facilitate personalized learning experiences (Zhang et al., 2020). Each learner's performance is constantly and in real-time evaluated, and a continuously changing individualized learning pathway is developed (Taylor et al., 2021). As such, adaptive learning settings that leverage AI learning applications and account for learners with different learning characteristics, distinct backgrounds, and differentiated learning needs are promising to realize for the improvement of learning outcomes.

Nevertheless, AIEd and the integration of adaptive learning technologies in educational contexts remain underexplored. There is still no consensus on what adaptive learning technologies can fully achieve and how they are implemented in practice (Kabudi et al., 2021; Özyurt & Özyurt, 2015; Zhang & Aslan, 2021), especially in the framework of vocational and continuing education (Petridou & Lao, 2024; Rott et al., 2022). A recent systematic literature review indicated that previous studies have primarily focused on improving learning performance in adaptive learning environments (Raj & Renumol, 2022). While there have been studies that did not find any significant impact on academic achievement and students' learning experiences (Akkoyunlu & Soylu, 2008; Wang et al., 2006), the review by Chiu et al. (2023) revealed that most studies reported significant improvements in learning outcomes due to the integration of AI technologies. Similarly, numerous studies have shown that personalized learning realized through adaptive learning systems enhances learning performance (El-Bishouty et al., 2019; Huang et al., 2016; Nakic et al., 2015; Tseng et al., 2008). Overall, even though predominantly positive effects have been demonstrated, personalized adaptive learning is considered a field in its infancy (Taylor et al., 2021), underscoring the need for further research in this promising area (Kabudi et al., 2021; Zhang & Aslan, 2021).

1.2 Relevance and Scope of the Thesis

This thesis contributes to the body of research by evaluating the effectiveness of the delivery of an AI course offered through an adaptive learning system designed to enhance AI learning in a real-world educational setting among individuals with different characteristics. In the framework of the project 'Bringing AI into Vocational Education' ('KI B^3—Künstliche Intelligenz in die berufliche Bildung bringen'), a comparatively new educational offer in Germany, an additional qualification on AI and machine learning (ML) was developed for learners in different professional sectors from VET and CVET institutions. The course was taught over two consecutive school years in a blended learning setting. It featured a combination of face-to-face and online classes and predominantly online self-learning sessions that were delivered in the learning platform of Moodle. An adaptive learning system supported by AI technologies was embedded in Moodle that incorporated interactive, adaptive, and gamification elements to support the heterogeneous group of participating learners, thereby enabling them to personalize their learning experience and improve their learning outcomes.

As learners' individual differences play a significant role in determining the extent to which and how effectively they engage in the learning process (Jonassen & Grabowski, 2012), the use of adaptive learning technologies that address these individual differences is crucial for learning success. Given the high heterogeneity of learners in VET and CVET, with differences in age, educational background, and professional experience, the integration of adaptivity and individualization features into adaptive learning systems, which can be tailored to the individual characteristics of each learner, can support individual knowledge acquisition while simultaneously accommodating these diverse learning profiles. These features can enable meaningful interactions between learners and the adaptive learning system. Such interactions have the potential to promote individual knowledge construction and thereby enhance learning outcomes. Several prior studies have underscored the achievement of higher scores within adaptive learning systems compared to non-adaptive learning systems (Cui et al., 2018; Kardan & Conati, 2015; Kommers et al., 2008; Ling & Chiang, 2022; Wang et al., 2020).

The attainment of successful learning outcomes can further be facilitated by instructional approaches that account for learners' prior knowledge. Prior knowledge refers to the existing knowledge, skills, or competences that learners bring to the learning process (Jonassen & Grabowski, 1993), facilitating the acquisition and construction of new knowledge (Schunk, 2012). Consequently, adaptive learning systems can enhance learning outcomes by tailoring the learning experience to the learner's existing knowledge base. This is particularly relevant in the context of an AI-focused additional qualification implemented in vocational and continuing education settings. In this learning context, learners possess varying levels of AI-related prior knowledge, depending on their educational background and the specific demands of their occupations. By taking individual differences in AI-related knowledge into account and offering targeted support, adaptive learning environments can help learners more effectively integrate the relatively new topic of AI into their existing knowledge structures. In addition, gaining AI knowledge and skills in contemporary blended learning settings, and especially with the aid of an adaptive learning system, necessitates familiarity with digital learning applications to facilitate the acquisition of knowledge and skills. Previous research has identified a positive association between digital experience and learning outcomes (Hasan & Ali, 2004; Pagani et al., 2016). Furthermore, individuals with extensive computer experience gain more knowledge from hypertext-based programs than those with limited computer experience (Brinkerhoff et al., 2001).

Therefore, not only learners' prior knowledge but also their experience with digital learning tools represents a critical factor in achieving successful learning outcomes within adaptive learning environments.

This empirical study aims to investigate how the adaptive system's features of adaptivity and individualization, in conjunction with the learner characteristics of prior knowledge and experience with digital learning applications, influence learning outcomes and contribute to greater success in AI learning. The aim is to examine whether these factors contribute to enhanced success in AI-driven learning environments. By investigating the effectiveness of these factors within an authentic adaptive learning environment supported by AI technologies, the study can yield valuable insights into how AI technologies can be leveraged to improve learning outcomes in contemporary educational settings. Suggestions can be further provided on how adaptive and individualized interventions can be designed to take into account learners' individual characteristics to promote their learning outcomes. To this end, the study places particular emphasis on learning styles as a key learning characteristic, according to which learners can be differentiated and enhanced learning outcomes can be achieved (Kinshuk, 2016; El-Bishouty et al., 2019; Karagiannis & Satratzemi, 2018; Tseng et al., 2008). Specifically, it examines whether learners with certain learning styles, namely learners with active, sensing, visual, or sequential preferences, demonstrate better learning outcomes within an adaptive learning environment than learners with reflective, intuitive, verbal, and global learning types. This strand of research has remained underexplored. By identifying which styles are linked with better outcomes, the study aims to contribute to the development of more personalized adaptive learning systems that cater to learners' diverse needs, thereby realizing AI-driven learning environments that are both inclusive and effective.

In addition, the study aims to outline key implications for integrating AI-related educational content and AI-driven learning technologies into VET and CVET settings, highlighting actionable insights for both educators and stakeholders in vocational and continuing education research and practice. Furthermore, this study seeks to propose guidelines for the optimal design of adaptive learning systems that could enable personalized learning experiences tailored to individuals with varying characteristics. By investigating AI's ability to tailor learning experiences to individual needs, learners who excel and strive in adaptive learning environments can be identified. Consequently, the current thesis can offer valuable recommendations for leveraging AI as a means to bridge educational gaps, thereby providing equitable learning opportunities for students with diverse learning characteristics. The insights gained could inform the development of AI tools that cater to a broad range of learning preferences and needs, potentially closing gaps in educational access and effectiveness. Furthermore, the application of adaptive learning systems in contemporary vocational learning environments can be instrumental in strengthening the integration of AI competences and skills in both VET and CVET institutions (Petridou & Lao, 2024; Rott et al., 2022). This integration can support lifelong learning by equipping learners with the necessary skills to thrive in an evolving job market and adapt to new technological advancements driven by AI. Finally, as limited studies have implemented AI technologies in authentic educational settings, this research also provides critical insights into how adaptive learning systems supported by AI technologies can be better aligned with educational theories and practices. By bridging the gap between technological capabilities and pedagogical frameworks, the study aims to contribute to the effective implementation of AI in education, thereby fostering a learning environment that is both theoretically grounded and aligned with pedagogical principles.

1.3 Structure of the Thesis

The thesis proceeds with Chap. 2, which details the study's theoretical background and presents the related theoretical concepts. It begins with framing the emergence and integration of AI applications in education, starting with a definition of AI and a brief explanation of its characteristics. An overview of AIEd is then provided. Next, the learning theories and conceptual frameworks underpinning AIEd are discussed. Adaptive learning systems are then defined, and their contribution to educational practice is highlighted. A description of the theoretical conceptualization of individual differences in learning follows, including the description of the concepts of adaptivity and individualization, along with prior knowledge and experience with digital learning applications. Particularly, the concept of learning styles is detailed in separate sections, explaining how this fundamental characteristic differentiates learners and influences learning outcomes within adaptive learning systems. The integration of AI into VET and CVET is subsequently described. In the following, the project 'Bringing AI into Vocational Education', in the framework of which the current study was initiated, is introduced. Subsequently, the blended learning environment, in which the course on AI and ML was delivered, is described. An emphasis is given on the integration of adaptive learning software into Moodle, whereby the implemented adaptive techniques are described. The chapter concludes with a summary of the theoretical framework of the thesis. In Chap. 3, the research questions and hypotheses of the thesis are outlined. Chap. 4 is devoted to the methodological approach of the thesis, including the research design, sample, procedure, research instruments, and a brief description of the data analysis. The results of the quantitative analysis are then presented in Chap. 5. In the following chapter, the results are critically discussed in relation to the research hypotheses along with the study's implications, acknowledged limitations, as well as directions for future research. The study's conclusions are drawn in Chap. 7 with respect to the study's contributions and its relevance for the field of education.

Theoretical Background 2

2.1 Definition and Characteristics of Artificial Intelligence (AI)

Even though AI recently gained extensive popularity, it does not constitute a recent development. AI was established as a field of study in the aftermath of the Dartmouth Summer Research Project on AI in 1955 in the United States of America. The original conception of AI stemmed from a proposal formulated as part of this initiative. The proposal referred to the initiation of a project that was based on the assumption that "every aspect of learning or any other feature of intelligence can in principle be so precisely described that a machine can be made to simulate it. An attempt will be made to find how to make machines use language, form abstractions and concepts, solve kinds of problems now reserved for humans, and improve themselves" (McCarthy et al., 2006, p. 12). Since its initiation, AI has seen significant growth, and a wide variety of AI applications and areas of research are still emerging today.

As a constantly evolving and inherently interdisciplinary field, AI has not been easy to define (Chen et al., 2020). According to the English Oxford Living Dictionary (n.d.) and Merriam-Webster Dictionary (n.d.), AI is presented as a machine-based system that is able to perform tasks for which human intelligence is required, by imitating human intelligent behavior, such as visual perception, speech recognition, decision-making, and translation between languages. This definition is congruent with the definition of an AI system provided by the European AI Act (Helberger & Diakopoulos, 2023) as well as the definition formulated by the group of experts on AI at the Organisation for Economic Co-operation and Development (OECD, 2019), who agreed that an AI system is "a machine-based system that can, for a given set of human-defined objectives, make predictions,

E. Petridou, *Personalized Learning in Vocational and Continuing Education*,
https://doi.org/10.1007/978-3-658-51517-1_2

recommendations or decisions influencing real or virtual environments" (Vincent-Lancrin & van der Vlies, 2020, p. 7). The power of AI systems lies in two key characteristics: the automation of processes and their calculation competency. As Turing (1950) emphasized: "Parts of modern machines which can be regarded as analogues of nerve cells work about a thousand times faster than the latter...machines take me by surprise with great frequency..., largely because I do not do sufficient calculation" (p. 455, 450). This observation underscores AI systems' ability to automate complex tasks, efficiently handling repetitive or intricate processes, as well as their remarkable speed in performing calculations compared to human cognitive capabilities. An extensive number of calculations can be processed by AI systems fast, enabling calculations that a human could hardly achieve and generating results that for human intelligence would not be feasible.

An AI system's lifecycle consists of the following critical phases: 1) *planning* and *design, data collection* and *processing,* and *model building* and *interpretation*; 2) *verification* and *validation*; 3) *deployment*; and 4) *operation* and *monitoring* (OECD, 2019; Vincent-Lancrin & van der Vlies, 2020). The initial phase involves outlining the objectives and requirements of the AI system. It includes designing the system architecture, defining the problem to be solved, and determining the necessary data inputs. Data collection and processing follow, wherein relevant data is gathered, cleaned, and prepared for analysis. Model building and interpretation involve developing algorithms and models that can analyze the data and provide insights or predictions. Once the model is built, it undergoes verification and validation processes to ensure its accuracy and reliability. Verification checks if the model meets the specifications and requirements set during the planning phase. Validation assesses the model's performance in real-world scenarios, ensuring it produces valid and useful results. After successful validation, the AI system is deployed into a production environment where it can be used to perform its intended functions. This phase involves integrating the system with existing infrastructure and making it accessible to end-users. The final phase focuses on the ongoing operation and monitoring of the AI system. Continuous monitoring is essential to track the system's performance, ensure its reliability, and make necessary adjustments or updates. This phase also includes addressing any issues that arise during operation and adapting the system to changing conditions or new data (Ameisen, 2020; Mitchell, 2019).

As a field of research and a multifaceted concept, AI has been defined in terms of three general dimensions: (a) as *applied philosophy*; (b) as a *method*; and (c) as a *tool* and *solution* (K. Porayska-Pomsta, personal communication, June 30, 2022). In the first case, AI as applied philosophy enables individuals to formulate fundamental questions such as how they think, how they perceive, and how they interact with the environment. As these questions can be addressed with the help of AI, AI can also serve as a method of inquiry. AI can support human learning through the construction of computational models, based on which theories can be tested, and the outcomes of this testing can be used to inform relevant theories. Lastly, AI can serve as a tool and solution in the sense that it can provide technological pathways to tackle challenges of the real world to improve people's lives. Based on this last dimension, AI is usually defined as an intelligent autonomous agent that "measures an agent's ability to achieve goals in a wide range of environments" (Legg & Hutter, 2007, p. 402). AI serves as an agent that interacts with the environment through observation and action by receiving and sending signals to the environment (see Fig. 2.1). AI has the ability to act on the environment and upon its actions to receive feedback in the form of a reward. The presence or even the absence of the reward allows the agent to evaluate its success based on a pre-defined objective. Therefore, the distinguishing feature of AI applications in comparison with other technologies lies in their autonomous ability to influence our environment by undertaking human actions and decisions (K. Porayska-Pomsta, personal communication, June 30, 2022).

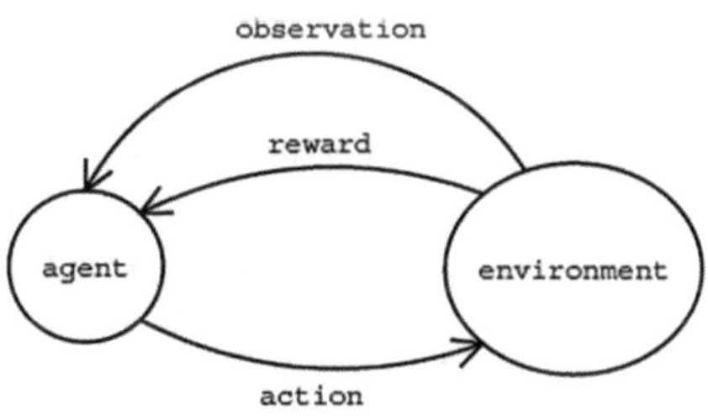

Fig. 2.1 AI as an Agent Interacting with the Environment. (*Note.* From "Universal intelligence: A definition of machine intelligence," by S. Legg, and M. Hutter, 2007. *Minds and machines, 17*(4), p. 407 (https://doi.org/10.1007/s11023-007-9079-x). Copyright 2007 Springer Nature and Copyright Clearance Center (SNCSC). Reproduced with permission from SNCSC)

Several prominent AI methodologies have been developed in the last few years, including *ML*, which is based on pattern recognition, *deep learning*, and *neural networks*, which are based on extracting higher-level features from vast amounts of data as well as *quantum computing*, which is rather probabilistic and implements concepts of quantum mechanics (Chen et al., 2020; Cope et al., 2020).

2.2 The Field of AI in Education (AIEd)

AI applications have significantly influenced not only computer science and related fields but undeniably educational science as well. Advancements in novel AI technologies, particularly in knowledge-based systems and expert systems models, have generated an increasing body of AI applications in education (Zhang & Aslan, 2021). In 1970, a new educational field was officially established, the field of AI in education (AIEd) (Brusilovsky & Peylo, 2003). The field of AIEd "is concerned with [the] development of AI techniques for the study of human teaching and the engineering of systems that facilitate human learning" (Woolf, 1991, p. 2). AIEd is grounded on the three dimensions that characterize AI as a whole. As *applied philosophy*, AIEd allows the formulation of questions regarding human learning, such as what learning is, what knowledge entails, and what is needed to support learning. AIEd is also defined as a *method*. AI models can be constructed that aim to respond to fundamental questions or even enrich our knowledge regarding human learning. Lastly, AIEd as a *tool and solution* refers to its ability to create AI-driven environments that support learners in their learning experiences and assist teachers in improving their practices through learning analytics (K. Porayska-Pomsta, personal communication, June 30, 2022).

How AI technologies can be leveraged to support human learning dates back to Bloom (1984). Bloom and his team found out that one-to-one instructional learning (tutoring) leads to greater learning gains than the two other conditions they tested. These were the conventional classroom and one-to-many mastery learning, which were based on the instruction of one teacher to 30 students. They demonstrated that "the average student under tutoring [condition] was about two standard deviations [=2sigma] above the average of the control class" (Bloom, 1984, p. 4), as it is depicted in Fig. 2.2. Bloom's 2-sigma effect addressed the necessity to devise one-to-one personalized learning solutions at scale that are practical and feasible in order to support a broader audience of students in achieving high levels of learning. As a result, the educational field endeavored to utilize and exploit AI technologies to realize one-to-one learning settings. By employing AI-based learning systems that autonomously adjust to individual learner needs, targeted and effective learning support can be delivered, enabling personalized learning experiences that promise to enhance learning gains.

To date, a plethora of AI applications have emerged in education and will still be emerging in the years to come. AIEd initially followed the conception of AI as an intelligent tutoring system (ITS) (Guan et al., 2020). An ITS, as it will be detailed below, can independently resolve the problems presented to the user in a

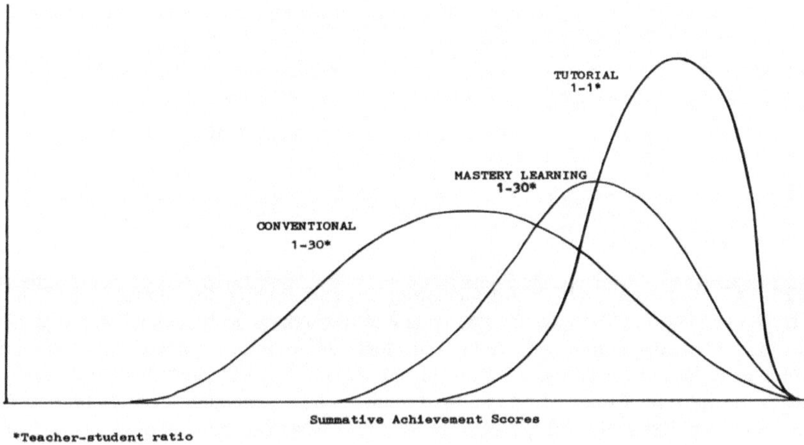

Fig. 2.2 Comparison of Student Achievement Distributions Across Conventional, Mastery Learning, and Tutorial Instruction. (*Note.* From "The 2 sigma problem: The search for methods of group instruction as effective as one-to-one tutoring," by Bloom, B., 1984, *Educational Researcher, 13*(6), p. 5 (https://doi.org/10.3102/0013189X013006004). Copyright 1984 by the American Educational Research Association. Reprinted with permission)

human-like way, engaging in reasoning about the solution process and providing commentary on that solution (Ross, 1987). A recent systematic literature review (Zawacki-Richter et al., 2019) distinguished four main categories of AI applications in higher education, based on the student life cycle framework developed by Reid (1995). This framework classifies AI-based services into two levels. The first is the level of the *institution* and *administration* and refers to matters such as admission, counseling, and library services. The second level is about *academic support*, which encompasses matters such as assessment, feedback, and tutoring. As shown in Fig. 2.3, the main AI applications in higher education that were identified in the comprehensive study of Zawacki-Richter et al. (2019) were the following: (a) *profiling* and *prediction*, (b) *ITSs*, (c) *assessment* and *evaluation*, and (d) *adaptive systems* and *personalization.*

The first category includes basic applications of AI, which are based on the development of learner models or profiles that allow predictions about learning. Usually, with the use of ML methods, learning patterns are recognized and classified. As a consequence, student profiles are modeled and predictions for their learning are made. For instance, based on students' academic achievement, the likelihood of their dropping out of a course can be estimated, and timely support

Profiling and prediction (admissions decisions and course scheduling; drop-out and retention; student models and academic achievement)

Intelligent tutoring systems (teaching course content; diagnosing strengths and automated feedback; curating learning materials; facilitating collaboration; the teacher's perspective)

Assessment and evaluation (automated grading; feedback; evaluation of student understanding, engagement and academic integrity; evaluation of teaching)

Adaptive systems and personalisation (teaching course content; recommending personalized content; supporting teachers and learning design; using academic data to monitor and guide students; representation of knowledge in concept maps)

Fig. 2.3 AI Applications. (*Note.* Adapted from Zawacki-Richter, O., Marín, V. I., Bond, M., & Gouverneur, F. (2019). Systematic review of research on artificial intelligence applications in higher education–where are the educators?. *International Journal of Educational Technology in Higher Education, 16*(1), p. 11 (https://doi.org/10.1186/s41239-019-0171-0), under the terms of the Creative Commons Attribution 4.0 International License (http://creativecommons.org/licenses/by/4.0/). Table 6 in this study was adapted by omitting the indication of the number of AI applications)

could be provided during the learning process. The second category comprises ITSs. ITSs have been extensively implemented in educational research. They usually refer to an intelligent agent or tutor that, based on learners' interests, aptitudes, and behavior profiling (Wang & Cheng, 2022), can deliver customized, timely, and appropriate materials, guidance, and feedback to learners (Zhang & Aslan, 2021). An ITS supports learning on the basis of four models: (a) the *learner model*, which provides information about the learner's knowledge level, cognitive ability, learning motivation, and learning style, (b) the *pedagogical model*, which represents the knowledge regarding effective teaching and learning approaches and involves the selection of the appropriate teaching practices as well as the provision of individualized guidance, (c) the *domain model*, which represents the knowledge that needs to be learned about a topic, and (d) the *diagnosis model*, which enables the evaluation of errors and flaws in student learning (Holmes et al., 2019; Huang & Chen, 2016). The third category of AI applications refers to the implementation of AI technologies in order to perform assessments and evaluations. For example, automated grading, which is based on an AI software system, can allow for large-scale assessments, reducing costly and time-consuming resources. Accordingly, corrective feedback may be provided automatically and support a wide range of students, enhancing their learning experiences (Zawacki-Richter et al., 2019). The last category of AI applications includes adaptive systems and personalization. As adaptive systems may have plenty of different functions they can perform, a common ground for their definition is difficult to be found. Following the long-standing work of Brusilovsky and his colleagues (Brusilovsky & Pesin, 1998; Brusilovsky & Peylo, 2003), a learning system is regarded as adaptive when it can adapt most of its fundamental functions to the learner's needs and knowledge. An adaptive system is able to collect information on learners' several cognitive and affective characteristics and build a learner's model based on the learner's interaction with the system. This allows the system to offer personalization, namely to personalize its learning support to learners' needs, including customized content presentation and tailored feedback provision. A more detailed presentation of these applications is provided in Section 2.4.

At the core of AIEd is the implementation of AI technologies in educational settings with the aim of achieving various educational purposes (Chen et al., 2020). Automation as a main function of AI can lead to more efficient schools and simplify teachers' tasks. AI-driven tools such as auto-grading systems (Wang & Cheng, 2022) can significantly reduce the time teachers spend on repetitive tasks, freeing them to focus on more complex and creative aspects of teaching. Beyond efficiency, AI holds the promise of making education more accessible and inclusive by providing the necessary support to students with different and special needs (Vincent-Lancrin & van der Vlies, 2020). AI's capacity to take into account learners' individual characteristics and requirements, and to adjust learning content and feedback, enables the realization of personalized and differentiated learning. Learning methods and strategies can be customized and optimized, leading to desired learning outcomes (Zhang & Aslan, 2021). Such personalized approaches can help address the diverse learning needs and preferences, ensuring that all learners can achieve their full potential. Thanks to AI, learning opportunities can extend beyond the traditional classroom setting by providing learners with AI tutoring systems and support (Al-haimi et al., 2021). These systems enable learners to engage in self-directed learning and provide assistance with homework and exam preparation without the presence of an instructor. Finally, the collaboration between teachers and AI has the potential to enhance the overall quality of teaching and learning (Al-haimi et al., 2021). Teachers can monitor student learning in real time as well as adjust their teaching practices based on students' needs. This dynamic feedback loop ensures that teaching practices remain responsive and effective, ultimately leading to improved educational outcomes. As such, the integration of AI into educational settings has demonstrated significant benefits. These technologies have not only the potential to significantly enhance access to learning opportunities and personalize learning experiences, but they also facilitate a diverse range of teaching and learning interactions. By tailoring educational content to the unique needs of individual learners, AI contributes to the improvement of educational outcomes, making it a powerful tool for modern education.

Nevertheless, along with the benefits of AI applications, the rapid implementation of AI applications in educational settings presents significant risks. Falsifications in the deployment of AI applications can lead to a variety of hazards, including substantial gaps in knowledge and ethical concerns. Key issues in this regard include equity of access and accessibility (Selwyn, 2019). Disparities in access can exacerbate existing inequalities, making it essential to ensure that all learners, regardless of their background, can benefit from AI-driven education. Accessibility challenges, particularly for learners with disabilities, are also concerning, as they can hinder equitable access to learning opportunities. The potential disruption of traditional pedagogies is another concern, as pedagogical approaches may be altered or dictated by AI systems. This shift could lead to an overreliance on AI and a reduced teacher autonomy. The balance of human-machine autonomy constitutes a pressing issue (De Visser et al., 2018). As AI takes on more roles traditionally held by educators, the question arises of how to maintain human oversight and ensure that the use of AI enhances, rather than diminishes, the role of teachers and human judgment in education. In addition, algorithmic fairness is another major concern, particularly with the emergence of different kinds of biases within AI systems (Holstein & Doroudi, 2021). These include representational bias, where certain groups may be misrepresented, allocative bias, which affects the distribution of resources or opportunities, measurement bias, where inaccuracies in data collection lead to flawed outcomes, and predictor bias, which occurs when certain predictors are given undue weight in decision-making processes. Such biases can result in unjust outcomes and perpetuate existing social inequalities. These issues, along with challenges in ensuring fairness, accountability, and transparency in data-driven AI systems, have been the most prevalent challenges in AIEd.

Ensuring that AI systems are fair, that there is accountability for decisions made by these systems, and that the processes by which AI operates are transparent to both educators and learners is crucial. However, as Holstein and Doroudi (2021) highlight, it is not enough to direct attention toward designing transparent and accountable systems within the field of AIEd, but rather it is necessary to engage the broad social-technical system. The key stakeholders need to be involved to confront the emerging hazards. To overcome such challenges and amplify the educational field with the potential that AI applications bring, AIEd needs to be co-designed with educational practitioners and learners. Since, as Wiener (1960, p. 1358) noted:

> "If we use, to achieve our purposes, a mechanical agency with whose operation we cannot efficiently interfere once we have started it, because the action is so fast and irrevocable that we have not the data to intervene before the action is complete, then we had better be quite sure that the purpose put into the machine is the purpose which we really desire and not merely a colorful imitation of it."

The ambition of AIEd to deliver high-quality education anytime and anywhere is well-documented in the literature (Khensous et al., 2024). However, to maximize the efficiency of AI applications in supporting learning and to identify areas where AI can add the most value to education, it is crucial to consider and integrate educational learning theories into AIEd.

2.3 Learning Theories and Conceptual Frameworks in AIEd

Although AIEd technologies have made significant strides, several recent literature reviews have emphasized the absence of educational perspectives in the field of AIEd (Chen et al., 2020; Hinojo-Lucena et al., 2019; Zawacki-Richter et al., 2019). Most AIEd researchers, having strong engineering backgrounds, often concentrate on technological design and development, neglecting the perspectives of educational researchers and teachers (Chiu et al., 2023). Given AI's inherently interdisciplinary nature, it is crucial for research to explore methods that actively involve teachers, students, and educational researchers (Holstein et al., 2019). As in other areas of education, AIEd needs to tackle the fundamental issues that characterize human learning, such as how to meet learners' needs, the timing and type of support required, and how to empower learners to regulate their own learning (Du Boulay, 2000). To be effective, the integration of AI applications into education needs to adhere to the educational and learning theories that underpin AI-based learning environments, thereby effectively guiding both instructional design and technological development (Bower, 2019).

According to a recent position paper by Ouyang and Jiao (2021), AIEd has since its birth undergone three paradigmatic shifts. The first paradigm is called AI-directed and is the least learner-centered paradigm. Based on the theory of behaviorism, the learner acts as a recipient of AI's guidance. In the second paradigm, which is defined as AI-supported, the learner is seen more as a collaborator with AI. The AI system adopts a less dominant role and becomes more of a supporting tool. The theoretical underpinnings of this paradigm can be found in cognitivism and social constructivism. The third paradigm stems from recent developments that have allowed more learner-directed AI systems that work on the basis of real-time data analysis of learning processes. It originates from the theory of human agency (Bandura, 2006), the assumption that AI can serve as a tool to augment human intelligence (Law, 2019), as well as the complexity theory (Mason, 2008). The AI system acts and interacts dynamically with the learners, who are seen as leaders. The synergetic collaboration that is enacted between the AI system and human intelligence promotes learners' augmented intelligence.

2.3.1 Behaviorism

The first paradigm, known as *AI-directed* or *learner-as-recipient*, involves AI entirely directing the learning process. Learning entails reinforcing knowledge acquisition through programmed instructions, which introduce new concepts in a logical and incremental manner (Ouyang & Jiao, 2021), as well as with immediate feedback. This paradigm is theoretically based on *behaviorism*, since the learner only acts as a recipient of AI's guidance and is expected to follow particular learning pathways and achieve learning goals, as the AI system predefines them. The system neither collects information on the learner's knowledge level and skills nor does it adapt its support to the learner's individual needs and characteristics. Instead, AI represents knowledge models and directs cognitive learning (Ouyang & Jiao, 2021), with the AI system determining and shaping the learning behavior according to behaviorist principles.

Behaviorism constitutes a theory of learning that originated from behavioral research in psychology. It was initiated from the idea that psychology's subject matter is behavior rather than subjective experience, aiming to establish psychology as an objective science (Moore, 1999). However, the idea of behaviorism culminated in defining behavior as not only externally-oriented acting but as subjective experience and emotions that are derived from publicly observable phenomena (Moore, 1999; Schmidt, 2004). Behaviorism was officially established with the publication of Watson's paper (Watson, 1913). In this paper, Watson stated that any kind of behavior is a result of experience and that any individual can be trained to behave in a particular way through appropriate conditioning. The act of conditioning in behavioral training was used as a means to monitor behavior and elicit desired behaviors. Two types of conditioning were implemented in behavioral research: *classical* and *operant conditioning.*

Classical conditioning can be traced back to Pavlov's and Watson's experiments (Pavlov, 1960; Watson & Rayner, 1920), whereby behavior is framed within the context of the stimulus-response reflex model. This model is based on the association of stimuli with particular anticipated responses. Based on the results of the experiments investigating animal behavior it was found that an organism has two types of responses to external stimuli: (a) *unconditioned/unlearned responses* that are elicited automatically as reflexive responses to natural triggers, as well as (b) *conditioned/learned responses* that are displayed when a neutral stimulus, namely a stimulus that at first elicits no response, is combined with a stimulus that automatically triggers an unconditioned response (Rehman et al., 2017). Over time, the neutral stimulus elicits a response similar to that of the naturally occurring stimulus, even in the absence of the naturally occurring stimulus.

However, classical conditioning was regarded by the behavioral psychologist Skinner (1978) as too simplistic to explain complex human behavior (Machado & Staddon, 2023). Hence, Skinner (1937) introduced operant conditioning, which he deemed more relevant for comprehending and shaping complex behaviors. Behavior is considered operant when it is controlled by its consequences (Staddon & Cerutti, 2003). That means that in operant conditioning, behavior is shaped by the outcomes that follow it. A behavior that is reinforced is likely to be displayed again, while a behavior that is punished is likely to be weakened or eliminated. Once an individual responds to an external stimulus by exhibiting a certain behavior, a consequence follows that either reinforces or punishes that behavior. Based on this principle, a behavior is more likely to be repeated if it is positively or negatively reinforced (Skinner, 1978). Therefore, behavioral consequences are seen as instrumental for displaying particular behavioral patterns, as the former affect the likelihood of the behavior recurring in the future.

In operant conditioning, there are four types of consequences. These are distinguished into two kinds of reinforcement, which aim to strengthen future behavior, and two kinds of punishment, which aim to weaken future behavior. *Positive reinforcement* is the presentation of a stimulus to strengthen a behavior, while *negative reinforcement* is the removal of a stimulus to increase the likelihood of the behavior in the future. *Positive punishment* is defined as the presentation of an aversive stimulus in order to weaken a behavior, while *negative punishment* is the removal of a stimulus to reduce the likelihood of that behavior in the future (Poling et al., 2002). However, the effectiveness of the reinforcements or punishments that are provided to strengthen or weaken a behavior depends on different factors, such as their frequency, suitability, the time point provided, as well as the clarity of the relation between the stimulus and the behavior meant to be modified. When a behavior needs to be weakened, such as replacing or eliminating an undesirable behavior, the intensity and consistency of usage, as well as the reinforcement of alternative behaviors, play a significant role (Schmidt, 2004).

Skinner (1978) made significant contributions to the reinforcement and strengthening of complex behaviors through a process known as *behavior shaping*. This technique involves the successive reinforcement of small partial achievements to ultimately exhibit a desired behavior. Having arranged suitable reinforcement contingencies, specific behaviors can be established and controlled by particular types of stimuli (Skinner, 1958).

Several behavioral characteristics present in contemporary adaptive learning systems can be traced back to Skinner's work, including his notable development of the *teaching machine* (Skinner, 1958). Originally designed as a testing device, once learning had occurred, the teaching machine functioned similarly to a private tutor. It allowed the constant interchange between the machine and the learner. This feature parallels the core functionality of adaptive learning systems that enable human-AI interaction. The teaching machine provided the students with the learning material once they were ready and demonstrated mastery of the current task, resembling the self-paced learning capabilities of modern adaptive learning systems. Additionally, it offered support through hints, prompts, and suggestions to help students achieve correct responses. Similarly, adaptive learning systems deliver personalized support through tailored learning paths, contents, and scaffolds, which can account for better learning gains (Zhang et al., 2020). Especially, the function of adaptive systems to provide immediate feedback to an individual student can be attributed to Skinner's notion of reinforcement. According to this view, learning involves forming, strengthening, or weakening associations between stimuli and responses through reinforcement or nonreinforcement (Greeno et al., 1996). Accordingly, in the context of adaptive learning systems and based on a form of individualized instruction, each student receives tasks and, upon responding actively to them, receives feedback specifically tailored to their individual responses.

Although adaptive learning systems are based on certain behavioral characteristics, they emphasize a more active and learner-directed role for the student. They do not strictly adhere to viewing learning with AI as a means to achieve predetermined learning goals, as seen by behaviorism (Burton et al., 2004). On the contrary, AI plays in reality the role of a support system, which realizes the individualized needs of the learner and provides the necessary support to an individual. Therefore, the other two paradigms, learner-as-collaborator and learner-as-leader, come into play.

2.3.2 Cognitivism and Constructivism

The second paradigm, known as *AI-supported* or *learner-as-collaborator*, renders the AI system as a supporting agent. Learners act as collaborators of the system, building communication with AI to achieve better or more efficient learning. This paradigm is theoretically grounded in *cognitivism* and *social constructivism* (Ouyang & Jiao, 2021). Following cognitivism, learning is guided by *componential analysis*, a principle that refers to the analysis of individual elements (Anderson, 2015) and involves breaking down and analyzing the meaning of concepts into their component parts. To perform a cognitive task, a particular set of information processes or components is necessary (Pellegrino & Lyon,1979). In this way, cognitive skills can be trained, and performance can be improved from learning opportunity to learning opportunity. This approach is grounded in the core approach of cognitive psychology, the *information-processing* approach. "Information-processing analysis breaks a cognitive task down into a set of abstract information-processing steps" (Anderson, 2015, p. 10). As soon as the tasks are practiced, they become an automatic process and demand an ever-decreasing cognitive ability.

In contrast with behaviorism, cognitivism sheds light on the cognitive processes of human thinking, indicating how an individual processes external stimuli and not only how the individual responds to them (Zhou & Brown, 2015). *Perception, representation of knowledge, human memory*, and *individual differences in cognition* are some of the central issues that concern cognitive psychologists. Understanding human perception predominantly revolves around the concept of information processing, which describes how information flows from the environment and is then processed before perception and object recognition are achieved. External stimuli, which are present in the environment that an individual perceives through the senses (input), undergo internal processing and then elicit a response exhibited through the individual's acting on the environment (output). As a vast quantity of information is constantly presented and received by the senses, the individual initiates the process of *filtering* (Anderson, 2015; Broadbent, 1958), whereby only the relevant information is kept and the rest information is filtered out. Sensory information is kept in the sensory register for a limited time. Here is where perception takes place, which is the act of attributing meaning to a stimulus input. Then, information is transferred to short-term or working memory (Schunk, 2012). Which information is selected is dependent quantitatively upon the performance capacity of the sensory organs and qualitatively upon the *Gestalt principles of organization* and *pattern recognition processes* (Schmidt, 2004). The Gestalt principles of organization explain how the visual world is organized into objects. As the information about visual scenes is processed by the neurons and delivered to the higher centers in the brain, visual scenes are classified based on their structure into particular object categories. Once the information from incoming stimuli is perceived, it needs to be identified and recognized as an object. Through visual pattern recognition, the individual can acknowledge forms and objects. A necessary prerequisite for these cognitive processes constitutes the *focus of attention*, whereby the individuals focus their attention only on pertinent information, on a part of their visual field (Anderson, 2015), based on their previous knowledge. Hence, "perception involves matching an input to known information" (Schunk, 2012, p. 165), meaning that perception can be regarded as a product of learning processes, as it can be influenced by already known information (Schmidt, 2004).

As denoted above, the sensory register keeps the sensory information only for a fraction of a second, and then it transfers it to *short-term memory*. As short-term memory is working memory, it is temporary and limited in capacity and duration. When new information is introduced and assimilated into working memory, it undergoes encoding, allowing it to merge with already known information retrieved from *long-term memory*, where both prior and new knowledge are permanently stored. According to this *dual memory model*, the stored information in memory forms knowledge, creating a reciprocal relationship with a person's learning and thinking processes. While knowledge influences learning and thinking, they, in turn, contribute to modifying knowledge (Schmidt, 2004). When a new premise is stored in long-term memory, *declarative knowledge* is gained. Declarative knowledge involves facts, definitions, and events. When verbal codes and images are stored in long-term memory, then *procedural knowledge* is enacted, which consists of processes, strategies, and skills (Schunk, 2012). Declarative knowledge essentially refers to the knowledge of various facts, while procedural knowledge refers to the knowledge of how to perform various tasks (Anderson, 2015). Both forms are interrelated, as procedural knowledge partly relies on existing declarative knowledge and facilitates the creation of novel declarative knowledge (Schmidt, 2004).

As cognitivists shed light on the cognitive processes of human thinking and learning, guidelines for information presentation in multimedia learning environments have been developed, which were based on two influential cognitive theories. According to the early works of Paivio on the *dual-coding theory* (1971, 1986), knowledge is stored in long-term memory in two independent but interrelated forms, the visual and the verbal. "Concrete objects (e.g., dog, tree, book) tend to be stored as images, whereas abstract concepts (e.g., love, truth, honesty) and linguistic structures (e.g., grammars) are stored in verbal codes" (Schunk,

2012, p. 185). Knowledge has the capacity to be stored in both visual and verbal formats. Therefore, an individual may have a pictorial representation in combination with a label of an object, being able to also describe it verbally. According to the dual-coding theory, individuals tend to have a preferred storage mode, either visual or verbal, which is more easily activated for a specific piece of knowledge. The knowledge that is encoded in both visual and verbal forms might be recalled more effectively, leading to significant educational implications. "When verbal and visual (e.g., narration and animation) information are combined during instruction, students benefit from dual coding" (Schunk, 2012, p. 327), as they are facilitated to form connections between verbal and pictorial information.

Following the insights of Paivio's theory (1986), Mayer (2001) developed the *cognitive theory of multimedia learning.* Based on the fundamental proposition that "people can learn more deeply from words and pictures than from words alone" (Mayer & Fiorella, 2022, p. 3), he proposed how multimedia learning environments should be designed in order to enhance learning. Multimedia learning takes place when individuals construct mental representations from words and pictures. Words incorporate material that is presented in verbal form, such as printed or spoken text, while pictures involve material that is presented in pictorial form, such as graphs, illustrations, and diagrams (Mayer & Fiorella, 2022). The cognitive theory of multimedia learning was based on the multimedia principle, a finding stemmed from 13 empirical studies according to which learners perform much better with the combination of words and pictures than from words alone on tests of problem-solving transfer, involving tasks that measure learners' understanding of the presented material (Mayer & Fiorella, 2022). This significant finding had implications for the instructional design of multimedia learning settings. To achieve effective learning when designing multimedia instructional messages, it is essential to consider how the human mind processes information. As such, Mayer's theory was developed based on three fundamental assumptions about human cognitive capabilities: the existence of *dual channels, limited capacity*, and *active processing.*

According to the cognitive theory of multimedia learning, humans have two information processing channels—one for auditorily/verbally represented material and one for visually/spatially represented material (Mayer & Fiorella, 2022). To conceptualize the distinction between the two channels, two approaches of cognitive processing need to be considered: the *representation modes* and the *sensory modalities.* The first approach refers to the format of the presented stimuli. Similar to Paivio (1986, 2006), who made a distinction between verbal and non-verbal systems, external stimuli can be either verbal, such as printed or spoken words, or non-verbal, such as illustrations, videos, or animations. They are processed in two different information systems, the verbal and the visual channel, respectively. In this sense, the representation modes refer to two different models that are constructed in working memory, the verbally-based and the pictorially-based model. The sensory-modality approach examines whether learners first engage with presented materials through auditory means, such as spoken words or background sounds, or through visual means, such as pictures, video, animation, or printed words. According to this approach, one channel—the verbal one—processes auditorily represented material, aligning closely with Baddeley's theory of working memory (1990; Baddeley et al., 2015), while the other—the visual one—handles visually represented content. While information initially enters the human information system through one specific channel (either auditory or visual), learners may have the capacity to transform the information for processing through the alternative channel (Mayer & Fiorella, 2022).

The second assumption of Mayer's theory, which is in accordance with Baddeley's (1990; Baddeley et al., 2015) *theory of working memory* and Sweller's (Sweller et al., 2011) *cognitive load theory*, posits that humans have limited capacity regarding the quantity of information they can simultaneously process within each channel. Upon the presentation of an illustration or animation, the learner can retain only a limited number of images in the visual channel of working memory at any given moment. This retention typically represents segments of the presented material rather than an exact representation of the entire content. The third assumption renders individuals as active processors of multimedia presentations, engaged in forming a cohesive mental representation of their experiences. In active learning, individuals engage in three cognitive processes: (a) *selecting*: focusing on pertinent incoming information, the appropriate words and images in the presented material, and then transferring this information to working memory, (b) *organizing*: mentally structuring incoming information into a cohesive cognitive framework in working memory, and (c) *integrating*: linking cognitive structures with one another by assimilating incoming information with relevant existing knowledge activated from long-term memory.

These three cognitive processes that represent the *human information processing system* are displayed in Fig. 2.4. The diagram depicts the three memory stores -sensory memory, working memory, and long-term memory- represented by boxes. Arrows indicate the cognitive processes of selecting, organizing, and integrating information. The top row signifies the verbal channel, while the bottom row represents the visual channel. Multimedia presentation consists of external stimuli in the form of words and pictures, which enter sensory memory through the ears and eyes, allowing brief retention as auditory or visual images.

Working memory, positioned centrally, temporarily holds and processes knowledge in active consciousness. It operates based on the auditory and visual sensory modalities for raw material intake -sounds and images- depicted on the left side of working memory, and on the verbal and pictorial representation models for knowledge construction, shown on the right side of working memory. Long-term memory acts as a repository of knowledge, with an arrow indicating the transfer of information to working memory for conscious processing, occurring when an individual engages in active thinking about the presented material.

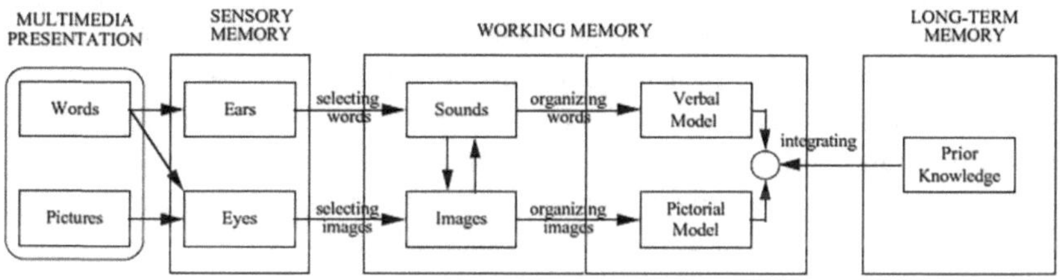

Fig. 2.4 Human Information Processing System According to the Cognitive Theory of Multimedia Learning. (*Note.* From "*The Cambridge handbook of multimedia learning* (3rd ed.)," by Mayer, R. E., & Fiorella, L., 2022, Cambridge University Press (https://doi.org/10.1017/9781108894333). This publication is in copyright. Subject to statutory exception and to the provisions of relevant collective licensing agreements, no reproduction of any part may take place without the written permission of Cambridge University Press. Copyright 2022 by Cambridge University Press. Reproduced with permission of Cambridge University Press through PLSclear)

Meaningful learning occurs when individuals actively engage in these cognitive processes. These processes are not strictly sequential and allow learners to transition between them in diverse ways. Effective multimedia learning requires the ability to orchestrate and monitor these processes actively, aiming to construct cohesive and meaningful mental representations. As such, active learning involves creating mental models or organizing knowledge to capture the key elements of the presented material and their interconnections. Consequently, the design of multimedia can be perceived as an endeavor to aid learners in their efforts to construct mental models (Mayer & Fiorella, 2022).

These fundamental cognitive approaches have significantly shaped instructional design by emphasizing principles for effective learning. Cognitivists' detailed work on information perception, processing, and storing has indicated how information should be presented for optimal learner processing, allowing didactical requirements to be derived for the development of effective AI-based learning environments. Learners, viewed as active seekers and processors of information (Schunk, 2012), require AI support to engage actively in the cognitive processes of selecting, organizing, and integrating information and to develop effective learning strategies that enhance their procedural knowledge. Recognizing cognitive load constraints is critical, requiring AI systems to adjust task complexity and pacing to avoid overwhelming learners. Leveraging the principles of dual coding and multimedia learning, AI systems need to incorporate both verbal and visual elements to enhance learning outcomes and cater to individual preferences. Furthermore, personalization is crucial, as cognitive capacities and prior knowledge, which influence knowledge construction, vary among learners. AI systems can support the creation of mental representations by offering adaptive feedback and monitoring learner interactions in real time, helping them integrate new information with existing knowledge. Ultimately, effective AI integration into multimedia learning design, guided by cognitivist principles, enables the continuous refinement of instructional materials, optimizing the learning experience and enhancing learning outcomes through personalization and dynamic adaptation.

In light of cognitivist principles, the application of cognitivism within AI systems becomes apparent when considering the similarity between computational processing and human information processing. AI technologies, designed to imitate human activities, perform cognitive functions analogous to those of humans. These systems receive and analyze information, determine how to store it in memory, and retrieve it when necessary (Schunk, 2012; Zhou & Brown, 2015). The foundational input-output model, which underpins cognitive approaches and explains learning processes, is similarly applied in AI-based learning. In essence, it was the proponents of cognitivism who first identified computers as tools for learning (Schmidt, 2004). Especially the application of ITSs, which resemble human tutors and work as instructional tools, serve to support learners in skill acquisition, following the principles of componential analysis. While learners engage in learning and problem-solving, ITSs support learners to incrementally acquire skills by interacting with them, monitoring individual skill components, and providing feedback to facilitate rapid mastery of complex skills. Given that learners' performance is shaped more by the amount of previously learned information and repeated practice rather than their native ability (Anderson, 2015), with tasks becoming automatic and requiring less cognitive effort, adaptive learning systems grounded in cognitivism can effectively customize learning experiences. By adapting to learners' prior knowledge, offering targeted practice, and reducing cognitive load, knowledge acquisition can be optimized.

The field of AIEd was substantially further influenced by the *social cognitive theory* of Bandura (1986, 1997, 2001). In the framework of social cognitive theory, human behavior is seen as a function of the triadic reciprocality model (Bandura, 1986), according to which there are reciprocal interactions among three factors: *behaviors*, *environmental variables*, and *personal factors*. There is a constant interplay among these interacting determinants, and all influence each other. However, at any particular moment, one factor might be more prevalent. This reciprocal model can be demonstrated in terms of the influential notion of perceived *self-efficacy* (Bandura, 1982, 1986, 1997), which refers to individuals' capacity to organize and execute the actions necessary to learn or perform behaviors at specified levels. Self-efficacy, as a personal factor, interacts with behavior, since self-efficacy beliefs have been found to influence various achievement behaviors, such as choice of tasks, persistence, effort expenditure, and skill acquisition (Schunk, 1991, 2001; Schunk & Parajes, 2002). The reciprocal nature of this interaction is prevalent when considering that students' actions can alter their own self-efficacy. As students observe their progress toward learning goals, their belief in their capability to perform well is enhanced, creating a continuous cycle of influence between behavior and self-efficacy. Further, the interplay between self-efficacy and environmental factors can be illustrated in research on students with learning disabilities (Schunk, 2012). Many students with learning disabilities tend to have a low sense of self-efficacy regarding their learning performance (Licht & Kistner, 1986). The social environment may react to them based on perceived attributes associated with learning disabilities, affecting their expectations. Teachers have been found to consider students with learning disabilities as less capable, even in subjects where they perform adequately (Bryan & Bryan, 1983), explaining the impact of personal beliefs on the environment. As a result, teachers' feedback, considered an environmental factor, can have an influence on students' self-efficacy, with positive reinforcement contributing to increased confidence in achieving success. Lastly, the reciprocal influence between environmental factors and behaviors can be illustrated in a common teaching situation. When the teacher imparts information and directs students to focus on the board, an environmental factor influences students' behavior as students gaze at the board without deliberate thought. Conversely, students' actions can impact the instructional setting. For instance, if students provide incorrect answers to teacher questions, it may prompt the teacher to revisit and reteach certain points (Schunk, 2012).

Contrary to Skinner's (1953) stance, which posits that learning is solely driven by the consequences of actions, social cognitive theory acknowledges that people's cognitions, such as thoughts, beliefs, and expectations, rather than consequences alone, affect the learning process. How individuals perceive and interpret the outcomes of their actions influences their future behaviors and learning outcomes. Understanding learning through the lens of social cognitive theory requires an examination of the social environments in which individuals act as well as the outcomes that arise from their behavior. Within the paradigm of social cognitive theory, learning is distinguished into *enactive* and *vicarious*. Enactive learning occurs through actual doing and stems from the consequences of one's actions. Consequences provide individuals with information about the correctness or suitability of their actions. Actions that yield positive outcomes are maintained, while those resulting in failures are adjusted or discarded. Success or rewards indicate effective performance, while failure or punishment signals the need for correction. The theory suggests that people are motivated to learn behaviors with desirable outcomes and avoid those with negative consequences. Vicarious learning involves observing or listening to models perform, without engaging in overt actions. Models can be either live models in person, symbolic representations, electronic media, or printed materials. When complex skills need to be acquired, a combination of observation and performance is necessary. Students observe models, such as their teachers, elaborating and illustrating skills, and then implement the learned behaviors in practice. Thus, in social cognitive theory, learning occurs primarily through performance but is significantly influenced by observation. Performing what we learn depends upon several factors such as motivation, interest, incentives, perceived need, physical condition, social pressures, and the nature of other competing activities. Performance is more influenced by reinforcement, or the expectation of it, rather than the actual process of learning (Schunk, 2012).

Instrumental for the learning process is the role of *self-regulated learning* in social cognitive theory. In the context of perceived self-efficacy, which significantly influences an individual's sense of agency, self-regulation is defined as a process in which individuals initiate and maintain behaviors, cognitions, and affects, systematically directed toward achieving their goals (Zimmerman & Schunk, 2001). Through self-regulation, individuals gain an enhanced sense of personal agency. Through the lens of social cognitive theory, the ability to self-regulate is enacted in learning settings when learners have choices to make (Schunk, 2012). The latter include choices to participate, choices of methods, outcomes, and social and physical settings. The choice to participate in tasks is influenced by learners' goals, values, and self-efficacy. During the execution of a task, learners have the choice to implement different learning strategies or to enact relaxation techniques in case they become anxious. While engaged in the task, learners have the choice of outcomes. They can assess their performance and determine if their efforts are progressing toward achieving the desired outcomes.

Lastly, learners have the option to select the social and physical environments in which they engage with the task. That means that they can arrange their surroundings to be supportive of learning and seek assistance when required. The learners' choices and the self-regulatory processes enacted may vary depending on the learning situations, such as the extent to which they are allowed to self-direct their learning. During the learning process, individuals not only regulate their actions to stay focused on achieving goals. They also self-regulate their thoughts and emotions, ensuring they maintain self-efficacy, value the learning experience, expect positive outcomes, evaluate goal progress, assess the effectiveness of their strategies, and adjust them as needed. Finally, they strive to maintain a positive emotional climate. In light of the classical social cognitive theory of self-regulation, three main self-regulatory processes are enacted in learning situations: *self-observation*, *self-judgment*, and *self-reaction*. Students approach learning activities with diverse goals, such as gaining knowledge and skills or completing assignments. On the basis of these goals, they continuously observe, judge, and react to their perceived progress toward these goals. This cyclical process underscores the reciprocal interactions among personal, behavioral, and social/environmental factors (Schunk, 2012).

These fundamental principles of social cognitive theory have influenced instructional design, offering key guidelines for developing effective AI-based learning environments. The focus on enhancing self-efficacy beliefs has led to striving for self-directed learning opportunities, whereby learners independently practice skills to build confidence in their abilities. Self-regulation is essential in this process, as learners need to set goals, implement learning strategies, and evaluate their progress. However, according to social cognitive theory, courses of action are not solely determined by one's efficacy judgments, namely, how well they think they will perform in given situations. Rather, the courses of one's actions are also heavily seen in the context of social interdependencies. They depend on the social reactions of one's environment. In this context, learning is understood as a result of the learner's transactions with the environment, whereby performance is determined largely by interpersonal judgments of efficacy. Therefore, social cognitive approaches emphasized the importance of social learning and underlined the value of group-based learning experiences. Through modeling, individuals modify their behaviors, cognitions, and emotions. To this end, contemporary adaptive learning environments can be designed to encourage peer learning, offering opportunities for ongoing exchange and communication among learners. In addition to creating such environmental conditions, effective instructional strategies and appropriate learning support are also crucial for enhancing learners' experiences in AI-driven settings. For instance, worked examples that guide learners step-by-step through problem solutions, along with rewards for positive behavior, can enhance learners' self-efficacy beliefs. Furthermore, combining textual explanations with graphical elements can foster learners' interaction with the AI system. Mentoring, integrated within AI learning environments, is also valuable, as it provides learners with role models they can observe and imitate, fostering increased self-efficacy and motivation. In summary, incorporating modeling into adaptive learning environments is highly beneficial. The key is to initiate instruction with social influences, such as role models, and progressively transition towards self-influences as learners internalize skills and strategies (Schunk, 2012).

With respect to the view of learners as collaborators with AI systems, another educational theory that had significant influence on AIEd is the *social constructivist view of learning* (Vygotsky, 1978). While cognitivism views the independent acquisition of knowledge as a process of independent discovery and comprehension of the real world within the individual's social environment, the constructivist approach is based on the fundamental notion of individual construction of the contents of knowledge (Schmidt, 2004). Constructivism is considered more of "an *epistemology,* or philosophical explanation about the nature of learning" (Schunk, 2012, p. 230) rather than a theory. It emphasizes the knowledge construction by the individuals and asserts a relative truth of knowledge. Each individual's constructions of knowledge are true for them, but not necessarily for others. Constructivist approaches pinpoint learning in terms of human factors and do not align with behaviorist approaches, which focus solely on environmental influences. This transition in the focus of learning theory was provoked by the emergence of cognitive psychology and its emphasis on learners' information processing as a primary factor influencing learning. Cognitivism challenged behaviorism's assertion that external stimuli, responses, and consequences were sufficient to elucidate learning. Constructivists' accounts went a step further than cognitivist approaches. Situating learning within the mind does not suffice for constructivists, but rather they emphasize the context in which learning takes place. This assumption is closely related to the social cognitive theory of Bandura (1986, 1997), according to which individuals, behaviors, and environments engage in reciprocal interactions.

The contribution of constructivism lies in the personal and subjective construction of knowledge and the consideration of the context of learning. In the framework of constructivism, it is assumed that individuals autonomously construct knowledge and are actively involved in learning situations (Geary, 1995; Schunk, 2012). Cognitions are predominantly constructed by individuals based on their experiences within various situations, indicating that thinking occurs within these contexts (Bredo, 1997). Essentially, constructivism is grounded in the premise that the acquisition of skills and knowledge is formed based on the interplay between individuals and situations (Cobb & Bowers, 1999). This is attributed to *situated cognition* (or *situated learning*), according to which cognitive processes, taking into account thinking and learning, are situated in physical and social contexts and are not confined exclusively to an individual's mind (Anderson et al., 1996; Cobb & Bowers, 1999; Greeno, 1998; Schunk, 2012). Thus, knowledge generation is attributed to beliefs and experiences within various situations, which are different among individuals (Cobb & Bowers, 1999; Schunk, 2012). The consideration of the interaction between individuals and the environment distinguished constructivism from cognitivism. Unlike constructivism, cognitivism diminishes the significance of situational context once external stimuli are received and processed in the mental structures.

These social constructivist perspectives have profound implications for instructional design and the development of learner-centered AI-based environments. Effective learning experiences should promote critical thinking, prompting learners to challenge their preconceptions and reassess existing beliefs. To achieve a deep understanding of learning materials, learners need to personally uncover underlying principles and study content from multiple perspectives (Schunk, 2012). However, enabling learners to actively engage with content is not sufficient. Collaborating with peers is also crucial for enhancing their ability to construct knowledge. Encouraging participation in peer groups fosters skill development through exposure to diverse perspectives and enriched social interactions. Especially in adaptive learning environments, features that facilitate meaningful human-AI interactions, collaborative peer learning, and opportunities for practice in diverse settings need to be incorporated. Such features not only support context-dependent learning but also promote the effective transfer of learning by fostering a deeper integration of knowledge and enabling learners to apply their understanding in diverse and practical situations.

There are three different constructivist views regarding knowledge development. *Exogenous constructivism* suggests that gaining knowledge involves reconstructing structures present in the external world. This perspective emphasizes the substantial impact of the environment on knowledge formation, including influences from experiences, teaching, and exposure to models. Proponents of this view assert that mental structures mirror reality and resemble contemporary information processing theories (Schunk, 2012). On the contrary, radical constructivists contend that the individual's mental world is the only reality. For *endogenous constructivism,* knowledge is not a mere reflection of the external world acquired through experiences, teaching, or social interactions. Instead, knowledge evolves through the cognitive process of abstraction, following a generally foreseeable sequence. The *theory of cognitive development* by Piaget (1970) aligns with this view, as indicated below. In the middle of the two contradictory views lies *dialectical constructivism,* which pinpoints knowledge construction in the interplay between individuals and their environments. Knowledge construction is not strictly tied to the external world, nor is it solely the product of mental processes. Knowledge rather mirrors the consequences of mental conflicts stemming from interactions with the environment. This viewpoint is closely associated with Bandura's (1986) social cognitive theory as well as the emphasis on the influence of the social environment in Vygotsky's (1978) social constructivism approach (Schunk, 2012), as explained below.

Piaget's theory of cognitive development (1970), which emerged in the field of human development, had a significant influence on constructivist approaches. Piaget identified four phases in children's cognitive development that take place in a fixed sequence: the *sensorimotor stage* (birth to 2 years old), where infants interact with their surroundings in spontaneous ways, grounding their understanding in present actions; the *preoperational stage* (2 to 7 years old), marked by the ability to envision the future and reflect on the past, though remaining mainly focused on perceptual experiences; the *concrete operational stage* (7 to 11 years old), characterized by substantial cognitive advancement and the development of abstract thinking; and the *formal operational stage* (11 years to adulthood), which extends to the capacity to contemplate hypothetical scenarios and multiple dimensions, with emerging idealistic thoughts during adolescence. Even though the main constructivist assumption of Piaget's theory lies in the position that children apply their own concepts to the world in order to comprehend it (Byrnes, 1996), the social environment plays an instrumental role in cognitive development (Schunk, 2012). Cognitive development depends on four factors: *biological maturation, experience with the physical environment, experience with the social environment,* and *equilibration.* Among these, the process of equilibration plays a central role. During this process, individuals urge to achieve an optimal balance or adaptation between cognitive structures and the environment (Duncan, 1995). During equilibration, individuals engage in the processes of *assimilation* and *accommodation.* Assimilation involves adjusting external reality to match pre-existing cognitive structures through interpretation and framing, thereby altering the perception of reality. Accommodation entails modifying internal cognitive structures to align with external reality, occurring when individuals adapt their ideas to better comprehend and make sense of the actual world. Learning occurs when disequilibrium arises or "when children experience cognitive conflict and engage in assimilation or accommodation to construct or alter internal structures"

(Schunk, 2012, p. 238). It is essential, though, that the conflict is not excessively intense, as it may fail to stimulate the process of equilibration, and that it occurs when the children are in the transitioning process of one developmental stage to the other.

The assumptions of Piaget's theory of cognitive development offer three key implications for instructional design (Schunk, 2012) that can be effectively integrated into contemporary AI-based learning environments. First, instructional tools should be designed to recognize and adapt to learners' current developmental stages, allowing for tailored instruction that meets their cognitive readiness. Learners in transitional stages can potentially benefit more from instruction at a slightly higher level, as the cognitive conflict won't be overly overwhelming for them. Second, learners can benefit from stimulating environments that encourage hands-on activities and active exploration, fostering the active construction of knowledge. A third implication stems from Piaget's suggestion to promote disequilibrium. To foster learning, it is beneficial to create environments that induce disequilibrium by providing learning materials challenging enough to prevent easy assimilation yet manageable enough to encourage successful accommodation. Furthermore, while solving problems, learners should not be hindered from giving incorrect answers, as such situations can promote disequilibrium, demanding instructional feedback, and thus leading to deeper understanding.

Another constructivist approach that influences applications of AIEd is Vygotsky's (1978, 1987) *sociocultural theory*. During his time, the predominant psychological theories were the behavioral theories and especially Pavlov's experiments that overlooked cognitive processes or the social context in which learning occurs. Challenging the essential perspectives of these theories, Vygotsky offered an alternative viewpoint by shedding light on the significant role of the social environment in shaping human cognition. Vygotsky argued that, unlike animals, which merely respond to their surroundings, humans possess the ability to modify their environments according to their needs, highlighting how humans learn through interactions within their social context (Schunk, 2012). Vygotsky's sociocultural theory posits that human development is influenced by the interaction of *interpersonal (social), cultural-historical,* and *individual factors* (Tudge & Scrimsher, 2003). Interpersonal interactions, such as engaging with others in the environment through activities like apprenticeships, trigger developmental processes and promote cognitive growth. As learners engage in these interactions, they transform their experiences by leveraging their existing knowledge and personal attributes, thereby reorganizing their mental structures. The theory's emphasis on the cultural-historical perspective underscores that learning and development are inherently linked to the context in which they take place. How learners interact with their surroundings, including people, objects, and institutions, plays a pivotal role in shaping their thought processes. The meaning of concepts evolves as they become linked with the external world (Gredler, 2009). Finally, the influence of individual factors on development refers to the unique inherited characteristics of each person, which contribute to creating distinct learning pathways.

Among the three key factors influencing human development, social interactions were regarded by Vygotsky as instrumental in transforming learning experiences. The core idea of his theory is that the influence of the social environment on cognition is mediated through the environment's "tools". These include cultural objects like cars and machines, as well as language and social institutions such as schools and churches. Social interactions play a pivotal role in coordinating the interpersonal, cultural-historical, and individual factors that affect development. The process of cognitive change unfolds as individuals employ cultural tools in their social interactions, leading to the internalization and mental transformation of these experiences (Bruning et al., 2004; Schunk, 2012). Vygotsky emphasized that social learning contributes to knowledge construction, underlining the significance of learners' cultures and the process of cultural transmission of the environment's "tools" in learning and development.

A key concept in Vygotsky's theory is the *zone of proximal development* (ZPD). ZPD has been defined as "the distance between the actual developmental level as determined by independent problem-solving and the level of potential development as determined through problem-solving under adult guidance or in collaboration with more capable peers" (Vygotsky, 1978, p. 86). It represents the potential learning capacity of a student under appropriate instructional conditions (Puntambekar & Hübscher, 2005) and sheds light on the developmental processes that have the potential to form, mature, and develop. It highlights the necessity of social interactions and the exchange with more skilled individuals, such as between a teacher and a learner or a master and an apprentice, to foster cognitive development. For cognitive change to happen, collaboration between the teacher and the learner is necessary by utilizing cultural "tools". This culturally mediated interaction leads to cognitive transformation when internalized by the learner (Bruning et al., 2004). Even though the concept of ZPD was incorrectly seen as synonymous with *scaffolding* (Tudge & Scrimsher, 2003), with which there are indeed some similarities, the importance of ZPD lies in the proposition that "learners bring their own understandings to social interactions and construct meanings by integrating those understandings with their experiences in the context" (Schunk, 2012, p. 244). Therefore, the role of the cultural-historical setting is instrumental, as the outcome of a learning situation can be significantly influenced by the experiences that an individual brings to this context, showing that engaging in the cultural world leads to a transformation in mental functioning.

Vygotsky's ideas are implemented in various educational applications (Schunk, 2012) and lay the ground for a promising integration in AI-based learning environments. The emphasis of Vygotsky's ideas on interpersonal interactions that enable and foster learning processes is reflected in the concepts of scaffolding and apprenticeships. Instructional scaffolding, which was initiated by Wood et al. (1976), involves managing task elements beyond learners' current capabilities, allowing them to concentrate on and master aspects of the task within their immediate grasp. This concept, which as denoted above is related to ZPD, reflects Vygotsky's urge to assist learners in gaining cognitive mediators from the social environment to enhance their learning. Closely related is the learning support received in the framework of apprenticeships. Collaborating with experts allows less skilled learners to cultivate a shared understanding of crucial processes and incorporate this knowledge into their existing understanding. In the context of AI-based learning environments, the AI system can serve as the more knowledgeable peer that offers tailored guidance according to learners' individual preferences and needs, enabling them to effectively construct knowledge and develop skills. Apart from these concepts, peer collaboration can fulfill a significant instructional role, enabling shared social interactions between learners. Adaptive learning environments can facilitate such collaboration by providing platforms for learners to interact, exchange ideas, and support each other, either through forums, collaborative activities, or interactions with AI tools. Lastly, the sociocultural theory pinpoints the importance of cultural-historical as well as individual characteristics of the learners that need to be considered in contemporary learning environments. In adaptive learning environments, support can be differentiated based on each learner's unique cultural background and individual characteristics, thereby creating a more personalized and contextually relevant learning experience.

In conclusion, constructivist perspectives underscore that knowledge cannot be merely transmitted between individuals but must be actively constructed by learners. Constructivist learning environments are therefore designed to facilitate this process by enabling learners to actively engage in the construction and acquisition of new knowledge and skills (Schuh, 2003). Learners' thinking is challenged to construct their own understanding of concepts and skills (Schunk, 2012). The design of contemporary learning environments needs to support the construction of new knowledge, which inherently maintains a certain degree of individuality (Schmidt, 2004). AI-based learning systems are particularly well-suited to incorporate constructivist principles. They can offer a richer and more supportive learning experience, enable learners to actively engage in learning and interact with AI, and allow for tailored and context-specific support. A key aspect of creating a constructivist learning environment is the provision of instructional support and peer-assisted learning. Instructional AI support should be carefully designed to optimize learning within each learner's ZPD, ensuring that the challenges presented by the AI system are appropriate to their current level of understanding. Peer-assisted learning, on the other hand, enables learners to undertake the role of active agents in the learning process, fostering higher levels of achievement within cooperative learning settings, such as through participation in forums or collaborative activities. According to the social constructivist view, learning constitutes a socially mediated process that occurs when learners become active knowledge constructors and engage in interactions with their immediate situation-specific learning environments. Knowledge is not transferred between individuals but is constructed or further developed through interaction (Schmidt, 2004). These interactions play a critical role in influencing learners' individual development (Liu & Matthews, 2005). Adaptive learning systems can build effective interactions with the learners and leverage these insights by collecting data on learners' interactions and activities. This data can be used to provide tailored instructional support and to enhance the efficacy of human-AI interaction. As such, learning can be optimized and become more personalized and learner-centered (Ouyang & Jiao, 2021). Finally, following constructivism, learners are expected to engage in learning activities from multiple perspectives and utilize multiple learning media, such as texts, videos, and computers (Honebein, 1996). This multifaceted approach not only enriches the learning experience but also ensures that it remains flexible and responsive to the diverse needs of individual learners.

However, what this pedagogical paradigm of mutual interaction and collaboration between the learner and the AI system lacks is the constant communication or coordinated interactions between learners and AI. While interacting with the AI system, learners engage in dynamically changing learning processes, which need to be captured by the system. The system receives constantly different input from the learners, necessitating the dynamic adaptation of the student model to accommodate these variations. As stated in previous research, "it is critical for the AI systems to offer real-time data analysis and immediate feedback to [the] learner and for the learner to use those [sic] feedback to enhance the ongoing, emergent learning processes" (Ouyang & Jiao, 2021, p. 3). These issues are addressed in the third pedagogical paradigm, as it is illustrated in the following section.

2.3.3 Human Agency and Complexity Theory

A third paradigm of AIEd has been determined, which is called *AI-empowered* or *learner-as-leader* (Ouyang & Jiao, 2021). This paradigm has its fundamentals in Bandura's (2006) concept of *human agency* as well as the *complexity theory* (Mason, 2008; Morrison, 2008). In the framework of the social cognitive theory (Bandura, 1986), which regards human functioning as the result of the reciprocal interaction among intrapersonal factors, behavioral patterns, and environmental influences, an agentic viewpoint is presented regarding human development, adaptation, and change (Bandura, 2001). Humans, through cognitive self-regulation, act as agents by intentionally influencing their course of life. Four fundamental characteristics define human agency. One key characteristic is *intentionality*, whereby individuals formulate intentions by developing action plans and methods for achieving them. The second element of human agency is *forethought*. Individuals establish goals for themselves and predict the potential outcomes of future actions, which serve to direct and inspire their efforts. The third characteristic of agency is *self-reactiveness*. Agents act as self-regulators, constructing suitable courses of action and motivating themselves while also regulating the execution of those actions. The fourth aspect of agency is *self-reflectiveness*. Individuals engage in self-examination of their own functioning. Using functional self-awareness, individuals reflect on their efficacy, the validity of their thoughts and actions, and the significance of their pursuits. Based on this metacognitive ability, they then make any required corrective adjustments (Bandura, 2006). Taking into account that human functioning occurs as a result of the mutual interactions between intrapersonal, behavioral, and environmental determinants (Bandura, 1986), the majority of human actions are seen as socially-situated (Bandura, 2006). In accordance with this theory, AI-based learning environments serve as the context in which human agency can flourish, enabling learners to actively shape their learning trajectories.

Paradigm three not only positions learners as leaders but also considers AI as a tool capable of enhancing human intelligence (Law, 2019), a view shaped by the principles of complexity theory (Mason, 2008; Morrison, 2008). Complexity theory describes the multivariate co-existence and dynamic interactions among multiple entities or agents that lead to the emergence of new phenomena and behaviors. At the core of this theory lie the notions of *continuity, change, emergence,* and *interconnectedness* that can be found in dynamic systems. Continuity and change can be understood in terms of the emergent phenomena, because "given a significant degree of complexity in a particular environment, or critical mass, new properties and behaviours emerge that are not contained in the essence of the constituent elements, nor can be predicted from a knowledge of initial conditions" (Mason, 2008, p. 32). New phenomena, properties, and behaviors emerge, and new patterns develop while old ones change, as a result of the dynamic interactions and adaptive orientation within a system. Although the exponential relationships and the interconnectedness among the multiple elements or agents are essential, the complexity theory sheds light on the significance of the individual, marginal, and seemingly irrelevant events. Even minor actions or agents within a system can significantly influence its overall dynamics, reinforcing the importance of considering all interactions in dynamic adaptive systems.

Education is considered a complex adaptive system, whereby different bodies such as students, teachers, information, and technology are connected and interact dynamically, contributing to learners' augmented intelligence. Learning is seen as a dynamic process characterized by the emergence and co-evolution of the individual, the social group, and the broader society (Morrison, 2008). Individuals and their environments interact dynamically in learning settings, influencing each other in an emergent and agent-based manner. Knowledge is continually being constructed and reconstructed through the process of assimilating and accommodating new information into existing knowledge frameworks. Key requirements of cognition are interaction, distributed control, diversity, and redundancy (Davis & Sumara, 2005). Cognition involves more than just acquiring new information; it encompasses motivation, personality, learning styles, dispositions, preferences, and the overall integration of the individual. Learning happens when both the instructors and the learners engage in mutual interactions, empowering learners to link new knowledge with their existing knowledge structures. Instructors are seen as co-learners and co-constructers of meaning, and learners ought to be ready to demonstrate autonomy, responsibility, ownership, self-direction, and reflection. Learning is enhanced by substantial and constructive communication between learners and instructors, changing both in a process of co-evolution (Morrison, 2008). However, the interactions of instructors with the learners are not sufficient. Further elements of knowledge or other educational entities that co-exist, such as information and technological systems, dynamically interact, affect, and shape each other, leading to a process of co-evolution of all parts.

Adaptive learning systems, as complex systems, need to achieve a synergetic collaboration between the AI system and human intelligence. In dynamically changing learning environments, uncertain and unexpected situations may come up in real time due to the complexity of learners' learning processes. In such situations, AI systems need to be able to face unforeseen events and act in dynamic situations. For AI systems to serve as autonomous agents, being able to make their own decisions, *human-AI interaction* is not sufficient, but rather, *human-machine cooperation* needs to be achieved (Hoc, 2000). Systems based on human-computer interaction are rather static, and only the user is in the position to control the computer. However, in contemporary complex and dynamic systems, control is allocated to both humans and machines, with the latter working as autonomous agents able to act autonomously in emerging learning situations and augment human intelligence (Law, 2019).

AI systems need to be designed based on a human-centered perspective. They need to be developed based on the prerequisite that "they are part of a larger system consisting of human stakeholders, such as users, operators, clients, and other people in close proximity" (Riedl, 2019, p. 2). AI systems not only need to be able to understand humans from a sociocultural perspective but also to facilitate humans to comprehend them. Intelligent systems must possess a commonsense knowledge of human actions and the underlying reasons behind them. A sophisticated intelligent system that considers sociocultural beliefs and norms can clarify ambiguous human behavior and make informed predictions about how to anticipate and address human requirements. This demands continuous adjustment of AI algorithms to align with human conditions and contexts, ensuring that machine intelligence is utilized to enhance human welfare (Yang et al., 2021). Such AI systems are less error-prone, fair, and safer. At the same time, AI systems need to generate explanations comprehensible to non-expert end-users, thereby building trust and familiarity between the user and the system as well as ensuring a high degree of accountability, transparency, and fairness (Riedl, 2019; Yang et al., 2021).

Considering the dynamic nature of learning environments, AI systems can function as personalized tools, providing real-time support to learners. *Precision education* and *smart learning analytics* can contribute to the transformation of one-size-fits-all learning environments to more individualized learning approaches. Precision education involves utilizing ML and AI-driven learning analytics to enhance the quality of teaching and the effectiveness of learning by dynamically diagnosing learning conditions and delivering timely interventions (Yang et al., 2021). Students' learning behaviors, learning environments, and learning strategies are analyzed following the four-step process of precision medicine. *Diagnosis*, *prediction*, *treatment*, and *prevention* are utilized to identify and implement tailored solutions (Yang, 2021). Through the analysis of individuals' learning status and behaviors, AI systems can offer tailored preventive and intervention measures customized to each learner. Acting as intelligent tutors, these systems integrate the expertise and intelligence of experienced teachers into their decision-making process (Hart, 2016). As such, they are able to identify students who may be at risk and provide timely interventions to support their academic progress (Yang et al., 2021). The potential for enhanced learning outcomes can be further achieved by smart learning analytics, which utilize big data and AI technologies to identify students who might be facing challenges and promptly provide interventions to assist them (Yang et al., 2021). By examining learning patterns, these systems foster the development of students' skills and knowledge, promoting continuous learning progress. Leveraging human-AI synergetic interaction and cooperation, adaptive learning systems can be designed to provide highly personalized and effective support that enhances learners' educational experiences and outcomes (Hwang, Xie, et al., 2020; Ouyang & Jiao, 2021).

2.4 Adaptive Learning Systems in Education

Adaptive learning systems have been among the most prominent applications of AI in educational settings. Such systems enabled by AI technologies have become increasingly relevant due to their capability to provide tailored learning material and adapt to learners' individual needs (Kabudi et al, 2021). Adaptive learning systems aim to enhance individual learners' learning experience by adapting several elements of learning systems, such as user interfaces, learning materials, or learning trajectories, to suit the unique needs and progress of each learner (Hwang, Xie, et al., 2020). Technologies based on adaptive learning date back to the early 1950s, when Pask (1982) first developed a truly adaptive system called SAKI, standing for self-adaptive keyboard trainer. SAKI, first implemented in 1956, served as an adaptive teaching machine facilitating the acquisition of keyboard skills by dynamically analyzing learners' input through an evolving probabilistic student model. This model used probabilistic methods to predict learners' understanding and skill level, enabling the system to tailor tasks to their individual performance (Holmes et al., 2019). As of that time, in the 1960s and 1970s, *computer-assisted instruction* (CAI) came into focus. The first AI techniques that were integrated into CAI were developed in the framework of the SCHOLAR system. This system could provide individual answers to learners' statements by making inferences from a semantic network, a structured representation of knowledge in which concepts are interconnected by relationships, enabling reasoning and context-dependent responses (Carbonell, 1970). The SCHOLAR system served as the first example of an ITS, which, as denoted in Section 2.2, functions as an adaptive agent able to adapt the learning sequence to each individual learner.

According to the pioneering work of Brusilovsky (1996), adaptive learning systems have evolved within the field of *adaptive hypermedia* in computer science, intending to support individual learning (Brusilovsky, 1998). "Adaptive hypermedia systems, which have seen rapid growth since 1996, build a model of the goals, preferences, and knowledge of the individual user and use this throughout the interaction for adaptation to the needs of that user" (Brusilovsky, 1996, p. 87). These systems are typically grounded in various AI technologies (Brusilovsky, 2001) and are considered adaptive when the following requirements are met: (a) they should function as a hypertext or hypermedia system, including classic hypermedia features, such as contextual links, indexes, local and global maps, as well as guided tours (b) they should incorporate a user model, which entails fundamental information about each user, and (c) they should have the capability to adapt the hypermedia content based on this model, namely by appearing differently to users depending on their individual models.

There is a variety of existing hypermedia systems. *Educational hypermedia systems* have gained the greatest attention and are the focus of this thesis. Educational hypermedia systems have relatively small hyperspaces dedicated to specific courses or sections of learning materials within a given subject. Learners typically aim to grasp the entirety or a significant portion of the material provided. A key factor in educational hypermedia is the user's familiarity with the subject matter being taught. *Adaptive hypermedia techniques* are instrumental in addressing several challenges associated with educational hypermedia. Learners' knowledge levels can vary significantly, and their individual understanding may be evolving rapidly. Consequently, the same content may be challenging for novices yet mundane for advanced learners. Novices often enter educational hyperspaces with limited prior knowledge, encountering mostly unfamiliar material. Further, some learners require navigational assistance to navigate through the hyperspace effectively. Without such guidance, they may become disoriented even within relatively small hyperspaces or resort to inefficient browsing strategies. Adaptive learning systems can take into account such learning differences and provide tailored learning support.

Figure 2.5 depicts how an adaptive learning system works, particularly how adaptation is provided on the basis of the user model. In the field of education, the term learner model is used, referring to user models specifically initiated in the framework of learning environments. The process of adaptation begins with the collection of users' data. Once a user interacts with an adaptive learning system, such as when they undertake a learning activity, their data are automatically collected and processed by the system, which consequently builds the user model. Various characteristics of the individual user are collected, identified, and represented in the system's user model, which is crucial for a user-adaptive system to provide the adaptation effect (Brusilovsky & Millán, 2007). In educational hypermedia, these characteristics are the learner's knowledge of the subject matter represented in hyperspace, the learner's learning goal, knowledge, background, experience, preferences (Brusilovsky, 1996), interests (Brusilovsky & Millán, 2007), as well as the learner's individual traits, such as learning styles (Brusilovsky, 2001). Based on the information obtained about the user, the system then engages in a decision-making process, whereby the appropriate adaptation techniques are selected and implemented by the system while the user engages in the learning process (Popescu, 2008). This ensures that the user receives learning support that is aligned with his/her individual needs and characteristics. For instance, based on the user's competency, the user receives recommendations concerning specific kinds of content. At the same time, specific types of navigation, as well as other facets of the learning experience, are tailored to the user's mental abilities and characteristics (Kinshuk, 2016). Paramythis and Loidl-Reisinger (2004) clearly state what distinguishes adaptive learning environments:

> a learning environment is considered adaptive if it is capable of: monitoring the activities of its users; interpreting these on the basis of domain-specific models; inferring user requirements and preferences out of the interpreted activities, appropriately representing these in associated models; and, finally, acting upon the available knowledge on its users and the subject matter at hand, to dynamically facilitate the learning process. (p. 182)

Adaptive learning is commonly considered a type of technology due to its foundation on AI and reliance on ITSs (Peng et al., 2019). It is the development of the learner model that enables the system to be adaptive, as it represents crucial information about an individual user, necessary for an adaptive system to tailor its behavior to each individual user, thereby achieving the adaptation effect. As Kinshuk (2016) highlights, "the better a learning environment is able to understand the student and their learning goals, the better it will be able to provide adaptivity and personalization" (Kinshuk, 2016, p. 6). An adaptive learning system collects data for the user model from multiple channels, which could involve passively observing user interactions and actively soliciting direct input from the user (Brusilovsky & Millán, 2007). Recommendations are made based on the inferences made by the system, making it possible to provide adaptive support to each individual learner. Various aspects of the presentation of learning material

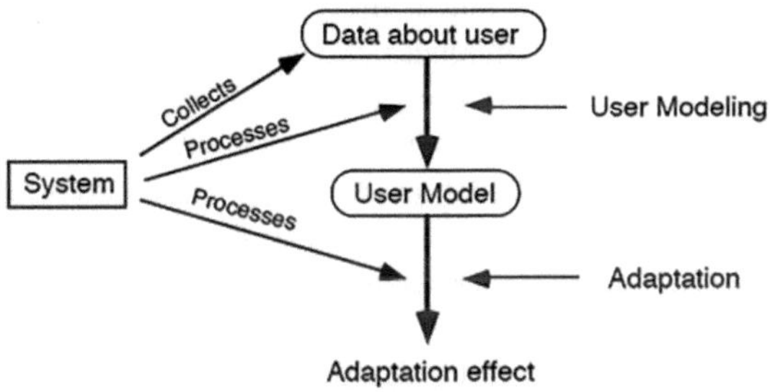

Fig. 2.5 How Adaptive Learning Systems Work. (*Note.* From "Methods and techniques of adaptive hypermedia," by Brusilovsky, P., 1996, *User Modelling and User-Adapted Interaction, Special Issue on Adaptive Hypertext and Hypermedia,* Springer Nature, *6*, p. 88 (https://doi.org/10.1007/BF00143964). Copyright 1996 Springer Nature and SNCSC. Reproduced with permission from SNCSC)

are aligned with the individual characteristics of learners. These functionalities make adaptive learning systems accountable for learners with different needs, goals, and preferences. This is manifested by the ability of the system to adapt the information presented to the current knowledge level of the learner, to provide navigation support, and to guide the user in the learning process (Brusilovsky & Pesin, 1998). Therefore, a modern adaptive learning system is mainly a learning system that is capable of adapting most of its key functional aspects, such as content presentation and navigation support, to the learner's needs and preferences by building a learner's model from interpreting the user's interaction with the system (Brusilovsky & Peylo, 2003; Kobsa, 1995; Magnisalis et al., 2011).

Several *adaptation techniques* have been proposed in previous literature. However, to the author's knowledge, no recent comprehensive review yet exists. Hence, a selective review of well-established adaptation techniques is presented below, which are aligned with the scope of the current thesis.

Following the earliest comprehensive work of Brusilovsky (1996, 2001), different individuals, each with their own goals and levels of knowledge, may be drawn to different pieces of information presented on a hypermedia page and may choose diverse links for navigation. Hypermedia comprise an array of via links interconnected nodes/pages or hyperdocuments, each of them containing local information and links to related pages. Hypermedia systems often incorporate an index and a global map, offering links to every accessible page within the system. In traditional hypermedia, there is not much room for adaptation. Users encounter static content where information is uniformly presented. Each hypermedia page offers predetermined links and information, lacking the flexibility to adapt to diverse user preferences. Adaptation integrated into hypermedia systems revolutionized user experience by adjusting the content of regular pages (*content-level adaptation*) and the links from regular pages, index pages, and maps (*link-level adaptation*). These adaptations are categorized into *adaptive presentation* and *adaptive navigation support*, representing adjustments to content and links, respectively. The taxonomy of adaptive hypermedia technologies, detailed below, is illustrated in Fig. 2.6.

Adaptive presentation refers to the adaptation of the content of a hypermedia node/page that a specific user accesses, aligning it with their current knowledge, goals, and other characteristics of the user. Adaptive presentation is further distinguished into three adaptation technologies. The first is *adaptive multimedia presentation,* according to which a standard page's content may consist not only of text, as seen in traditional hypertext systems, but also of a collection of various multimedia elements. The second adaptation technology, *adaptive text presentation*, encompasses both *canned text adaptation*, including techniques such as stretch text, inserting or removing fragments, altering, sorting, and dimming fragments, and *natural language adaptation*, which has recently seen incredible growth with the development of advanced natural language generation systems, such as the Chat Generative Pre-Trained Transformer (ChatGPT) (Wu et al., 2023). Lastly, *adaptation of modality* offers a range of media options for presenting information to the users, adjusting it to the user's preferences, abilities, learning styles, and work context (Brusilovsky, 2001). In a system featuring adaptive presentation, pages are not static but are dynamically generated or assembled to suit each individual user (Brusilovsky & Peylo, 2003).

Adaptive navigation support, as the second major adaptation technique, assists users in navigating through hyperspace by customizing the appearance of visible links based on the individual user's goals, knowledge, and other characteristics (Brusilovsky, 2007). Adaptive navigation support is further subdivided into different adaptation technologies: *direct guidance, adaptive link sorting, adaptive link hiding, adaptive link annotation, adaptive link generation,* and *map adaptation.* Direct guidance provides global guidance by recommending the next optimal node/page for the user to visit based on their goals, knowledge, and other parameters stored in the user model. In particular, the link to the "best" node may be visually highlighted, or a dynamic next link may be generated to steer the user towards it. Adaptive link sorting involves arranging all the links on a specific page based on the user model and certain user-relevant criteria. Links are organized in order of priority, with those deemed more relevant to the user positioned closer to the top of the page. Adaptive link hiding ensures global and

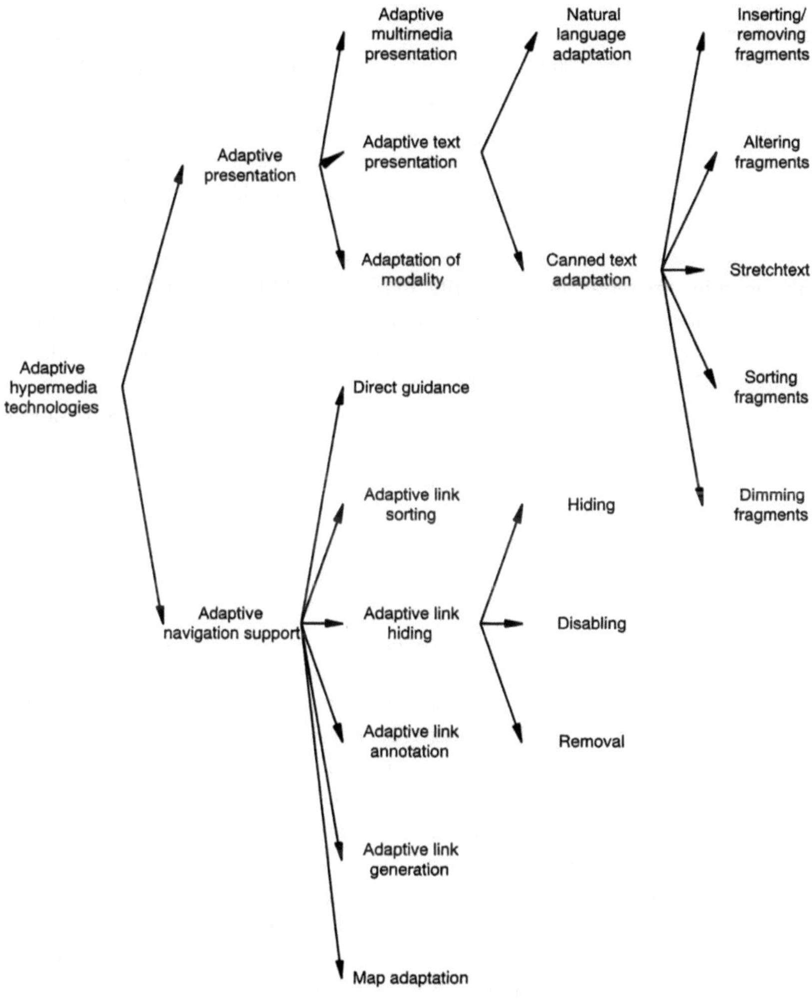

Fig. 2.6 Taxonomy of Adaptive Hypermedia Technologies. (*Note.* From "Adaptive hypermedia," by Brusilovsky, P., 2001, *User Modelling and User-Adapted Interaction, 11*(1), p. 100 (https://doi.org/10.1023/A:1011143116306). Copyright 2001 by SNCSC. Reproduced with permission from SNCSC)

local guidance, as well as local orientation support, focusing on smaller, specific parts of the hyperspace. It essentially involves narrowing down the navigation options to the most relevant nodes to visit by hiding, removing, or disabling links to pages that are deemed irrelevant to the user's current context or goals (Brusilovsky, 2001). A page might be deemed irrelevant for various reasons, such as if it doesn't align with the user's current learning objective or contains materials beyond the user's current level of comprehension. Hiding such pages serves to protect users from the complexities of the entire hyperspace, thereby reducing cognitive load. For instance, the system may initially present only a portion of the learning material and gradually introduce additional components as the learner advances through the course. Adaptive link annotation provides global and local orientation support. It aims to enhance links by providing additional information through comments regarding the current state of the nodes. Relevant links can be highlighted, while non-relevant ones can be dimmed. Annotations can take the form of textual explanations or visual cues, such as distinct icons or varying font sizes, to offer users more insight into the content behind the annotated links. Adaptive link hiding and adaptive link annotation serve not only to reduce cognitive load but also facilitate personalized access to information and aid learners in following an individualized learning path (Brusilovsky, 2007; Brusilovsky, 1999; Brusilovsky & Peylo, 2003). Adaptive link generation refers to the generation of new, non-authored links for a page and encompasses the following occurrences: identifying valuable new connections between documents and permanently incorporating them into the existing set of links; creating links for navigation based on similarity between items; and dynamically suggesting pertinent links to users. The last adaptation technique, map adaptation, involves utilizing maps to visually depict either hyperspace or a localized region of hyperspace as a network of nodes interconnected by arrows, representing concepts and their relationships. Through maps, users can conveniently navigate to any visible node by simply clicking on its representation. Map adaptation is implemented by adjusting the presentation form of local and global hypermedia maps available to users. Local maps provide a focused view of a specific area in the hyperspace, aiding detailed exploration, while global maps offer an overview of the entire structure for broader orientation. These adjustments serve both to enhance usability and to optimize orientation within the hyperspace by tailoring the map's complexity and layout to the user's needs or current context.

For a more detailed explanation of user modeling and an in-depth presentation of adaptation technologies implemented in adaptive hypermedia systems, interested readers are advised to consult the studies of Brusilovsky (1996, 2001, 2007). An updated and further developed taxonomy of adaptation techniques was provided by Knutov et al. (2009). A more recent study by Papadimitriou and Gyftodimos (2017) also presented the adaptive and intelligent techniques that are implemented in contemporary adaptive educational hypermedia systems. However, an exhaustive enumeration of these techniques is above the scope of the current thesis.

Adaptivity in contemporary learning environments can be manifested in different ways. Courses and materials can be tailored to learner characteristics in order to provide personalized learning spaces (Chang et al., 2015). Adaptive presentation and adaptive navigation support are applied in a wide range of recent studies on adaptive learning systems (Papadimitriou & Gyftodimos, 2017). Additionally, at the system's interface, an important adaptation technique that is implemented is *adaptive interaction* (Paramythis & Loidl-Reisinger, 2004). Adaptive interaction, resembling adaptive link annotation, entails adjustments occurring at the system's interface to enhance the user's interaction with the system, without altering the learning content itself. Representative examples of this kind of adaptation are the implementation of different graphical or color schemes, adjusting font sizes, and other modifications to accommodate users' preferences and needs. Another manifestation of adaptivity is the technique of *content discovery and assembly* (Paramythis & Loidl-Reisinger, 2004). It involves utilizing user-specific data to find and organize learning materials from various sources, particularly focusing on tailoring content selection based on individual learners' past learning experiences. This approach addresses the complexity of personal learning preferences and experiences to enhance the relevance and effectiveness of the educational content presented. A further adaptation technique found in modern learning environments is *adaptive collaboration support* (Paramythis & Loidl-Reisinger, 2004) or *adaptive group formation* (Papadimitriou & Gyftodimos, 2017). Through this technique, adaptive support is initiated in learning scenarios characterized by communication among multiple individuals. Thanks to collaborative opportunities, social interaction can be achieved, and common objectives can be set among different users. For instance, forums and group learning activities can be tailored to the characteristics and needs of users, facilitating cooperation among users. Additionally, leveraging knowledge about potential collaborators allows for the formation of groups that are well-suited to the nature of the collaborative task. Lastly, according to a recent study (Taylor et al., 2021), there are additional tools in adaptive learning environments that authorize the learners to evaluate and personalize their learning. *Self-assessments*, offered when completing each lesson, enable learners to metacognitively control their learning progress. This pedagogical approach is usually combined with the so-called *"chunking" of content*, whereby the content is divided into small, manageable "bite-sized" chunks

(Mayer, 2005). This technique aims to facilitate cognitive information processing by reducing cognitive load and making adaptive learning content delivery possible. At the same time, the method of *retrieval learning*, namely requesting learners to engage in free recall while learning (Bae et al., 2019), allows learners to practice retrieving relevant information and realize their current knowledge state, thus enabling the system to assess their ongoing performance and promote an individualized learning pathway.

Adaptive technologies offer numerous benefits, including reducing information overload (Knutov et al., 2009), enhancing learning experiences, providing flexibility in learning time, offering timely feedback, enabling flexible management of learning experiences, promoting learner-centered learning and faster learning progress (Kabudi et al., 2021), as well as ensuring success for all learners (Kurt, 2021). Learners are provided with the opportunity to construct their knowledge (Kabudi et al., 2021) and take control of their learning (Taylor et al., 2021) by determining their learning path and making decisions about their learning. Therefore, in adaptive learning environments, the core of the learning process becomes the learner. Learners are facilitated to make their own decisions in learning (Taylor et al., 2021) and become capable of progressing independently, without the presence of the instructor (Kabudi et al., 2021). Assessment of adaptation techniques such as adaptive navigation support has revealed their capability to facilitate users in achieving their objectives, diminish navigational complexity, and enhance overall satisfaction levels (Brusilovsky, 2007). Among these advantages, one major benefit of integrating adaptive techniques in contemporary learning systems is the development of personalized and individualized learning settings and their provision at scale (Taylor et al., 2021).

Personalized learning, regarded as a key objective in modern educational systems (Zhang et al., 2020), lies in the consideration of three aspects: individual differences, personal needs, and personal development (Peng et al., 2019). A learning environment that promotes personalization, aims to "engage each learner in the learning process in the most productive and meaningful way to optimize each learner's learning potential and success" (Thyagharajan & Nayak, 2007, p. 829). Adaptive learning systems are inherently personalized learning platforms in which the individual learner's perspective is considered (Kabudi et al., 2021; Kinshuk, 2016). In adaptive learning environments, "content, activities, navigation, presentation, interaction and other aspects of the course are adapted and personalized to the real-time context of the individual student" (Kinshuk, 2016, p. 4). By assessing learners' current knowledge and skills, delivering feedback and educational content, and continuously tracking learners' progress, adaptive learning systems enhance each student's learning (Taylor et al., 2021).

For instance, adaptive learning environments can accommodate diverse learning styles. Learners exhibit varying preferences in how they approach learning. While some learners prefer gaining an overview of the entire material before delving into details, others prefer a sequential progression through the material, opting for an overarching view to prevent feeling overwhelmed by the content (Kinshuk, 2016). Tailored support, aligned with these preferences, not only ensures a personalized experience but also enhances engagement and comprehension. Thanks to personalized adaptive learning, both individual learner's interests and desires are recognized as relevant to educational settings (Peng et al., 2019). By customizing instruction to individual learners (Taylor et al., 2021), learners' individual differences are considered, and their personal development is achieved by meeting their personal needs. In essence, it is the adaptation techniques that can "support personalized access to information" (Brusilovsky, 2007, p. 263). Flexible individualized learning support allows learners to follow their individual learning path, enabling them to progress independently (Kabudi et al., 2021). Thus, adaptive learning environments enable the development of *individualized learning* at scale (Taylor et al., 2021), which would not be feasible through traditional learning approaches (Kurt, 2021).

Even though there is to date no clarity on what adaptive learning technologies can fully achieve and how they are effectively implemented in practice (Kabudi et al., 2021; Özyurt & Özyurt, 2015; Zhang & Aslan, 2021), the integration of adaptivity into contemporary learning environments is seen as advantageous. Not only is the continuous assessment of individual students' learning processes supported, but also one of the key measures of a learning environment's effectiveness, namely the level of learning achievement, is enhanced (Kinshuk, 2016; Yilmaz-Soylu & Akkoyunlu, 2009). Although some studies found no notable effects on academic achievement or students' learning experiences (Akkoyunlu & Soylu, 2008; Wang et al., 2006), the review by Chiu et al. (2023) highlighted that the majority of research reported substantial enhancements in student academic performance as a result of incorporating AI technologies. Recent studies employing innovative adaptive techniques within adaptive learning systems have demonstrated promising results. Hwang, Sung, et al. (2020) developed an adaptive learning system that took into account both the cognitive and the affective status of the students. Their research revealed that students who learned with a system integrating cognitive and affective analysis of their performance exhibited superior learning outcomes compared to those in conventional learning systems or systems solely based on cognitive state analysis. Similarly, Gomede et al. (2021) implemented an adaptive recommender system that effectively enhanced learning outcomes. Chrysafiadi et al. (2023) demonstrated that incorporating adaptivity in an ITS significantly enhanced learners' satisfaction, knowledge acquisition, recommendation accuracy, interaction efficacy, and engagement in the learning process. Ristić et al. (2023) further found that students using an adaptive e-learning module experienced enhanced learning effectiveness, satisfaction, and motivation, with sustained knowledge retention over time.

Another key advancement in investigating the effectiveness of adaptive learning environments to enhance learning outcomes sheds light on the consideration of specific learner characteristics when providing adaptivity. A substantial body of research has focused on the construct of learning styles, yielding promising results (El-Bishouty et al., 2019; Graf & Kinshuk, 2007; Karagiannis & Satratzemi, 2018; Özyurt & Özyurt, 2015; Tseng et al., 2008), as demonstrated in the following section.

2.5 Individual Differences and Learning Outcomes in Adaptive Learning Environments

Learning constitutes a complex endeavor, which necessitates learners' ability, motivation, and willingness to learn. At the core of learning success is the consideration of learners' *individual differences*. Individual differences play a significant role in determining to what extent and how effectively an individual can engage in the learning process. As learning tasks come along with mental processing demands, acquiring various skills and knowledge while engaging with these tasks requires the application of different sets of learning traits (Jonassen & Grabowski, 2012). Russell (1997) emphasized that educators should identify and acknowledge learners' differences and leverage available technology to address them accordingly. "However, the majority of current implementations of learning environments lack the support individual students need to achieve success in their learning" (Kinshuk, 2016, p. 3). Especially, in web-based learning environments, where learning may take place anytime and with the absence of an instructor, the significance of learners' individual characteristics increases and may essentially influence learners' success or failure (Nakic et al., 2015).

According to the *Handbook of individual differences, learning, and instruction* (Jonassen & Grabowski, 2012), learners' individual differences stem from learners' individual learning traits, which are studied in the framework of differential psychology of learning and instruction. There is an array of learning traits that affect learning behavior and learning processes. These learning traits are entailed in five main categories: *intellectual aptitudes of learning, cognitive controls and cognitive styles, learning styles, personality,* and *prior knowledge.*

Intellectual aptitudes of learning essentially refer to intelligence, the general mental abilities, including both primary mental abilities, such as verbal comprehension, and secondary mental abilities, such as creativity. Cognitive controls and cognitive styles refer to the ways in which an individual interacts with and gathers information from their surroundings, structures knowledge, and subsequently utilizes that knowledge. Learning styles delineate individual preferences regarding different methods and activities of learning. Personality comprises a set of mental tendencies that guide behavior in certain ways, shaping how individuals interact with their environment and in particular, with other people. Prior knowledge constitutes "the knowledge, skills, or ability that students bring to the learning process" (Jonassen & Grabowski, 1993, p. 417). It is regarded as one of the strongest predictors of learning achievement. As a multifaceted concept, prior knowledge involves not only the prerequisite knowledge that is necessary for learning a new skill or comprehending new information but also the general knowledge that a learner utilizes when acquiring new knowledge. Prior knowledge encompasses both structural knowledge and prior achievement. Structural knowledge refers to what individuals know and how knowledge is organized. Prior achievement involves the skills and learning abilities individuals have previously accomplished, both directly related and less related to the content. Both forms of prior knowledge constitute significant indicators of an individual's capacity to learn new concepts and skills (Jonassen & Grabowski, 2012). As described in cognitivism, prior knowledge facilitates knowledge construction and acquisition (Schunk, 2012). However, prior knowledge may also hinder learning. Three determinants have been identified that can foster learning outcomes. Prior knowledge needs to be activated to facilitate the retrieval of information from memory, to be relevant for the current learning task, and congruent with the learning content (Brod, 2021).

Individual differences act as learning filters. "They mediate the process of learning in overt and subtle ways" (Jonassen & Grabowski, 2012, p. 12). Learners' abilities or preferences impact their capability to achieve different learning outcomes. In order to maximize learning outcomes, instruction needs to be adapted in such a way that it takes into account the learners' differences in ability, personality, and preferences. Adaptive instruction serves the purpose of tailoring the form of instruction to the individual needs or desires of the learners to enhance their learning outcomes (Jonassen & Grabowski, 2012). Adaptive instruction in web-based learning environments is provided in the framework of adaptive learning environments. As described in Section 2.4, learner characteristics are collected by the adaptive system, stored in the user model, and utilized by the learning environment to provide relevant adaptive and personalized support (Kinshuk, 2016). It is the learner characteristics to which the system is adapted in order to account for learners' individual differences. User modeling in adaptive hypermedia systems is based on considering the following learner characteristics to provide adaptive support: learner's knowledge of the subject being taught, interests, goals, experience, preferences, background, and individual traits (Brusilovsky, 1996; Brusilovsky & Millán, 2007). Based on the classification of Brusilovsky and Millán (2007), individual traits refer to learner characteristics that delineate the learner as a unique individual. They include personality traits, cognitive styles and factors, and learning styles. Individual traits constitute stable attributes of a learner that either remain unchangeable or can only be altered gradually over an extended period of time.

In a recent comprehensive review of users' individual characteristics, utilized as sources of adaptation in adaptive learning systems, 22 user individual characteristics were determined, and 17 among them were further identified as sources of adaptation (Nakic et al., 2015). Based on these findings, the effectiveness of adaptive learning systems is notably enhanced when tailored to one or more of the following learners' attributes: learning styles, background knowledge, cognitive styles, preferences (for specific learning materials), and motivation. Kinshuk (2016) introduced another classification of learner characteristics, attributing individual differences to these characteristics and emphasizing their consideration to achieve effective adaptivity and personalization. These were distinguished into *behavioral, performance, cognitive,* and *physiological attributes.* Behavioral attributes refer to learners' personal behaviors, such as their preferences and their familiarity with the exploration process and various types of multimedia objects. Performance attributes regard learners' levels of competency in a domain, including current comprehension and experiences within a domain, and their proficiency in relevant skills. Cognitive attributes describe learners' cognitive load capacities and necessitate comprehension of learners' cognitive abilities, such as working memory capacity and inductive reasoning ability. Physiological attributes refer to learners' physical conditions, which can be assessed by measuring various physiological parameters, such as monitoring heart rate variability to assess learners' stress levels (Kinshuk, 2016). By considering learners' differences, each learner can exhibit mastery and achieve better learning outcomes (Kinshuk, 2016; Schunk, 2012).

Learning outcomes encompass all the effects of the learning process (Lehmann, 2010). These include *skills, cognitive outcomes, affective outcomes,* and *metacognitive knowledge* (Bloom, 1956; Gupta et al., 2010). When it comes to computer-based learning processes, skills are defined as the ability to operate the system to be learned, including command-based knowledge, namely knowledge of the commands and their syntax, and tool-procedural knowledge, which refers to the ability to apply a sequence of commands to accomplish specific tasks. Cognitive outcomes describe the learners' attitudes and insights, which include knowing which processes the learned software can be used for, comprehending the software's capabilities, and applying the acquired knowledge in novel situations. Affective outcomes relate to learners' perceptions and motivation, such as evaluating the software's utility, fostering motivation to explore the software further, and ensuring satisfaction with the learning process while addressing issues such as computer anxiety. Metacognitive knowledge pertains to an individual's knowledge about their own learning and information processing, including self-efficacy, namely the confidence in one's ability to perform specific tasks. These dimensions collectively contribute to a comprehensive understanding of the multi-faceted effects of the learning process and the various factors influencing learning outcomes in online learning environments.

Significant endeavors to establish a common ground for comprehending learning outcomes have been made, including the highly relevant example of the European qualifications framework (EQF). Adopted on April 23, 2008, by the European Parliament and Council, the EQF serves as a common European reference system designed to enhance the clarity and comprehension of qualifications across various countries and systems. Encompassing qualifications at all levels and within all educational and training sub-systems, the EQF offers a thorough overview of achievements and abilities expected in qualifications in the 41 European countries participating in its implementation. It essentially consists of eight reference levels that define learning outcomes in terms of knowledge, skills, and autonomy-responsibility. Knowledge is defined as theoretical and/or factual. Skills are defined as cognitive, including the use of logical, intuitive, and creative thinking, as well as practical, including manual dexterity and the ability to use methods, materials, tools, and instruments. Autonomy and responsibility refer to learners' ability to apply knowledge and skills autonomously and with responsibility. The different levels denote what a learner knows, understands, and can apply at the end of a learning process, from basic (Level 1) to advanced (Level 8) learning outcomes (Cedefop, n.d.; Europass, n.d.).

As previous research indicated, multiple factors influence learning outcomes in computer-based learning environments. Computer self-efficacy, attitudes, and experience directly impact learning outcomes in computer-based learning (Hasan & Ali, 2004). Individuals with extensive computer experience have been found to gain more knowledge from hypertext-based programs than those with limited computer experience (Brinkerhoff et al., 2001). Digital competence encompasses a range of digital skills and acquired knowledge essential for ongoing use of digital technologies to achieve personal objectives (Semeniako et al., 2024). Learners possessing digital competence are able to effectively interact with information technology, including digital content, computers, media information, and online venues. Digital competence is recognized as an essential skill for both digital learning and employability (Lucas et al., 2022). Its acquisition and development need to be prioritized for learners to succeed in a rapidly evolving digital job market. While previous research is scarce investigating differences in digital competency levels of learners from different fields of education and training (Chaw & Tang, 2024; Wild & Schulze Heuling, 2020), it has been shown that vocational learners possessing proficiency in digital competences have enhanced their academic achievement (Pagani et al., 2016).

In the framework of computer-based systems, learning outcomes are further significantly influenced by the software's learning support. According to findings from Wambua et al. (2021), a learner support system has been shown to positively and significantly impact the academic performance of distance learning students. While learning support can enhance recall and performance, its integration with instructor guidance is more beneficial for fostering comprehensive understanding and practical application of the material (Tzur et al., 2021). In adaptive learning systems, a promising approach for enhancing learning outcomes is implementing adaptivity within learning support. Learners who utilized learning systems with embedded adaptive support have been shown to achieve better learning outcomes and higher scores in comparison with learners using non-adaptive systems (Kardan & Conati, 2015; Kommers et al., 2008; Ling & Chiang, 2022; Wang et al., 2020). Tailored domain-specific support strategies have been demonstrated to improve acquisition of domain knowledge and task efficiency (Karakostas & Demetriadis, 2011). Specifically, tailoring content to a learner's prior knowledge in adaptive learning systems enhances both performance and perceptions, particularly for those with limited prior knowledge (Mampadi et al., 2009). Similarly, Mitchell et al. (2005) found that participants with lower domain knowledge exhibit greater improvements in learning performance compared to those with higher domain knowledge. In another study, in which learners watched online video lectures, learners with high prior knowledge demonstrated more positive attitudes, used more viewing strategies, and achieved better learning outcomes compared to those with low prior knowledge (Li, 2019). Collectively, these findings underscore that familiarity with digital applications, adaptivity, and prior knowledge have a substantial impact on learning outcomes across different educational contexts.

Furthermore, research suggests that individualized and personalized learning approaches can notably improve learning outcomes and contribute to more effective learning experiences. A recent literature review of 25 studies supported that individualized learning can significantly and positively influence learning outcomes (Mirari, 2022). In addition, a recent meta-analysis revealed that academic performance is greatly affected by learning scores, future aspirations, and support from peers and family (Li et al., 2023). In addition, the implementation of interactive strategies and individualized learning tasks has been found to positively influence academic performance, socialization, and social-emotional skills development in pre-university education (Manea et al., 2023). In blended learning environments, individualized interventions have been found to significantly improve learning behaviors, motivation, self-confidence, and overall course outcomes compared to uniform approaches (Zhang et al., 2019). These studies cumulatively emphasize the positive effects of individualized learning approaches, showing they significantly enhance overall learning outcomes across diverse educational settings.

Following the insights from previous research, this thesis investigates the impact of experience with digital learning applications, adaptivity, prior knowledge, and individualization on AI learning outcomes. As the evaluation of adaptive and personalized learning environments should primarily focus on how these systems cater to the unique characteristics and needs of individual students (Kinshuk, 2016), special attention is further attributed to the construct of learning styles as a main source of personalizing information (Kinshuk, 2016; Tseng et al., 2008). Therefore, this thesis places additional emphasis on exploring the influence of different learning preferences on AI learning outcomes within adaptive learning environments. The consideration of learning styles in adaptive learning environments has been extensively investigated in recent research, examining their relationship with learning outcomes and demonstrating their ability to enhance learning outcomes (Alshammari & Qtaish, 2019; Bajraktarevic et al., 2003; Chang et al., 2016; El-Bishouty et al., 2019; Karagiannis & Satratzemi, 2018; Tseng et al., 2008). The significance and detailed explanation of learning styles are discussed below.

2.5.1 Learning Styles

One significant parameter according to which learners can be differentiated is *learning styles* (Özyurt & Özyurt, 2015). The concept of learning styles is a scientific construct that operationalizes a wide range of personality traits relevant to one's learning (Lehmann, 2010). There have been many definitions for learning styles by researchers who have extensively investigated the concept. For Felder (1996), learning styles are the distinctive strengths and preferences in the methods individuals use to intake and process information. For Honey and Mumford (1992), learning styles mainly refer to the attitudes and behaviors that shape students' preferred ways to learn. Following recent studies, the concept of learning styles encompasses the "learning choices and learning differences of an individual" (Özyurt & Özyurt, 2015, p. 350). Schunk (2012) makes a concrete distinction between abilities and styles by underlining that "abilities refer to capacities to learn and execute skills; styles are habitual ways of processing and using information" (p. 478). As "different students have different preferred ways to learn" (Truong, 2016, p. 1185), some students are more familiar with reading texts while others may opt for visual representations of information, such as images and graphs. Some may learn better with theories and mathematical models; others may prefer practicing through experiments and examples. Some individuals prefer to engage in active and interactive learning, while others tend to function more effectively through retrospective and individualized methods. "When learners interact with various modes of instruction, they develop preferred patterns for engaging the physical, mental, and emotional requirements imposed by those learning modes" (Jonassen & Grabowski, 2012, p. 9). Hence, the construct of learning styles entails a specific set of individual preferences in the way learners perceive and process information (Lehmann, 2010) that essentially affect the learning process of each individual (Jonassen & Grabowski, 2012).

As learning styles provide valuable insights into learners' preferences, learning styles can serve as a guide for learners to identify the most suitable learning approach or for instructors to realize the most appropriate instructional methods (Fasihuddin et al., 2017). To this end, tailoring instruction to learners' learning styles and developing supportive learning environments has the potential to enhance learning processes (El-Bishouty et al., 2019; García et al., 2008; Schunk, 2012). In contrast to other learner characteristics, the construct of learning styles is considered a process-oriented adaptation criterion, as it has a direct relation to learning processes (Nistor et al., 2008). Such learner characteristics determine, to some extent, whether and how effectively an individual can learn (Jonassen & Grabowski, 2012).

Providing adaptive support based on learning styles stems from "the assumption that matching the instructional strategy to learning styles of the learners leads to better learning performance" (Nakic et al., 2015, p. 464). As Jegatha Deborah et al. (2014) emphasize: "especially, in an e-learning environment, the impact of the learning style causes a greater effect on the performance of the learners and in the design of the e-learning systems" (p. 804). Therefore, learning systems that consider students' different learning styles can be beneficial for all learners and have already been found to have a positive influence on their learning outcomes (Felder & Spurlin, 2005; García et al., 2007; Graf et al., 2010; Popescu, 2010). Mismatched teaching approaches and learning styles can result in unsatisfactory learning experiences and outcomes (Felder & Silverman, 1988; Pritchard, 2013). Learners who strongly prefer specific learning styles may encounter difficulties if the instruction doesn't align with their preferences (Felder & Silverman, 1988). Therefore, adapting instruction to learning styles can not only facilitate learning but also enhance learning efficiency (García et al., 2007).

Learning styles are key characteristics for creating highly successful adaptive systems (Nakic et al., 2015). Filippidis and Tsoukalas (2009) implemented adaptive presentation support tailored to students' distinct learning styles, underlining the positive results of the adaptive support provided. Chang et al. (2016) implemented a learning styles-based adaptive learning system, demonstrating its effectiveness in enhancing learning outcomes. In another study, the integration of an adaptive tool tailored to accommodate learning styles resulted in enhancing course design, improving learning support, and shedding light on overall learning performance (El-Bishouty et al., 2019). Numerous studies have further demonstrated that considering learning styles can be effective in supporting learning and attaining improved learning outcomes (Alshammari & Qtaish, 2019; Bajraktarevic et al., 2003; Chang et al., 2016; El-Sabagh, 2021; Graf & Kinshuk, 2007; Graf et al., 2010; Popescu, 2010; Tseng et al., 2008). According to a comprehensive review of 51 studies (Truong, 2016), e-learning systems that adapt to students' learning styles can optimize students' learning processes. Recent studies have focused on the investigation of adapting learning support to different learning styles in order to accomplish personalized learning (Alshammari & Qtaish, 2019; El-Sabagh, 2021; Essalmi et al., 2015; Nafea et al., 2019; Röpke et al., 2018). This approach enables learners to create a flexible learning environment by creating individualized learning paths that align most closely with their needs and preferences, allowing each learner to engage in the learning process (Hussein & Al-Chalabi, 2020).

To accommodate individual learning styles, learners' preferences have been mapped in learning styles models that integrate instructional approaches to match learning styles. The theoretical landscape of learning styles' theories and models is vast. Yet there is no single universally accepted method of classifying learning styles. Instead, various models and classifications are employed (Romanelli et al., 2009). According to a review from Coffield et al. (2004a), 71 models of learning styles have been identified, while 13 of them have been regarded as major, due to their convention, significance, and influence on other models. In the framework of adaptive learning environments, a wide variety of learning styles models have been employed. Based on recent reviews (Özyurt & Özyurt, 2015; Truong, 2016) and a content analysis (Akbulut & Kardak, 2012), the most preferred learning style model in adaptive learning environments was the Felder-Silverman learning style model (FSLSM) (Felder & Silverman, 1988), which has also been regarded as a source of adaptation in adaptive learning systems (Nakic et al., 2015), followed by Kolb's learning style inventory (Kolb, 1985) and the VARK learning style inventory (Fleming & Mills, 1992), which stands for visual, auditory, read, kinesthetic learning styles. Other prominent learning styles' models that have been investigated in previous research are the Myers-Briggs type indicator (MBTI, Myers & Myers, 1980) and the Honey and Mumford (1992) learning style questionnaire. A detailed description of these models, except for the FSLSM that was utilized for the current investigation, was considered beyond the scope of this thesis. A reference and a short description of the models closely related to the FSLSM are provided below.

2.5.2 Felder and Silverman Learning Style Model

For the scope of this thesis, the FSLSM (Felder & Silverman, 1988) is adopted. Previous literature reviews, as well as empirical studies, have shown that the FSLSM is the most preferred and widely used model in adaptive learning environments (Filippidis & Tsoukalas, 2009; Karagiannis & Satratzemi, 2018; Özyurt & Özyurt, 2015), in technology-enhanced systems (Soflano et al., 2015), as well as in e-learning (Jegatha Deborah et al., 2014; Kuljis & Liu, 2005). It has been utilized in learning styles research for decades (Akbulut & Cardak, 2012). This is mainly attributed to its detailed and in-depth description of the different dimensions of learning styles (Carver et al., 1999; Graf et al., 2007), grounded in learners' psychological attributes. Providing detailed information about learning styles improves user modeling, which leads to more precise modeling of the learners and facilitates the delivery of more appropriate adaptive learning experiences (Graf et al., 2007). Further, as illustrated below, the FSLSM incorporates elements from various other learning style models, suggesting its broad applicability and generalizability (Soflano et al., 2015).

According to the FSLSM, learners are distinguished based on the way they prefer to receive and process information (Felder & Silverman, 1988; Truong, 2016). As depicted in Table 2.1, learners' preferences are classified into four dimensions. Two types of learners are identified for each dimension.

Table 2.1 The Felder and Silverman Learning Style Model

Dimension	Learner Type	
Processing	Active	Reflective
Perception	Sensing	Intuitive
Input	Visual	Verbal
Understanding	Sequential	Global

The first dimension, called *processing*, signifies how learners prefer to process information and practice their learning. *Active learners* comprehend and retain information best through active experimentation, by trying things out, applying the learning material, engaging in discussions, and working actively with others or in groups. *Reflective learners*, on the other side, learn through introspection and reflective observation, by thinking things through and reflecting on the learning material. They, rather, prefer to work alone or with a single familiar partner. Therefore, active learners tend to learn less in situations where they are expected to be passive, while reflective learners struggle to learn in contexts devoid of opportunities for contemplation on the presented information. The second dimension, called *perception*, specifies the kind of information that learners prefer to receive and learn from. *Sensing learners* learn best from concrete learning material, which is based on facts, data, and examples. They tend to be more practical and careful with details, while surprises and complications irritate them. *Intuitive learners* tend to be innovative and imaginative and prefer to learn from abstract learning material, such as theories and concepts. The third dimension is *input* and indicates the approach learners prefer to use in order to engage in learning. *Visual learners* remember best and prefer to learn from visual representations, such as pictures, diagrams, and flow-charts. If information is merely stated to them, they are likely to forget it. On the other hand, *verbal learners* prefer to learn from textual representations, which are either written or spoken. The last dimension is *understanding* and identifies how learners progress in the comprehension of information. *Sequential learners* achieve a good comprehension of a subject when the learning material is presented to them in small incremental steps and are able to follow linear learning paths. They usually infer from parts to the whole. They engage in linear reasoning processes in problem-solving, and they comprehend the content best when it increases in complexity and difficulty throughout the learning process. Sequential learners often excel in convergent thinking and analysis. *Global learners*, on the other side, may demonstrate proficiency in divergent thinking and synthesis. They learn in large leaps without seeing connections in the learning material and find it challenging to articulate how they arrived at solutions. They sometimes achieve better results by directly engaging with more complex and challenging material. Once they comprehend the learning material, they suddenly get the whole picture (Jegatha Deborah et al., 2014; Fasihuddin et al., 2017; Filippidis & Tsoukalas, 2009; Graf et al., 2006; Graf et al. 2010). Therefore, based on this conceptual framework, which encompasses two possible learner types in each dimension, there are 16 different learner types possible.

Following this conceptualization, concrete suggestions for the instructional design are drawn (Felder & Silverman, 1988). For active learners, instruction should involve alternating lectures with brief discussions or problem-solving activities. Learning material based on practical problem-solving tasks should be provided. CAI may also benefit active learners. For reflective learners, instruction should incorporate frequent pauses for thought during lectures and provide opportunities to comprehend fundamental concepts. For sensing learners, the material should consist of concrete information, such as facts, data, observable phenomena, hypothetical examples, and their results. In addition, CAI can provide significant support for them. For intuitive learners, the material should focus on abstract concepts, principles, theories, and mathematical models. To accommodate visual learners, visual aids, such as pictures, diagrams, process flow charts, graphs, and films of live demonstrations, should be utilized. For verbal learners, written and spoken explanations need to be provided. In addition, working in groups to exchange with other learners and writing summaries could be beneficial for them. Sequential learners are profited from sequential learning materials and by following a linear learning path. To accommodate sequential learners, theoretical material can be presented using the scientific method, starting with concrete examples of phenomena outlined in the theory, then developing the theory or model, validating it, deducing its consequences, and ultimately showcasing practical applications. Global learners can benefit when the overarching learning goal of a course is presented, establishing the context and relevance of the subject matter and demonstrating its relevance to learners' experiences. They should be allowed to employ their own strategies to solve problems and grasp the content instead of adhering to a single presented solution pathway. Assigning creativity exercises that entail generating alternative solutions and integrating material from various courses or disciplines can be a beneficial approach for both global and sequential learners.

The FSLSM includes elements from several major learning style models and psychological theories. The active/reflective dimension bears similarity to the dimensions of active experimentation and reflective observation of Kolb's learning style model, in his *theory of experiential learning* (Kolb, 1984; McCarthy, 1987).

According to experiential learning, learners' experience assumes an instrumental role in learning (Boyatzis & Kolb, 1991). "Learning is the process whereby knowledge is created through the transformation of experience" (Kolb, 1984, p. 38). Two types of experiences are investigated in this model: *grasping* and *transforming experience*. Grasping encompasses concrete experiences and abstract conceptualization. Transforming experience involves reflective observation and active experimentation (Jegatha Deborah et al., 2014). For effective learning to occur, the learner needs to go through a continuous cycle of experience, reflection, conceptualization, and experimentation. Kolb's learning styles inventory is based on the *experiential learning cycle*, a four-stage learning process that classifies learners' preferences into four categories: *accommodating, diverging, converging, and assimilating*. Accommodating learners prefer active experimentation and rely on concrete experiences for their learning process. Divergent learners prefer to learn through concrete experiences and reflective observation. While convergent learners also prefer learning through reflective observation, they additionally prefer abstract conceptualization and enjoy active experimentation. Lastly, assimilating learners depend their learning on both reflective observation and abstract conceptualization (Kolb, 1984). In an ideal learning cycle, learners engage with all four styles to varying degrees, with one style typically preferred for understanding and processing experiences. An effective learner can employ each of the four styles in various learning contexts, rather than relying exclusively on a single preferred style (Van der Lingen et al., 2020). The active and reflective preferences are also closely related to the extravert and introvert learner of the Myers-Briggs model (Lawrence, 1982). Especially the active learner presents some commonalities with the kinesthetic learner, as presented in the modality theory (Barbe et al., 1979) and neurolinguistic programming literature (Bandler & Grinder, 1979). Additionally, the sensing/intuitive dimension is based on the *theory of psychological types* from Jung (1971), whereby the notions of sensing and intuition were introduced and presented as the two primary ways in which people tend to perceive the world. Sensing involves gathering data through direct observation using the senses, while intuition involves indirect perception through the unconscious, such as speculation, imagination, or hunches (Felder & Silverman, 1988). The sensing and intuitive preferences are also measured with the Myers-Briggs type indicator (Myers & Myers, 1980), which constitutes a psychometric questionnaire developed to gauge psychological preferences in how individuals perceive the world and make decisions (Jegatha Deborah et al., 2014). In the framework of their theory, Myers and Myers (1995) distinguished two types of perception: the use of the five senses, named as sensing, and indirect perceptions, named as intuition. Therefore, the instrument they developed, assessed an individual's preference for sensing or intuition, among other factors (Felder & Silverman, 1988). Further, the consideration of concrete material from sensing learners and abstract material from intuitive learners is closely related to the concepts of concrete experience and abstract conceptualization of Kolb's experiential learning model (Kolb, 1984). The visual/verbal dimension presents some similarities with cognitive theories on information processing (Crowder & Wagner, 1992; Felder & Henriques, 1995; Martin, 1978). Lastly, the sequential/global dimension stems from the theory of approaches to learn, which explores how individuals adopt different strategies when acquiring knowledge (Pask, 1976). This theory differentiates between serialist approaches, focusing on step-by-step progression, and holist approaches, which emphasize a broader, integrative understanding. Sequential learners align with the serialist approach, processing information methodically, while global learners resemble the holistic approach, synthesizing larger concepts before addressing more specific aspects.

2.5.3 Measurement of Learning Styles

In order to assess the model, Felder and Soloman (1997) developed a research instrument to identify learning styles. The *index of learning styles* (ILS) was initially used in the educational context to identify the preferred learning profiles of engineering students and to facilitate the instruction of engineering professors (Felder & Silverman, 1988). From the instrument's inception, the ultimate goal was to match instruction and learning. Its application was then extended beyond engineering education, finding adoption among educators across diverse disciplines. ILS is a self-scoring 44-item web-based questionnaire aimed at extracting student's learning preferences across various scenarios such as problem-solving, entertainment, group work, writing, thinking, and memorization (Fasihuddin et al., 2017; Limongelli et al., 2011). It consists of 11 forced-choice questions corresponding to each of the four dimensions of processing, perception, input, and understanding. The calculation of the ILS relies on a bipolar scale, with mutually exclusive responses to items (Fasihuddin et al., 2017). Therefore, two answer options (a or b) are provided corresponding to the two opposite categories of one dimension (e.g., a) active scale, b) reflective scale). Due to the odd number of items on each scale, scoring items as $+1$ and -1 respectively, the cumulative score ranges from -11 to $+11$. This range reflects an emerging preference for the given modality (Zywno, 2003). Scores falling within ± 1 to ± 3 suggest a balanced learning style for that dimension. A score within ± 5 to ± 7 indicates a moderate preference, while a score within ±9 to ±11 indicates a strong preference for a particular style in that dimension (Fasihuddin et al., 2017). As the model is based on the assumption that each learner has a personal preference for each of the four dimensions (Graf, 2007), the resulting preferences suggest learning style types/profiles.

Learning styles in the FSLSM model are considered flexibly stable indicators (Coffield et al., 2004a), which may change over time (Truong, 2016). Learning preferences are not seen as fixed but rather as behavioral tendencies, since learners may act differently in some situations (Graf, 2007). Therefore, learning preferences do not constitute predictors of behavior. The learning styles scales are not considered as fixed categories but rather are continua. As Felder and Silverman (1988) state in their original work, "these characteristics [of each dimension] are tendencies of the two types, not invariable behavior patterns: any individual—even a strong sensor or intuitor—may manifest signs of either type on any given occasion" (p. 676). And as was later specified by Felder and Spurlin (2005), "when students experience a large and diverse assortment of learning situations, those classified as sensors will behave in a manner characteristic of sensors more often than they will behave like intuitors -much more often if their preference for sensing is strong, slightly more often if their preference is mild" (p. 104). Hence, an individual learner's manifestations of each of these styles should not be regarded as lifelong preferences, but rather as variable ones, contingent upon the learning context (Beckmann et al., 2015). This characteristic makes the ILS suitable for use in combination with a behavioral analysis in an adaptive learning environment, as it allows for behavioral changes even when learners show high preferences for certain behaviors (Graf et al., 2007, 2008, 2010). A more thorough explanation and clarification of the ILS is provided in Section 4.4.3.

The ILS questionnaire has been revised only once. An additional dimension, called organization, was initially integrated into the FSLSM and categorized into the inductive/deductive scales. This integration recognized induction and deduction as distinct learning preferences and teaching approaches. As such, the model initially consisted of five dimensions and 32 learning types in total. However, the inductive/deductive dimension was later eliminated. Felder (2002/1988) wanted to prevent instructors from relying on traditional deductive teaching approaches on the premise that these approaches do not foster deeper understanding. He wanted to promote the inductive method as the most effective method for teaching, including problem-based learning, discovery learning, and inquiry learning. At the same time, the dimension of input, which constitutes part of the final version of FSLSM, was modified. This dimension initially consisted of the learning types visual and auditory. The visual type referred to visual information, including pictures, diagrams, charts, and other visual information. The auditory type referred to auditory information, including spoken words and other sounds. However, as Felder (2002/1988) states, written prose was not included in the dimension, and it would not correspond either to the visual or the auditory learning type. Therefore, the dimension was revised following the cognitivist assumption that written words are converted into and processed by individuals as spoken ones. In this sense, the auditory learning type was renamed to verbal to include both spoken and written words within a single learning type, distinguishing it from visual information.

The ILS has been extensively used in previous research, especially in the framework of adaptive learning environments and embedded into learning platforms like Moodle (Graf, 2007; Graf et al., 2010; Karagiannis & Satratzemi, 2018; Özyurt & Özyurt, 2015). It constitutes a robust research instrument (Akbulut & Cardak, 2012) with an established reliability and validity (Felder et al., 2005; Felder & Spurlin, 2005) that further supported its generalizability (Soflano et al., 2015). Several previous studies have shown that its psychometric properties are satisfactory. Its test-retest reliability was found to be strong to moderate for all scales (Zywno, 2003). Its internal consistency was acceptable (Litzinger et al., 2007; Livesay et al., 2002; Zywno, 2003) and its construct validity was supported (Felder & Spurlin, 2005; Litzinger et al., 2007; Zywno, 2003). Further, the ILS questionnaire is easily available online and at no cost for research purposes (Felder & Soloman, 1997), which further facilitated its implementation in the present thesis.

There are various ways that learning styles can be detected. Employing a specially designed psychological test was indicated as the optimal method to measure learning styles (Filippidis & Tsoukalas, 2009). Learning styles are generally assessed with self-report instruments (Jonassen & Grabowski, 2012). Participants are asked to self-assess their preferences by answering a questionnaire (Truong, 2016). The ILS questionnaire elicits individuals' perceptions of their preferred ways to learn. Although implementing such a questionnaire does not provide a direct link to mental abilities, this approach taps into learners' overall self-perceptions. These self-perceptions are indirectly associated with mental abilities, as most individuals tend to favor the mental abilities and cognitive styles to which they are more proficient and accustomed (Jonassen & Grabowski, 2012). Self-report measurements are utilized not only in traditional learning settings, such as a regular classroom, but they have been extensively implemented in web-based and adaptive learning environments (El-Bishouty et al., 2019; Filippidis & Tsoukalas, 2009; Karagiannis & Satratzemi, 2018; Özyurt & Özyurt, 2015). However, their implementation is connected to various drawbacks. As with all self-report measurements, the answers can be biased by participants' arbitrary responses, which may lead to inaccurate results that do not reflect the actual learning preferences (Karagiannis & Satratzemi, 2018). Further, most learning styles' questionnaires, as is the case with the ILS questionnaire, are administered only once. Therefore, they reflect just a static, at a specific time point, representation of participants' learning preferences, while according to most learning style theories, learning preferences may change over time (Truong, 2016).

The rise of big data technology and the integration of innovative AI applications in education have made the implementation of innovative ways of measurement necessary. *Learning analytics* and *educational data mining* technologies enable the comprehensive recording of diverse learner data, facilitating the assessment of individual learning processes to enhance teaching and learning practices. Thanks to these measures, information on students' learning processes and behaviors can be collected in online learning environments, revealing significant insights into their learning styles (Truong, 2016). Learning analytics encompass the assessment, processing, interpretation, and presentation of data pertaining to students and their backgrounds, intending to enhance understanding and optimize learning outcomes within the contexts in which they occur (Siemens, 2012). As outlined by Khalil and Ebner (2015), the learning analytics approach comprises the following stages: firstly, recognizing the sources that generate data, including massive open online courses (MOOCs), learning management systems (LMSs), and virtual learning environments; next, identifying datasets containing learner information; then, analyzing these datasets; and finally, intervening through the provision of personalized support. Along with learning analytics, the area of educational data mining has seen significant growth in contemporary adaptive learning environments aimed at achieving personalized learning (Peng et al., 2019). Research utilizing educational data mining has indicated that the vast amount of learning data captured by contemporary learning systems enables identifying latent learning patterns in learners' behaviors, clustering learners into groups exhibiting similar behaviors, and making predictions regarding learning outcomes (Akçapinar & Bayazit, 2019; Akhuseyinoglu & Brusilovsky, 2022). Classification, modeling, and prediction constitute fundamental components of educational data mining (Phani Krishna et al., 2018). A typical data mining cycle in a web-based learning system involves the following phases: collecting and preparing data, identifying patterns and assessing them, and ultimately employing the acquired insights in real time to mediate the interaction between the user and the web (Mobasher, 2007).

Throughout the years, researchers have created mechanisms and tools to automatically identify traces of learning styles present in LMSs using the FSLSM (El-Bishouty et al., 2019). Numerous techniques have been proposed for automating the classification of learning styles, including approaches like Bayesian networks, decision tree methods, and neural networks (Gambo & Shakir, 2021). Especially in adaptive learning environments, collecting information on learning preferences enables effective personalization of learning content and can lead to optimized learning processes (Truong, 2016). This allows an automatic detection of learning styles, which are inferred from learners' behavioral data, such as actions of interaction with the system and their duration (Karagiannis & Satratzemi, 2018). Schiaffino et al. (2008) developed an intelligent agent that identified learning styles from learners' actions based on the FSLSM using Bayesian networks. They subsequently offered tailored support aimed at enhancing learning experiences. Karagiannis and Satratzemi (2018) implemented an adaptive mechanism that automatically detected learning styles based on learners' responses to the ILS and analyzed learners' interaction behavior. Their system provided adaptive presentation and navigation support tailored to individual learning styles, positively affecting learners' motivation and performance. Gambo and Shakir (2021) devised a learning agent leveraging artificial neural networks to classify students' learning styles based on the ILS. This approach was intended to tailor learning content to students' learning behavior, enhancing personalization and providing a self-regulated smart learning environment. Joseph et al. (2022) utilized a learning analytics approach by analyzing learners' log data in online courses. They offered learning support by recommending personalized learning trajectories tailored to individual learning styles and based on the FSLSM, which contributed to improved learning performance. Log data are promising in the sense that they can be error-free (Feldman et al., 2015), as they constitute real-time objective data captured directly by the learning system. Nevertheless, Soflano et al. (2015) advocated for the use of questionnaires to assess learning styles, demonstrating that measuring learning styles prior to system use is more stable and preferable than assessing them within online learning environments, where learners' styles tend to fluctuate to meet course objectives.

2.5.4 Relationship Between Learning Styles and Learning Outcomes in Adaptive Learning Environments

Although there is a need to determine which learning styles have a greater impact on individuals' academic performance (Kinshuk, 2016), research findings remain inconclusive regarding the relationship between certain learning styles and learning outcomes. Brown et al. (2006) assessed students' learning styles with the ILS and provided personalized content based on the visual/verbal dimension of the FSLSM in an adaptive learning environment. No significant difference was found in achievement scores between students possessing different learning styles. Similarly, in a more recent study, no significant influence was found based on individual learning style on study time and learning outcomes, but rather on learner satisfaction and motivation (Beckmann et al., 2015). Nevertheless, it was emphasized that the substantial impact of style-matched learning materials on intrinsic motivation, combined with the well-established influence of intrinsic motivation in fostering learning success (Schiefele & Schreyer, 1994), suggests an indirect relationship between learning style and learning success. Furthermore, Chang et al. (2016) implemented an adaptive learning system based on the ILS to accommodate learners' preferences and a mashup search engine to provide access to additional learning materials to enhance learning outcomes. Sequential learners had the highest learning outcomes, followed by global learners, while the lowest learning outcomes were observed in active and visual learners. El-Bishouty et al. (2019) used the ILS to develop an online course analyzer tool, intending to facilitate teachers in supporting diverse learning styles. Their results indicated that tailoring a course to accommodate particular learning styles can enhance students' learning outcomes to varying degrees. More specifically, they found that the learning materials and the instructional methods tailored to learning styles supported learners on average by up to 31%. Most supported were sequential learners at 68%, and the least supported were global learners at only 15%. The research group concluded that significant learning outcomes can be achieved by tailoring instruction to learning styles, such as enhanced knowledge acquisition, better communication between teachers and learners, as well as better feedback provision, and improved quality of assignments. However, which learning styles were related to higher learning outcomes were not investigated. Overall, previous studies presented varied findings regarding the relationship between specific learning styles and learning outcomes, suggesting the need for further investigations on the influence of learning styles on learning outcomes measures.

2.5.5 Critique and Potential of Learning Styles in Adaptive Learning Environments

Even though it is not the predominant stance on learning styles, the construct of learning styles has been criticized for its conception and contribution (Kirschner,

2017). The criticism was based on three primary reasons. First, it was underlined that a disparity exists between learning preferences and what truly fosters effective learning. Previous research has shown that students' self-reported learning preferences do not always align with the most effective instructional strategies for enhancing learning outcomes (Hattie, 2008; Pashler et al., 2009), indicating that educational interventions may need to focus more on evidence-based strategies to enhance learning outcomes. Second, the preference for learning methods was criticized for not necessarily reflecting an individual's true learning style, as many learning style models categorize individuals into discrete groups, a framework that lacks substantial support from objective research. Third, it was indicated that the majority of studies supporting learning styles fail to meet the fundamental criteria for scientific validity. However, the extensive critique of learning styles conducted by Kirschner (2017) did not address the FSLSM. Another study highlighted that learning styles may be limited in their efficacy due to a lack of robust empirical evidence and the questionable reliability of measurements used to assess them (Coffield et al., 2004b). Nevertheless, these studies criticizing the concept of learning styles have not considered the potential of learning styles in adaptive learning environments. Thus, as Akbulut and Cardak (2012) underline "the empirical evidence regarding the pedagogical value of learning styles has been questioned, but the research on the issue continues" (p. 835). The vast body of research that continues to investigate the concept of learning styles and their significance in contemporary adaptive learning environments (Graf et al., 2010), as detailed in previous sections, endorses its implementation and further investigation in the framework of the current thesis. Based on the theoretical framework of the concept of learning styles and the presented empirical studies, it is prevalent that the consideration of learning styles is promising for learning success, especially in adaptive learning environments. It has been shown that learners achieve better learning outcomes when they learn according to their preferences, concluding that optimal learning outcomes can be achieved when instructional learning environments are tailored to learning styles.

2.6 Integrating AI into Vocational Education and Training (VET) and Continuous Vocational Education and Training (CVET)

As one of the megatrends of the 21st century, AI is expected to disrupt occupations, leading to the emergence of new job structures and skill positions (Cedefop/OECD, 2021). The ever-increasing implementation of AI technologies necessitates that entire industries and their workforce adapt and evolve accordingly. In order to navigate the evolving landscape effectively, continuous training in AI is essential to ensure that employees can readily adapt to new challenges and changes in their roles (Twomey, 2018). With the integration of AI into various application-based scenarios, there is a rising demand not only for IT specialists but also for skilled workers with different specializations who possess AI-related knowledge and competences (Cedefop/OECD, 2021; Rott et al., 2022). The challenge for vocational and continuing training lies in effectively integrating AI-related knowledge and skills in existing curricula and establishing suitable training opportunities for proficient employees, as well as contributing to the development of emerging AI professions (Rott et al., 2022).

Along with the rapid technological change brought by AI technologies, learning settings are pivotal aspects in shaping the alternative possibilities in future employment. To keep up with the rapid technological growth, learning environments in VET and CVET need to be constantly adapted and enhanced through AI-driven tools to improve vocational and continuing education learners' learning outcomes effectively. According to the United Nations Educational, Scientific, and Cultural Organization (UNESCO, 2019), AI can expedite the attainment of global education objectives by diminishing obstacles to learning access, automating administrative tasks, and refining methodologies to enhance learning outcomes. In this context, learning both with and about AI is considered vital for equipping individuals with the required skills needed to address the challenges arising from the digital transformation driven by AI (Dignum 2021; Rott et al., 2022; Stadelmann et al., 2021). This requirement can be adequately met within the framework of VET and CVET, within which the adjustment to emerging changes in professional tasks and roles is addressed. To date, the integration of AI in vocational and continuing training settings is a field in its infancy. Even though the possibilities of AI in VET have been discussed since the 1980s (Aleksander et al., 1988; Lipson, 1984), in many companies, the prospect of a new work environment, characterized by AI technologies and complete digitalization, remains a vision for the future. Thus, preparing young professionals for future workplaces driven by AI and digitalization presents a significant challenge, as the exact nature of these workplaces remains uncertain (Rott et al., 2022).

Based on the recent work of Attwell et al. (2020), AI can be incorporated into VET through two primary approaches: (a) *AI-based tools for teaching and learning*, and (b) *training for an AI-based working environment.* AI-based tools involve AI-based assessment tools, intelligent learning systems, or robots that can be incorporated into learning settings. At the same time, learners necessitate training to comprehend AI technologies and obtain essential AI skills tailored to an AI-driven professional environment. This has prompted a greater emphasis on exploring how AI can be effectively utilized in VET, highlighting the importance of integrating AI as a learning component into various VET curricula. Nevertheless, in Germany, AI topics have predominantly been taught in higher education institutions, while the incorporation of AI areas of study into VET and CVET has only recently started to emerge (Rott et al., 2022). This results in apprentices and experienced workers who may not yet possess the qualifications to effectively utilize AI technologies in their workplaces, as well as a teaching workforce that requires substantial preparation to impart AI knowledge and competences in VET. Consequently, subjects and applications related to AI remain relatively unexplored territories for both learners and educators (Petridou & Lao, 2024).

According to a recent study regarding the needs and requirements for an additional training offer in AI delivered in vocational schools (Rott et al., 2022), vocational teachers expressed readiness to teach AI content even though they lack extensive knowledge and training in the subject. Further, teachers viewed AI topics as relevant and necessary prerequisites for training future employees. Apprentices not only regarded AI topics as highly important for their professional development but also showed strong interest in AI, irrespective of their school qualifications and academic achievement. However, apprentices demonstrated little to no prior knowledge of AI. This was further supported by previous studies that indicated students' limited understanding and proficiency in AI, which further highlighted the shortage of AI courses and the necessity for a teaching workforce that is more knowledgeable and proficient in the subject (Chao et al., 2021; Stamenković et al., 2023). In this sense, teachers' willingness to teach AI content does not suffice, but rather, comprehensive training and constant teacher support are required to effectively incorporate AI into their teaching practices and subsequently educate apprentices on the subject of AI (Kim et al., 2022; Lindner et al., 2019). Overall, recent findings highlighted the need to embed AI topics in the curricula of different VET programs, which has yet to be implemented (Attwell et al., 2020; Rott et al., 2022).

Based on a survey by the Federal Ministry for Economic Affairs and Energy in Germany, AI has not yet been widely established across the different training companies, as only 5.8% of the surveyed companies reported utilizing AI (BMWi–Bundesministerium für Wirtschaft und Energie, 2020). According to the dual vocational training system in Germany, there are three different approaches to how AI content can be embedded into apprenticeship programs (Rott et al., 2022). The first possibility is to revise existing training regulations of each training profession to accommodate evolving workplace demands. Such a process would be lengthy and complex, necessitating modifications to legal statutes, curricula, and examination frameworks, alongside securing consensus among stakeholders. At the same time, all apprentices, regardless of their intended profession or workplace, would be obliged to undergo the AI qualification program. An alternative approach would be to assign the responsibility of AI qualification to employers, thereby placing it within the domain of workplace-related vocational training. This approach enables apprentices to acquire practical AI competences and skills directly applicable to their specific workplace. However, such an approach could potentially restrict the acquisition of theoretical knowledge in AI and lead to discrepancies in apprentices' AI proficiency across different enterprises. A third viable option is to offer supplementary AI qualifications within vocational schools, allowing interested apprentices to include AI-related courses in their curriculum. Such courses could be structured as conventional classroom instruction or self-directed learning modules, or a combination thereof. A potential difficulty in this approach is that the apprentices might not be able to find opportunities to apply their acquired knowledge in the companies in which they work. In addition, for this approach to work, vocational schools need to be willing to offer an AI additional qualification, and a significant number of apprentices need to be actively engaged in these programs. This last approach was implemented in the project (Rott et al., 2022), in the framework of which the current thesis was developed. A detailed description of the project and the implementation of the AI additional qualification is provided in Section 2.7.

The emergence of imparting AI knowledge and familiarizing future professionals with AI applications does not only concern VET. To adequately respond to the rapid changes brought about by AI, AI needs to be effectively integrated into the context of CVET as well. As CVET encompasses educational initiatives provided after initial education or entry into the workforce, it aims to assist individuals in enhancing or updating their knowledge and skills, acquiring new skills for career advancement or retraining (Cedefop & Tissot, 2014). Essentially, it lies in the core of CVET to cultivate AI literacy and ensure an accessible AI education to all individuals across all age groups (Kong et al., 2021). Positioned at the intersection of VET and CVET, additional qualifications play a pivotal role in bridging these domains and thus facilitating lifelong learning (Gutschow & Lorig, 2022). "An AI additional qualification can lay the foundation for creating CVET programmes that foster lifelong learning in an emerging AI-based society" (Petridou & Lao, 2024, p. 13). Additional qualifications seem promising to create sustainable learning opportunities.

Sustainable learning is apparent when learners possess a sense of well-being and confidence in the knowledge, skills, attitudes, and values they have attained, enabling them to apply them proficiently and expand upon them as they engage in continuous learning throughout their lives. Sustainable learning is crucial for an individual's future in a rapidly evolving world (Graham et al., 2015) and even more in an AI-influenced emerging world. CVET institutions play a pivotal role in sustainable learning by promoting professional growth, increasing adult participation in lifelong learning endeavors and elevating employment rates. Following the rapid advancements in AI, it is essential that CVET institutions integrate the acquisition of AI knowledge and skills into their curricula to equip future professionals for AI-driven workplaces, as experts anticipate that technological advancements and the skills required to navigate these new technologies will be pertinent across all industries (Jagannathan et al., 2019). Therefore, as companies are already indicating a demand for their skilled workforce, the AI additional qualification, the implementation of which is evaluated in the framework of the current thesis, establishes a foundation for pursuing additional professional qualifications in AI and can serve as a solid framework for an AI curriculum design in both VET and CVET (Petridou & Lao, 2024).

2.7 Description of the Project KIB³ and the Learning Environment

2.7.1 Project KIB³: Bringing AI into Vocational Education

The current thesis was developed in the framework of the project KIB³, which stands for 'Künstliche Intelligenz in die berufliche Bildung bringen', namely 'Bringing AI into Vocational Education'. This project was implemented from December 1, 2020, to November 30, 2024, within the framework of InnoVET, Germany's federal innovation competition, with the main goal of 'Shaping the Future—Innovations for Excellent Vocational Education and Training' ('Zukunft gestalten—Innovationen für eine exzellente berufliche Bildung'). It was funded by the Federal Ministry of Education and Research in Germany (Funding reference number 21IV005F, Bundesministerium für Bildung und Forschung, n.d.-a). The primary objective of the project was to develop, implement, and evaluate various continuing education certificates focusing on AI and ML. This need emerged from the changing conditions driven by rapid digital transformation and the growing use of AI in technical and commercial sectors, demanding new competences from employees to effectively adapt to evolving job requirements. Initially, the implementation of the project was based on the regional legislation of Baden-Württemberg, with subsequent plans to create standardized national legislation. The project was conducted by the Ludwig Maximilian University of Munich (LMU) at the Chair of General Pedagogy and Educational Research ('Allgemeine Pädagogik und Bildungsforschung'), which was responsible for the scientific guidance and evaluation, in cooperation with five partners. These partners included the Chamber of Industry and Commerce in Reutlingen, which had the joint project management, the Chamber of Industry and Commerce in Karlsruhe, which was responsible to identify company requirements and needs for AI specialists, and the Chamber of Industry and Commerce in the region of Stuttgart that ensured the permeability and eligibility of the qualifications. Additionally, the Technical University of Munich, which developed an adaptive learning software supported by AI technologies, and the University of Stuttgart, which created the digital learning modules, were involved.

Within the framework of the project, a modular format was devised that combined a cross-sector additional qualification on AI and ML and two advanced training certificates at the DQR-5 and -6 levels. The classification into the DQR levels ('Der Deutsche Qualifikationsrahmen für lebenslanges Lernen') refers to the German Qualifications Framework for Lifelong Learning that classifies qualifications within the German education system and renders them comparable across Europe. According to the Federal Ministry of Education and Research in Germany (Bundesministerium für Bildung und Forschung, n.d.-b), DQR level 5 denotes competences required for independently planning and executing comprehensive professional tasks within a complex, specialized, and evolving learning area or professional field. DQR-6 refers to competences necessary not only for planning, executing, and evaluating comprehensive professional tasks and problem scenarios but also for independently managing processes within specific areas of a scientific discipline or professional field. The additional qualification was designed to offer an additional qualification certificate on AI and ML for industrial-technical and commercial traineeships. The advanced training certificate at the DQR-5 level was developed to provide a Specialist Professional Degree, while at the DQR-6 level to provide a Bachelor Professional Degree.

The present thesis focused on the implementation of the additional qualification, which was essentially a course on AI and ML developed for vocational and continuing education learners from different sectors in industrial-technical and commercial professions. This qualification was considered necessary to provide early and ongoing AI training to specialists and executives, preparing them for the substantial and long-standing transformations in the economic value chain due to AI adoption. Given the dual system of VET in Germany, which relies on collaboration between companies providing vocational training and vocational schools, apprentices have the opportunity to enhance their skills beyond the compulsory VET program through additional qualification initiatives. Such additional qualifications can serve as a means of acquainting apprentices from various vocational sectors with the fundamentals of AI. Importantly, they represent a feasible avenue through which all interested individuals can delve deeper into AI concepts and applications (Rott et al., 2022).

The course comprised 100 learning hours of 45 minutes and was delivered twice: from September 2022 to July 2023, and from September 2023 to July 2024. The learning content was assessed through a 60-minute written exam. The participating vocational schools and CVET institutions were located in the region of Baden-Württemberg. Initially, the course was offered at four vocational schools and one CVET institution during the school year 2022/23. Subsequently, it expanded to eight different vocational schools and two CVET institutions during the school year 2023/24. Participation in the course was voluntary. Learners completed and obtained the qualification alongside their mandatory VET program. The learning materials were developed as digital learning modules. These modules were designed to be used by teachers either exclusively or in conjunction with additional learning materials. Besides the digital learning materials, there were also worksheets available. The implementation of the additional qualification varied across participating schools and institutions. While some teachers opted to solely utilize the provided learning materials, others supplemented them with their own materials and worksheets. The extent to which teachers incorporated additional materials and whether they utilized the readily available worksheets in face-to-face and online sessions was not systematically investigated. The content development was based on needs assessments conducted with companies and subsequently discussed within the framework of the 'Legal Provisions' working group. This committee included representatives from all three Chambers of Industry and Commerce involved in the project, as well as representatives from large enterprises, social partners, vocational schools, and training providers (Lao et al., 2024). The following learning topics were delivered: Basic Concepts of AI, Data Handling, Basic Concepts of Data Analysis and ML, and

Opportunities, Challenges, and Ethical Issues of AI. The investigation of the current thesis was conducted within the context of the project evaluation undertaken by the research team from the LMU of Munich. The author of this thesis was actively involved in evaluating the course, which enabled the data collection necessary for the scope of this thesis.

A student-centered, action-oriented learning setting was selected by the research team as the ideal didactical setting for the additional qualification, which was further supported by previous research (Tramm & Naeve-Stoß, 2020). This decision was in line with teachers' preferences, as interviews with the teaching staff showed (Rott et al., 2022). This teaching approach is rooted in the constructivist learning theory. Learners in action-oriented classes collaborate to collectively address, discuss, and assess potential solutions to problems within group settings. These solutions aid in clarifying the underlying theoretical concepts. By facing authentic problems that could arise in their future professional roles, learners incrementally enhance their vocational competence (Rott et al., 2022; Straka & Macke, 2003).

The course was delivered in a blended learning setting, which allowed learners to take responsibility for their learning. Per preliminary findings obtained before implementing the additional qualification, teachers, foreseeing potential challenges with exclusive online learning due to apprentices' incomplete development of self-regulation skills, advocated for a supervised learning format to impart AI knowledge (Rott et al., 2022). Although learners expressed interest in both online and face-to-face learning, the blended learning approach was implemented to reconcile the preferences of both groups. This approach facilitated independent learning alongside teacher assistance and guidance. Courses took place in a face-to-face manner at the vocational schools as well as online. Teachers met with learners on average once a month, either in person or online. The number of meetings varied between the different schools. Learners had the flexibility to engage in self-directed learning at their own pace and convenience and were offered opportunities for personalization. They were provided with the opportunity to ask questions, receive personalized feedback, and seek guidance on their individual performance. At the same time, teachers supported them in sustaining their motivation (Rott et al., 2022).

A dedicated adaptive learning software was developed to facilitate knowledge acquisition, leveraging learning progress tracking and offering individualized support. The course was embedded and delivered within an LMS, as LMSs are considered well-established in the context of higher education (El-Bishouty et al., 2019) and facilitate the integration of additional functions (Akbulut & Kardak, 2012). Moodle was selected as the most appropriate learning platform for several reasons. An extensive literature review of the state-of-the-art e-learning platforms (Akçapinar & Bayazit, 2019; Al-Ajlan & Zedan, 2008; Campo et al., 2021; Chang et al., 2019; Chavan & Pavri, 2004; Kika et al., 2019; Suartama et al., 2020) highlighted its advantages. First, Moodle follows the open-source paradigm, as it constitutes a plugin-based platform with a wide number of already-developed plugins. Second, Moodle's functionalities met most of the project's basic requirements, and its architecture allowed for the integration of adaptive learning software. Additionally, Moodle is developed based on pedagogical principles and has a solid foundation in the constructivist approach. Finally, its widespread use globally and in Germany further supported its selection. Several plugins were integrated into Moodle for the scope of the project, rendering the software learner-centered, interactive, and adaptive. AI features, including adaptivity, facilitated learners not only to acquire knowledge about AI but also to utilize AI assistance in their learning journey (Rott et al., 2022). A list and card format layout was implemented to deliver the learning content.

To ensure the optimal design of the course tailored to the target group, learners were surveyed in a pilot study (Rott et al., 2022). The survey focused on identifying the most relevant target group for the AI content and considerations for the didactic structure of the learning modules. While apprentices expressed strong interest in AI, they lacked a fundamental understanding of the subject. Based on the perceptions of the interviewed teachers and the surveyed apprentices, both investigated groups agreed that the primary focus of the content delivery of an AI qualification should be on the basic theoretical principles of AI alongside job-related practical examples. In addition, suggestions were formulated by both groups regarding an effective instructional design of an AI training program. Learners showed a clear preference for a traditional, teacher-centered approach and interest in online and face-to-face instruction. Teachers advocated for a learner-centered approach and considered a blended learning format as ideal for an AI additional qualification. On the one hand, online learning could enable apprentices to learn flexibly and independently. On the other hand, solely learning online could not be beneficial for apprentices, as they are not yet adequately familiar with self-regulated learning. Therefore, blended learning was deemed suitable as a supervised learning format, whereby apprentices can learn in their own way by additionally receiving the necessary teacher support and guidance. Teachers further endorsed the use of learning software to facilitate self-directed learning and a self-learning setting. Likewise, apprentices have shown their preference for employing educational software, underscoring the significance of integrating explanatory videos as a primary aid for learning.

Based on the findings of a second study conducted in the framework of the project, which evaluated the delivery of the course during its first round, learners have shown the strongest interest in ML and a rather strong interest in programming tasks, even though the latter are considered challenging and complex AI topics (Petridou & Lao, 2024). In addition, learners and teachers alike acknowledged the importance of well-functioning learning software that incorporates visually stimulating resources, such as videos, animated graphics, and interactive quizzes, to improve comprehension and engagement with complex AI assignments, such as programming tasks. Similarly, both groups agreed on the necessity to integrate profession-related practical examples that could not only aid in comprehending abstract and complex topics but also lead to more effective transfer of knowledge to job-related tasks. Regarding the didactic implementation of the qualification, learners encountered challenges with self-regulating their learning, aligning with teachers' expectations (Rott et al., 2022). Furthermore, learners' communication with their instructors was limited. They avoided communicating their progress and difficulties to their teachers, hindering teachers from offering sufficient support. These findings further reinforced the importance of blended learning settings for the successful implementation of AI additional qualifications, highlighting the necessity for easily accessible teacher support, either online or face-to-face, to monitor learning progress and address emerging issues. A final key finding was the challenge learners faced in balancing their existing vocational responsibilities, work commitments, and AI coursework. This highlighted the necessity for AI course designs to be flexible and considerate of participants' varying time constraints and learning requirements.

2.7.2 Blended Learning Environment

A *blended learning* approach was adopted, as elaborated above, to deliver the AI additional qualification. Blended learning formats are gaining prominence in educational settings, as they have been found to contribute to better learning outcomes (Badrus & Arifin, 2021; Kiviniemi, 2014). Blended learning environments are constructed on the idea of the combination of instructor-led learning sessions, conducted in face-to-face or online formats, with digital learning settings based on the concept of independent self-learning. In this sense, blended learning represents an innovative pedagogical approach that combines the strengths of traditional classroom teaching with the benefits of technology-supported learning, whether offline or online (Lalima & Dangwal, 2017). In face-to-face sessions, learners have the opportunity to directly address their problems to teachers and engage in interactive discussions with peers. Online learning offers learners the flexibility to decide when, where, and at what pace they engage with the material, empowering them with greater autonomy in their learning journey (Wright, 2017).

Blended learning offers numerous benefits for learners. While face-to-face learning settings encourage deeper engagement in learning (Hubackova & Semradova, 2016), incorporating online learning provides learners with greater flexibility to shape their learning trajectories (Nafea et al., 2019). Online learning enables learners to personalize their learning experiences, catering to individual needs that are often challenging to address in a traditional classroom setting (Kunze & Frey, 2021). Learners can regulate their learning pace, determine task duration and timing, and tailor their involvement in specific tasks (Steib & Stoffers, 2022). Blended learning settings foster a collaborative learning environment, as learners can actively cooperate with their peers online or in person, pose questions, elaborate on their understandings, and exchange ideas. Learners benefit from structured support while navigating their educational journey, eliminating the need to manage the entire learning process independently (Steib & Stoffers, 2022). Blended learning further supports the diverse learning needs of students with various personality types and learning styles (Caravias, 2018), providing a flexible framework that allows for the adaptation of learning units to individual preferences and requirements. Especially in the context of VET and CVET, the implementation of blended learning settings provides learners with the flexibility to engage with course materials at their own pace and convenience as well as address their issues in person, allowing them to balance their educational pursuits with their professional engagements. Overall, blended learning enables a richer, more flexible learning experience. Learners are encouraged to take an active role in their learning, engage with course materials according to their needs, receive instructional support, and collaborate with peers, thereby deepening their understanding and enhancing their learning experience.

Nevertheless, blended learning may pose challenges for students' learning. Learners must fulfill certain criteria to effectively participate in blended learning environments, primarily encompassing self-regulation strategies, digital proficiency, and workload management (Kintu et al., 2017). When learners struggle with self-regulation (Rott et al., 2022), they may require additional support from their instructors. Therefore, teachers must offer appropriate feedback and learning assistance tailored to individual student needs (Klímová & PraŽák, 2019). However, students' interaction with teachers in online learning may be limited (Tu & McIsaac, 2002). Hence, teacher support needs to be readily available to monitor progress and address emerging issues, thus fostering learners' independence and autonomy (Petridou & Lao, 2024). Furthermore, in case only scarce opportunities for students to contact and communicate with their peers are provided, self-learning may become isolating and could even result in students dropping out of the program (Willging & Johnson, 2009). In addition, as proficient use of technology is essential for online learning environments, limited experience in digital learning may potentially result in significant obstacles to students' learning progress. At the same time, access to digital devices and a stable internet connection is crucial for successful participation in digital learning, which may not be readily available for all students (Rott et al., 2022). Selecting the appropriate learning arrangement greatly influences how learners behave and their overall success in learning (Rienties & Toetenel, 2016). Thus, it is teachers' responsibility to design blended learning settings in a manner that allows students to benefit from the combination of instructor-led and self-learning approaches. They are tasked with minimizing the drawbacks of this instructional format by providing the necessary support and guidance. Conclusively, it's important to underscore that the success of blended learning hinges not just on the quality of the course content and the learning platform, but also on students' preparedness and enthusiasm to actively participate in the online learning environment (Hubackova & Semradova, 2016).

2.7.3 Integration of Adaptive Learning Software into Moodle

Moodle, which stands for modular object-oriented dynamic learning environment, constitutes an LMS that has been extensively used in higher education due to its flexibility and at-no-cost availability (Morze et al., 2021). It has been introduced among other learning environments to support different learning activities (Kinshuk, 2016). Moodle facilitates instructors sharing course materials like documents, quizzes, and videos. It enables tracking of learners' progress, assessment of learning outcomes, and evaluation of assignments and quizzes. The platform supports various content types, including text-based materials and video lectures. Additionally, it promotes collaborative learning through online discussion forums and provides a logging system to monitor student activity, offering a comprehensive solution for online education (Shrestha & Pokharel, 2021). When creating a course in Moodle, teachers are assigned the role of dividing the course into learning units, defining the order of learning, providing quizzes, and creating discussion forums for the learners. On the other side, learners are usually restricted by this teacher-driven design of the course. All learners have access to the same content, navigation, and other aspects of the course, despite possessing different characteristics and interests, prior knowledge, and competence levels. While online courses in such learning platforms can include various learning resources, little or most often no intelligent or adaptive support is provided (Graf et al., 2010).

Recent developments in adaptive learning have sparked an array of innovative tools, which are integrated into LMSs, particularly in Moodle, aimed at delivering personalized learning tailored to individual learners' needs (Kabudi et al., 2021; Morze et al., 2021). Adaptivity in these environments may be implemented through one or several elements, including: (a) *content*, (b) *sequence*, (c) *assessment*, and (d) *interactions* (EdSurge, 2016; Morze et al., 2021; Taylor et al., 2021). Adaptive content is implemented when individualized learning materials, such as feedback, scaffolding, additional material, or learning activities, are provided as a response to learners' specific knowledge level. For instance, a response to a learner's specific misunderstanding may serve not only as corrective feedback but also as provision of subsequent targeted support for immediate remediation. When it comes to adaptive sequence, which could be static, dynamic, or a combination of both, a continuous collection and analysis of learners' real-time data is realized. Learners are provided with the order of skills and the type of content they need to receive next. For instance, upon assignment completion, an adaptive learning system analyzes learners' performance and learning behaviors and then matches them to a new set of skills based on their performance. Adaptive assessment is implemented when learners' knowledge level is evaluated by receiving specific assessment questions with a level of difficulty based on learners' answers to previously asked questions. Finally, adaptivity is implemented through learners' interaction not only with instructors and the learning system, but also through the combination of these interactions (EdSurge, 2016; Morze et al., 2021; Taylor et al., 2021).

Different modes of content delivery are applied to realize adaptivity. According to Bloom's taxonomy of cognitive goals (Anderson & Krathwohl, 2001) and the hierarchical structure of learning content in personalized adaptive learning environments (Peng et al., 2019), the following materials could be provided: (a) *materials for learning*, such as text, video, audio, animation (b) *materials for practice*, such as problem sets, tool kits, and exercises, and (c) *materials for creation*, such as cases, virtual experiments, and simulation scenarios. These diverse materials allow learners to engage deeply with content by actively constructing knowledge through tailored resources that match their needs and goals. The adaptive framework also fosters autonomy, enabling learners to choose preferred materials that support the development of personalized learning experiences. By aligning materials with individual learning paths, personalized experiences not only facilitate the comprehension of learning materials but also increase learner motivation (Limongelli et al., 2011).

Following a needs analysis conducted by project partners responsible for the development of the AI additional qualification, Moodle was chosen as the preferred learning platform. LMSs, including Moodle, provide several benefits such as "constant availability and accessibility to course materials, cost savings, collaboration amongst students and lecturers, improved performance, feedback from users and effective communication" (Kabudi et al., 2021, p. 1). The suitability of Moodle was further supported by findings from studies conducted within the project framework. According to initial study findings, vocational school teachers are already acquainted with Moodle and endorse its utilization for delivering AI-related content. Learners have also been found to advocate for the utilization of a learning software that entails explanatory videos to support their learning (Rott et al., 2022). Based on further findings from the AI course evaluation, learners expressed particular satisfaction with the support provided by explanatory videos, quizzes, PDF slides, and image-based books within Moodle (Petridou & Lao, 2024). However, the technical aspects of the platform posed significant challenges, hindering both the teaching process and the overall learning experience. Instructors had to address technical issues instead of focusing on the AI content, while participants' learning was disrupted, affecting their learning experience and motivation. Therefore, regular troubleshooting was recommended to address these challenges, ensuring the platform's functionality. The importance of utilizing learning software tools for delivering AI contents is further emphasized in a recent review (Stamenković et al., 2023) and supported by several previous studies that have shown promising results by employing various software tools to facilitate AI learning (Grivokostopoulou & Hatzilygeroudis, 2013; Naser, 2008; Zhou et al., 2020).

An adaptive learning software supported by AI technologies was embedded into Moodle to provide individualized adaptive support, as denoted in Section 2.7.1. At its core, the AI-based learning system employed a sophisticated intelligence engine that functioned as a personalized tutor for each learner, assessing their knowledge levels and tailoring the learning experience to their individual needs. AI-driven mechanisms, including learner modeling to monitor and interpret learners' interactions, behavior-based clustering to dynamically group similar learners, and dynamic recommendation systems, enabled personalized learning paths and automated assignment evaluations, as well as adjustment of content difficulty based on learners' performance. Interactive and adaptive functions were incorporated in the form of plugins, rendering Moodle learner-centered. These plugins, which serve as extensions of a technical entity, adding new features to an existing software, were utilized to account for the varied needs, backgrounds, and knowledge of the heterogeneous group of learners. Several elements allowed the interactivity of the software. Gamification elements included a simulation-based ice cream sales estimation game and motivating performance-based rewards/ badges. Self-assessment H5P quizzes, which are interactive, browser-based quiz modules using the open-source H5P software, were available after each learning unit and included various question types such as drag and drop into text, flashcards, multiple choice, and fill-in-the-blanks. An interactive programming environment was further utilized, including Jupyter Notebooks, which constitute interactive, web-based computing environments that allow users to work on practical projects containing coding in Python with standard libraries for ML.

The adaptive functions entailed adaptive presentation and adaptive navigation techniques, following Brusilovsky's (2001) taxonomy of adaptive hypermedia technologies (see Section 2.4). These techniques monitored individual learning progress, assessed learners' knowledge level and performance, and provided individualized support, thereby enabling a personalized learning path. Various adaptive techniques were utilized. A *non-fixed sequence of learning modules* enabled personalized learning paths. This approach allowed learners to select what to learn next while guiding them towards the learning goal of acquiring the entire set of domain concepts, thereby preventing them from feeling overwhelmed with the learning tasks. A further adaptive element was the possibility of *specifying prior knowledge* by allowing learners to indicate learning units as already known, thereby avoiding redundant content. In addition, the feature of *disabling learning units/materials* was available. When learners did not fulfill the current section's requirements, subsequent learning units or materials were not accessible. It was regarded that the specific units did not belong to their current educational goal. The relevant links remained visible, but access to particular learning materials was restricted until individual learners were prepared to understand them. Moreover, *the availability of learning materials in different formats* and *the automatic flagging of their completion* provided learners with a selection of learning materials, including explanatory videos, image-based books, and PDFs. Once they selected their preferred format, the system automatically flagged non-selected materials as completed. Further adaptive features were the *assessment of performance* and *regulation of learning progress* through self-assessments via automatically evaluated and reported back quizzes. In addition, learners could mark content already mastered as completed. The system then automatically dimmed irrelevant content and highlighted the relevant learning units. A color-based mechanism indicated relevant links in green color and irrelevant ones in grey. Learners could also check their learning progress through a progress-based annotation that was constantly updated to show their current progress in the course. Therefore, based on adaptive presentation, particularly *adaptive multimedia presentation, adaptive text presentation,* and *adaptation of modality*, the learning pages in the course were not static but rather adaptively assembled for each learner (Brusilovsky & Peylo, 2003) and served to facilitate the learning process. Adaptive navigation support, primarily realized through *adaptive hiding* and *adaptive annotation,* enabled learners to take control of their progress in the entire course. By aiding learners in identifying their optimal learning path through the learning materials, this technique served to decrease their cognitive load and facilitated learners to focus on the most relevant learning materials (Brusilovsky, 1999). Overall, the adaptive features empowered learners to independently acquire AI knowledge and skills, promoting a personalized learning experience tailored to their individual needs and preferences.

Except for the above-mentioned adaptive functions that were integrated into Moodle, learners benefited from several basic supportive features. Worksheets were made available for group work, either face-to-face or online. These facilitated learners to deepen their understanding while working collaboratively. Interaction between learners was further enabled through the discussion forum or the chat function. Learners could also communicate via email with their peers and with their instructors, who periodically sent them learning updates. Besides, learners received push notifications, which were generated once new assignments were available or when forum posts and learning materials were updated. Learners were also encouraged via an automatically-generated question at the end of each learning unit to provide feedback on their comprehension and highlight aspects they found particularly engaging in the specific unit. In addition, a search function allowed them to locate materials related to specific keywords, concepts, and definitions. Moreover, they could check their profile, calendar, reports, messages and notifications, grades, badges, glossary, downloaded files, additional learning materials, and graphs with statistics, which allowed them to compare their progress with that of their peers.

The design of the learning environment draws upon several pedagogical and psychological theories. *Behavioral aspects,* such as *individual reinforcement* and *behavior shaping,* are integral to the use of badges and quizzes. Individual reinforcement occurred as both badges and quizzes were provided at a designated time, upon completion of learning sections, tailored to learners' current knowledge. Quizzes, in particular, shaped learners' behaviors by reinforcing partial achievements and contributing to the ultimate goal of acquiring AI knowledge and skills. The course design further facilitated *self-paced learning.* Learners had the possibility to specify prior knowledge and determine learning sequence, by setting learning modules as known and selecting the next learning module, features that reflect behavioral principles. The ability to answer quizzes after each learning unit to test learning gains, providing reinforcement and helping learners solidify their understanding, aligns with Skinner's central learning concepts. As described in Section 2.3.1, Skinner's *teaching machine* allowed learners to proceed at their own pace by presenting learning material incrementally based on readiness and requiring learners to demonstrate mastery of one step before moving to the next. Besides, Skinner emphasized the importance of *immediate feedback* for learning. In addition, the course was structured to engage learners with the learning content in a motivating game-based manner (Gee, 2003), leveraging behaviorist principles through *rewards* and *reinforcing feedback* to encourage consistent engagement and mastery of concepts. Learners had the possibility to actively participate in activities or quizzes, which were offered incrementally and provided relevant feedback, reflecting further behaviorist principles rooted in *programmed instruction* (McDonald et al., 2005).

Further, cognitivists' approaches and constructivist principles were pivotal in developing the learning environment as a *self-learning platform.* At the core of its development was to encourage learners to self-regulate their learning and independently construct AI knowledge and practice skills, complemented by system support through interactive and adaptive functions that stimulated active participation and peer collaboration. To mitigate *cognitive load*, learning units were designed to facilitate step-by-step progression, leveraging the system's capability to consider learners' prior knowledge and facilitate personalized learning trajectories. Quizzes were provided at sophistically determined intervals throughout the course. This approach aimed to achieve the *spacing effect* as developed in the framework of experimental psychology by Ebbinghaus (1885). The spacing effect posits that revisiting learning material at gradually increasing intervals enhances content retention and promotes learning success. Learners were further provided with the possibility to determine their learning path and make decisions about their learning. This feature aligns with the constructivist principle that learners are not passive recipients of information but *active participants* in the learning process, taking responsibility for their learning and *self-constructing knowledge.* Learner-centered and interactive approaches were prioritized to encourage learners to actively engage in learning, construct knowledge autonomously, thereby offering a *"learning by doing" experience* (Schimanke et al., 2014). In addition, the platform promoted *peer-to-peer communication* and interaction through features like the discussion forum and collaborative activities embedded within the course structure. These practices can be dated back to social cognitive theory and social constructivism, particularly the notion of *situated cognition*, which emphasizes how cognitive processes are situated within physical and social contexts. Lastly, *multiple learning media* were made available, aligning with constructivist principles. This variety supports *learners' autonomy* by allowing them to select materials that align with their individual preferences and engage with content from multiple perspectives, thereby enhancing motivation and contributing to better learning outcomes.

2.8 Summary of the Theoretical Framework

Following the presentation of theoretical concepts and recent research developments pertinent to this thesis, the key insights from the theoretical framework will be summarized.

The integration of AI into various fields is at present indisputable, necessitating that VET and CVET institutions not be left behind. In Germany, AI topics have primarily been taught at higher education institutions, with their integration into VET and CVET programs only beginning to develop recently. Specialists and emerging professionals often lack the necessary qualifications to effectively utilize AI technologies in their workplaces. To cope with the new job requirements in their workplaces, they need to receive adequate AI training. The course on AI and ML developed in the project 'Bringing AI into Vocational Education' addressed this gap by imparting AI knowledge to young adults from diverse occupations. This course employed an adaptive learning software supported by AI technologies, leveraging interactive and adaptive functions to enhance learning outcomes and ensure individualized learning trajectories. The objective of this course, to learn about and with AI, theoretically positions this research in the field of AIEd. The field of AIEd encompasses the study of AI technologies in educational settings to foster human learning and achieve a range of educational objectives. As demonstrated, AI's value in education lies in its ability to offer individualized learning solutions that cater to a broader range of learners and account for their diverse characteristics.

To optimize the effectiveness of an adaptive learning environment in VET and CVET settings and thereby enhance learning outcomes, it is crucial to ground its implementation in established educational theories. Despite the growing integration of AI into education, there are still no precise educational guidelines for developing an AI-based learning environment that aligns with well-established theoretical frameworks in VET and CVET settings. While fundamental principles of behaviorism remain integral to AI-based learning systems, key functionalities of such systems are deeply rooted in cognitivism and social constructivism. Behaviorist approaches, including individual reinforcement and behavior shaping, can be effectively integrated into AI-based adaptive learning environments through mechanisms like quizzes, badges, and automated feedback provided at strategic time points. These elements serve to reinforce incremental achievements and support knowledge acquisition in AI-related competences. However, achieving effective knowledge acquisition necessitates that learners assume an active role rather than functioning merely as passive recipients of AI guidance. Learners need to actively engage in a dynamic learning process, whereby collaboration with the AI-based learning system takes place. This requires establishing an interactive learning environment in which AI functions as a supportive agent, realizing learners' distinct learning needs and preferences and facilitating them in effectively constructing knowledge and developing skills.

Since individual learning differences determine to what extent and how effectively learners engage in the learning process, leveraging adaptive technologies to address these variations plays a pivotal role in fostering learning success. A fundamental role in adaptive technologies is the adaptation to prior knowledge. Following cognitivist principles, learners' performance is shaped more by their existing knowledge and repeated practice than by innate ability. Therefore, an adaptive learning environment has the potential to enhance learning by customizing learning experiences to learners' prior knowledge. Considering prior knowledge is crucial, as prior knowledge constitutes a significant indicator of an individual's ability to acquire new concepts and skills and is a strong predictor of learning achievement. Learners need to actively select and organize relevant information, integrating it with existing knowledge to effectively construct a cohesive mental representation of their learning experiences. This process is facilitated by a stimulating learning environment that promotes the active construction of knowledge and incorporates both textual and visual representations to enhance content recall and comprehension, following the principles of dual coding and multimedia learning. Personalization constitutes an essential feature in this context, as instructional support needs to be adapted to learners' cognitive readiness to enhance knowledge acquisition. This is particularly relevant in the context of an AI training qualification implemented in VET and CVET institutions. In these learning settings, learners have acquired varying levels of AI-related knowledge based on their educational backgrounds as well as the specific demands of their professions. By accounting for differences in AI knowledge levels and providing tailored support, adaptive learning environments can facilitate learners to integrate the relatively new topic of AI into their existing knowledge more effectively.

In this regard, the delivery of an AI training course in a blended learning environment is considered beneficial. This learning format enables learners to take responsibility for their learning process and seek support from instructors when they encounter difficulties. Independent online study is combined with periodic in-person or online teacher assistance, thereby fostering personalized learning and sustained motivation. However, as blended learning relies on technology-supported instruction, particularly when an adaptive learning system is implemented, learners' digital proficiency constitutes a prerequisite. Learners need to possess the ability to efficiently use the digital learning applications embedded in the course. Essentially, familiarity with these tools enables learners to interact with the learning system, thereby constructing AI knowledge and skills. Learners with extensive experience in digital learning applications have been found to achieve superior learning outcomes. This is particularly evident in vocational and continuing education, where learners' digital skills positively influence their academic achievement, thereby improving their professional prospects. Hence, considering learners' prior knowledge alone is insufficient. Learners' existing experience with digital learning applications is also a critical factor for successful learning outcomes in an AI course delivered in VET and CVET institutions.

A key distinction between traditional or online learning environments and adaptive learning environments is the integration of human-AI interaction in the latter. One-to-one instructional learning realized in adaptive learning environments through AI technologies can lead to greater learning gains by enabling personalized learning experiences. Rooted in constructivist approaches, meaningful interactions between learners and the AI-based adaptive learning system have the potential to facilitate deeper knowledge integration and application in practical learning contexts. Drawing from the constructivist perspective of situated cognition, knowledge generation is enacted within adaptive learning systems when learners actively engage with the learning system. These interactions are facilitated through adaptive features that promote individualized learning. Content presentation and navigation support are the core elements that can be adapted in the framework of adaptive learning systems. AI-based support can be differentiated based on each learner's individual characteristics, creating a personalized and contextually relevant learning experience. This is particularly beneficial in vocational education, where learners acquire job-specific skills that require both theoretical knowledge and hands-on practice. Through adaptive learning pathways, adaptive learning systems can facilitate the application of theoretical knowledge in practical contexts by simulating real workplace scenarios, offer targeted guidance that helps apprentices and professionals develop practical competences required in their respective fields, and provide training aligned with industry demands.

Following the concept of ZPD, which emphasizes that learners benefit from instructional support of more capable peers tailored to their current level of understanding, the AI-based learning system functions as the knowledgeable peer that provides guidance tailored to learners' individual needs and preferences, particularly their existing knowledge. This personalized support enables learners to effectively construct AI-related knowledge and skills. Given the high diversity of learners in vocational and continuing education, varying in age, educational background, and professional experience, the AI-based learning system needs to facilitate independent knowledge acquisition while adapting to these diverse learning profiles. By offering tailored support, a personalized learning experience is fostered that accommodates individual learning needs and equips vocational and continuing education learners with job-relevant skills. Through individualized guidance, real-time feedback, and adaptive support tailored to specific professions, adaptive learning environments can help apprentices and continuing education learners bridge the gap between theoretical instruction and workplace application, ultimately enhancing their employability and job readiness in an AI-emerging world where digital competences and human-AI collaboration are becoming essential across industries.

Nevertheless, while recent research suggests that adaptive technologies hold promise for enhancing knowledge and skill acquisition, there is still limited empirical evidence regarding their effectiveness in improving learning outcomes, particularly within vocational and continuing education settings. Therefore, this thesis examines whether the features of adaptivity and individualization embedded into adaptive learning systems, alongside prior knowledge and experience with digital learning applications, can exert any influence on AI learning outcomes. These factors are investigated as significant determinants of AI learning success, contributing to closing the research gap on the impact of personalized adaptive learning on learning outcomes.

Among the most influential learning characteristics for enhanced learning achievements, the role of learning styles has been extensively examined in the framework of adaptive learning environments. Learning styles encompass individual preferences in the way learners perceive and process information, influencing their approach to learning tasks and content. Learning styles affect individuals' learning processes, influencing their engagement with learning content and determining how effectively they acquire knowledge. By aligning instructional methods with learners' preferred styles, learning experiences become more personalized and effective, leading to enhanced learning outcomes. Various learning style models are utilized in adaptive learning environments, with the FSLSM, which was developed by Felder and Silverman (1988), being prominently employed in adaptive learning environments and technology-enhanced systems due to its adaptability and detailed psychological dimensions for precise user modeling and adaptive learning. Based on the way learners prefer to receive and process information, this model distinguishes learners into active and reflective learner types, sensing and intuitive, visual and verbal, as well as sequential and global learner types. The different learner types reflect differentiated approaches to learning, influencing how learners engage with and comprehend educational material.

Since an adaptive learning environment developed for AI training primarily relies on cognitivist and constructivist learning approaches, thereby fostering active engagement and active construction of knowledge, learners with active learning styles are probably favored to a higher degree than reflective learners. Similarly, sensing learners may be better supported than intuitive learners, as the system prioritizes concrete learning materials, including practice-oriented exercises, worksheets, and collaborative activities. Furthermore, a strong emphasis is placed on visual representations to facilitate knowledge construction and integration with prior knowledge, potentially benefiting visual learners more than verbal learners, who primarily depend on spoken or written explanations. Lastly, an AI-based learning system that promotes a sequential learning path to facilitate progressive knowledge acquisition is assumed to support sequential learners better than learners with global learning styles, who learn in large leaps and do not necessarily profit from a sequential learning order. However, the extent to which learners with specific learning styles achieve better learning outcomes in adaptive learning systems designed for vocational and continuing education remains largely unexplored. This thesis further seeks to address this gap by investigating which learning styles are related to improved learning outcomes in an AI training course.

In summary, there has been a significant gap between the potential capabilities of AIEd technologies and their actual implementation in authentic educational settings, especially in the framework of VET and CVET. At the same time, employing adaptive learning systems and personalizing support to individual learning characteristics holds great potential for improving the learning outcomes of learners in VET and CVET institutions, who constitute a highly heterogeneous group often lacking sufficient AI-related knowledge and skills. This thesis serves to address this research gap by shedding light on the learner characteristics and the learning system's features that contribute to enhanced AI learning outcomes in vocational and continuing education settings.

Research Questions and Hypotheses 3

Based on the framework that was derived from the theoretical background of this thesis, the following research questions (RQs) along with their hypotheses (Hs) are formulated:

RQ1: Do adaptivity, individualization, prior knowledge, and experience with digital learning applications have an effect on learning outcomes?

H1: Previous research has demonstrated that these factors are expected to have a positive effect on learning outcomes (Gomede et al., 2021; Jonassen & Grabowski, 2012; Kinshuk, 2016; Kurt, 2021; Mirari, 2022; Nakic et al., 2015; Schunk, 2012; Taylor et al., 2021).

More specifically, adaptivity realized through the system's adaptive techniques is expected to have a positive effect on learning outcomes. While no consensus has so far been achieved regarding the full potential of adaptive learning technologies (Kabudi et al., 2021; Özyurt & Özyurt, 2015; Zhang & Aslan, 2021) and individual studies did not demonstrate positive results on academic achievement (Akkoyunlu & Soylu, 2008; Wang et al., 2006), substantial previous research has indicated positive effects on learning outcomes (Chiu et al., 2023, Chrysafiadi et al., 2023; Gomede et al., 2021; Karakostas & Demetriadis, 2011). Further studies have demonstrated that learners achieve better learning results when learning with the aid of adaptive techniques compared to learning in a non-adaptive learning environment (Cui et al., 2018; Kardan & Conati, 2015; Ling & Chiang, 2022; Wang et al., 2020). The potential of adaptivity to enhance learning outcomes was also theoretically supported by thorough theoretical endeavors (Jonassen & Grabowski, 2012; Kinshuk, 2016; Taylor et al., 2021).

E. Petridou, *Personalized Learning in Vocational and Continuing Education*,
https://doi.org/10.1007/978-3-658-51517-1_3

Individualization of the learning environment and through the learning software to the learners' needs is further expected to positively affect learning outcomes. Previous research has indicated not only that individualized adaptive learning instruction can lead to greater learning gains (Wang et al., 2020) but also that individualized learning strategies and tasks can have a positive impact on learning outcomes (Manea et al., 2023). Particularly in blended-learning environments, individualized interventions have been shown to significantly enhance learning outcomes (Zhang et al., 2019). Based on the findings of a recent review, a positive and significant influence thereof is expected (Mirari, 2022). These positive results are further theoretically supported by several previous studies. Customizing instruction to individual learning needs facilitates each learner to achieve mastery and better learning outcomes, as individual characteristics are significant determinants of learning effectiveness (Jonassen & Grabowski, 2012; Kinshuk, 2016; Schunk, 2012; Taylor et al., 2021).

Adaptivity and individualization are expected to positively influence learning outcomes, as the design of the learning environment was based on prominent learning theories. The provision of individualized immediate reinforcement of partial achievements at designated times following behaviorism is expected to have a positive influence on acquiring AI knowledge and skills. In addition, following cognitivism and constructivism, adaptive functions enable learners to self-regulate their learning as well as independently and actively construct knowledge via a step-by-step progression, reducing their cognitive load. Besides, adaptive functions allow learners to create their individual learning path and learn with the aid of practice-oriented exercises and peer-to-peer collaboration, thereby further contributing to better learning outcomes.

Prior knowledge has been identified in previous research as a significant determinant of learning outcomes. "Prior skills and knowledge transfer directly to new learning" (Jonassen & Grabowski, 1993, p. 421), both significantly influencing the learning process. Previously acquired knowledge and skills contribute to the construction of new knowledge and the development of more advanced skills. Therefore, following cognitivist principles, prior knowledge is believed to foster knowledge construction (Schunk, 2012). Particularly, in adaptive learning systems, tailoring content to learners' prior knowledge has been shown to enhance learning outcomes (Li, 2019; Mampadi et al., 2009). However, prior knowledge may sometimes hinder learning if it is not activated, relevant, and congruent with the content to be learned (Brod, 2021). The adaptive learning software utilized in this thesis allowed for the specification of learners' prior knowledge and adaptation to their needs, aiming to optimize learning outcomes. Consequently, it is expected that prior knowledge will have a significant positive impact on learning outcomes.

Experience with digital learning applications is further expected to positively affect learning outcomes, as familiarity with these tools enables learners to navigate the AI course more effectively than those with little experience, thereby enhancing their learning outcomes. While research on the relationship between digital competency and learning performance remains limited (Chaw & Tang, 2024), previous studies have shown that computer experience directly impacts learning outcomes (Brinkerhoff et al., 2001; Hasan & Ali, 2004). Specifically, for vocational learners, proficiency in digital competences has been found to positively affect academic achievement (Pagani et al., 2016). Thus, a positive effect is hypothesized.

RQ2: Do learners with different learning styles achieve different learning outcomes?

H2: Learners with certain learning styles are expected to achieve higher learning outcomes, as it is hypothesized that the adaptive functions of the software better accommodate certain learning styles.

RQ2.1: Do learners with active learning styles achieve higher learning outcomes than learners with reflective learning styles?

H2.1: According to Chang et al. (2016), active learners were found to be among the lowest performers. Nevertheless, based on Felder and Silverman's (1988) assumption that CAI benefits active learners and given that the course was designed as an action-oriented learning setting, including practice-based exercises and collaborative activities that required active learning, active learners are expected to achieve better learning outcomes than reflective learners. While there are no prior data on the size of such an effect, a moderate effect size is expected following Hattie's (2008) comprehensive analysis, which identified moderate effect sizes for educational interventions aiming to improve learning outcomes.

RQ2.2: Do learners with sensing learning styles achieve higher learning outcomes than learners with intuitive learning styles?

H2.2: Based on Felder and Silverman's (1988) assumption that CAI is beneficial for sensing learners, sensing learners are expected to perform better than intuitive learners. In addition, the learning materials include worksheets, exercises, and collaborative activities, which involve practice-oriented examples and detailed information about abstract concepts that favor sensing learners, thereby facilitating their learning. Although prior data on the exact effect size is not available, a moderate effect size is expected in line with Hattie's (2008) findings, which demonstrate that educational interventions typically yield moderate effect sizes in influencing learning outcomes.

RQ2.3: Do learners with visual learning styles achieve higher learning outcomes than learners with verbal learning styles?

H2.3: Previous research presents mixed findings. According to Brown et al. (2006), there is no significant difference in learning outcomes between visual and verbal learners. Chang et al. (2016) found that visual learners were among the lowest performers. However, since the learning content within the adaptive learning environment is primarily designed for self-directed learning, visual learners have more opportunities, such as diagrams and explanatory videos, while verbal learners have fewer opportunities due to the limited face-to-face instruction and spoken explanations. Therefore, it is hypothesized that visual learners will achieve better learning outcomes than verbal learners. As in previous similar studies, the effect size is not reported, a moderate effect size is anticipated based on Hattie's (2008) synthesis of educational interventions, which consistently reported moderate effect sizes on learning outcomes.

RQ2.4: Do learners with sequential learning styles achieve higher learning outcomes than learners with global learning styles?

H2.4: Based on the findings of El-Bishouty et al. (2019), which indicated that sequential learners were the most supported by the implemented adaptive system while global learners were the least supported, and the study by Chang et al. (2016), which found that sequential learners were the highest performers, it is hypothesized that sequential learners will achieve better learning outcomes than global learners. In addition, the learning software, despite allowing learners to follow individual learning paths, restricts access to content that is considered advanced or identified as unfamiliar to the learners, thereby predominantly supporting a sequential learning order. Considering the lack of an exact effect size in previous research, a moderate effect size is expected, drawing on Hattie's (2008) findings of average moderate effect sizes of educational interventions on learning outcomes.

Methodology

4

At the core of the project 'Bringing AI into Vocational Education' was the evaluation of the delivery of an additional qualification on AI and ML designed for learners in industrial-technical and commercial sectors of VET and CVET institutions in Germany. The course was delivered in a blended learning format, combining face-to-face instruction with an adaptive learning software designed for the course's online delivery. To enhance the learning outcomes of the diverse learner group, the software incorporated adaptive techniques that tailored support to learner characteristics and fostered individualized learning. This thesis examines whether the software's features of adaptivity and individualization, alongside the learner characteristics of prior knowledge in AI and experience with digital learning applications, positively influence AI learning outcomes. In addition, emphasis is placed on learning styles as a key factor influencing learning outcomes within adaptive learning systems. Hence, it is further investigated whether learners with certain learning styles achieve better learning outcomes in the course. The following sections outline the methodological approach that was followed to systematically investigate these research questions and their hypotheses, as described in Chap. 3. First, the survey design and data collection process are described, followed by details on participants and the sampling procedure. Subsequently, the cognitive interview used to refine the implemented instruments is presented. Section 4.4 provides an overview of the instruments utilized to measure the key constructs of the thesis, including prior knowledge in AI, experience with digital learning applications, learning styles, individualization, adaptivity,

Supplementary Information The online version contains supplementary material available at https://doi.org/10.1007/978-3-658-51517-1_4.

E. Petridou, *Personalized Learning in Vocational and Continuing Education*,
https://doi.org/10.1007/978-3-658-51517-1_4

and learning outcomes. Finally, the last section reports the data analysis methods applied to assess the hypotheses of the thesis.

4.1 Survey Design and Data Collection

A methodologically robust quasi-experimental research design was implemented (Campbell & Stanley, 1963), incorporating elements of both cross-sectional and time-sequenced data collection. Two rounds of data collection were conducted. These were coordinated with the delivery of the AI qualification during the regular school period in Germany over two consecutive years from 2022 to 2024. The survey method was adopted to collect learners' perceptions throughout the AI course via self-report questionnaires. Standardized online surveys were conducted at three time points in each school year. The first survey (t_0) was conducted before the beginning of the course. A mid-course survey (t_1) followed during the implementation of the course, as well as a final survey (t_2) was implemented at the end of the course. While each participant provided data at specific time points (pre-, mid-, and post-course) within a single school year, the study did not track individual change across multiple years. Instead, data were aggregated across the two consecutive cohorts (2022–2024), enabling a larger sample size and enhancing statistical power. The design allowed for the temporal sequencing of predictor and outcome variables, although it did not meet the criteria for a fully longitudinal study.

Table 4.1 outlines the exact time periods for each survey conducted across data collection rounds. At the beginning of each survey, participants were informed that their data would be handled confidentially and utilized solely for the scope of scientific endeavors. To ensure participants' anonymity, participants were asked to fill in a personal code by combining specific digits and letters at the start of each survey (see Appendix E in the electronic supplementary material). As each participant filled out more than one survey, and it was necessary to make comparisons across questionnaires, the personal code also served to allocate the questionnaires to individual participants. Participants were encouraged to participate in the surveys by the provision of incentives, including the chance to win vouchers, an iPad, and virtual reality glasses in a prize draw.

Table 4.1 Survey Time Periods Across Data Collection Rounds

Survey	Time period
First data collection (school year 2022/23)	
t_0	August 2022—December 2022
t_1	January 2023—February 2023
t_2	March 2023—September 2023
Second data collection (school year 2023/24)	
t_0	September 2023—March 2024
t_1	January 2024—May 2024
t_2	June 2024—August 2024

4.2 Participants and Sampling Procedure

The research sample consisted of learners from industrial-technical and commercial sectors at vocational schools and CVET institutions in the region of Baden-Württemberg. In the first data collection round, participants were recruited from the AI course conducted at four vocational schools and an in-house training program at a company. As the schools did not provide the exact number of learners, the total number of registered learners was estimated to be approximately 70. The second data collection round expanded to include new participants from the participating schools of the first data collection, participants from four additional schools, and one additional certification course offered by a Chamber of Industry and Commerce. The total number of registered learners in these courses was estimated to be 180, as the schools did not provide exact figures. The research team, consisting of the author and three educational researchers, contacted the instructors and provided them with the survey links. The learners were then instructed to participate in the online surveys at the start of their class, prior to beginning the AI course. The surveys were hosted on Unipark, an online survey provider specializing in survey and feedback solutions for scientific research and other purposes. A total of 222 learners who expressed interest in the study participated in the surveys voluntarily. Table 4.2 provides an overview of the response rates across the two data collection rounds. A decline in learners' willingness to participate in the surveys can be clearly observed over the course of the qualification. Response rates were particularly high at the beginning of the traineeship program (t_0). While a substantial number of participants remained engaged in the t_1 survey, a notable decline in participation was observed in the last survey

(t_2). This trend reflects a common pattern in longitudinal surveys, where participation decreases over time (Lao et al., 2024). This decline in participation can be attributed to learners' increasing demands, who had to balance their involvement in the course with occupational and school responsibilities. Additionally, the surveys' distribution method, which relied on instructors for dissemination and reminders, may have contributed to the decline, as the instructors' ability to consistently encourage participation could have diminished over time. Finally, learners' initial motivation may have decreased over time, further influencing their participation. Overall, the response rates ranged between 43% and 97%, which are regarded as adequate for educational studies (Hage, 1996).

Table 4.2 Survey Participation and Response Rates Across Data Collection Rounds

Survey	Participant who registered for the course	Participant who completed each survey	Response rate
	n	n	%
First data collection			
t_0	70	47	67
t_1	70	43	61
t_2	70	30	43
Second data collection			
t_0	180	175	97
t_1	180	131	73
t_2	180	104	58

The sociodemographic data of the participants were collected in the t_0-surveys. The sample consisted of 43 females (19.4%), 177 males (79.7%), and two learners who were identified as diverse (0.9%). Participants ranged in age from 16 to 47 years ($n = 220$), having a mean age of 21.5 years ($SD = 4.7$). Almost half of the participants (46.4%) had a higher education entrance qualification (A-levels) (Abitur), 28.8% had an intermediate school certificate (mittlere Reife), 20.7% had an advanced technical college certificate (Fachhochschulreife), and only 2.3% had a secondary school certificate. Three participants had other certificates, and one participant had no certificate. Most learners were in their second traineeship year (70.7%). The rest were either in the third (18.0%) or in the first traineeship year (10.4%), while only two participants (0.9%) were in the fourth traineeship year. Most participants were employed in a large company with 500 and more employees (68.6%), particularly in the first data collection, where almost all of the participants worked in large companies (91.3%). Participants coming from companies with 50–249 employees accounted for 16.8% of the total sample. Participants employed in companies with 10–49 employees and those with 250–499 employees each represented 5.9% of the total sample, while participants in small companies with 1–9 employees constituted only 2.7% of the total sample. Regarding the professional sectors in which the vocational and continuing education learners were employed, the industrial sector constituted the largest portion of the sample (60.9%). This trend was consistent across both data collections: in the first data collection, 71.7% of the learners were employed in the industrial sector, and although this proportion decreased to 58.0% in the second data collection, it remained the largest. Other sectors were less represented in the total sample, including other services (15.9%) and the sector of Information, Communication, and Software (10.5%). Much less represented sectors involved the sectors of Wholesale and Foreign Trade (4.5%), Transport/Logistics (3.6%), Retail (1.4%), Banking and Finance (1.4%), Management Consulting (1.4%), and Construction Industry (0.5%). In total, 22 different traineeship occupations could be identified. The most reported traineeship occupation in the industrial-technical sector was mechatronics technician (25.2%), and in the commercial sector was IT-Specialist (16.2%). For a detailed overview of the learners' sociodemographic characteristics, differentiated by first and second data collection, interested readers may refer to Tables A1 and A2 in Appendix A in the electronic supplementary material.

4.3 Cognitive Interviewing

Cognitive interviewing was conducted during the developmental phase of the questionnaires to ensure they effectively capture the intended constructs. The interviews evaluated the clarity, comprehensibility, and suitability of the survey questions for the target group of vocational and continuing education learners. The pretesting process aimed to identify any potential issues with wording, phrasing, and question formulation that might hinder participants from responding accurately. Items were selected from the questionnaires on learning styles, individualization, and adaptivity, as detailed in Sect. 4.4. The cognitive pretesting included questions that were translated or adapted from other questionnaires, as well as questions that were developed specifically for this study.

Cognitive interviewing is utilized as a diagnostic method to test survey instruments before they are administered to the respondents (Collins, 2003). Cognitive interviewing was developed during the 1980s and included two main techniques: *think-aloud* and *verbal probing* (Willis, 1999). The purpose of using the think-aloud method, which stems from psychological procedures, was to obtain information concerning the comprehensibility of the questions, potential difficulties in answering the questions, as well as to find out how interviewees interpreted terms (Lenzner et al., 2016). The think-aloud process requires the interviewees to verbalize their thoughts while solving tasks, shedding light on the response process and highlighting any issues in resolving tasks. Respondents may also be encouraged by the interviewer to continue speaking to express what they are thinking (Van Someren et al., 1994). However, interruptions are in principle not allowed, whether they are suggestions, prompts, or questions. This ensures that the interviewees maintain their flow of verbalizing their thoughts, without leaving room for the interviewer to make any interpretations or explanations. The think-aloud method is implemented either while resolving tasks, known as *concurrent think-aloud*, or after the tasks have been resolved, referred to as *retrospective think-aloud*. The second main technique, verbal probing, is derived from cognitive research and enables the interviewer to guide the respondents to elaborate upon their responses. *Cognitive probes* are utilized to elicit responses to specific questions, such as comprehension or retrieval questions (Collins, 2003; Willis, 1999). Follow-up questions allow the interviewer to gain deeper insights into respondents' understanding and reasoning. *Concurrent probes* are utilized once respondents answer the survey questions, while *retrospective probes* are administered once respondents have answered the whole questionnaire (Lenzner et al., 2016). Both the think-aloud technique as well as verbal probing can be effectively combined to optimize survey instruments (Collins, 2003; Willis, 1999).

The cognitive interview conducted for this thesis combined both methods and was held in July 2022, before administering the questionnaires in the first data collection round. An interview protocol was developed, including the scope of the interview, instructions on the interview procedure, the probing questions, and space for the interviewer's notes and comments. Six female apprentices from the Chamber of Commerce and Industry in Reutlingen voluntarily participated in the interview. The interview was conducted in pairs (two apprentices and the interviewer) in a quiet setting. Each pair was provided with selected items from three questionnaires utilized in the study. The apprentices gave their written consent for processing their data and were informed that their data would be handled confidentially. They received a short introduction about the purpose of pretesting. They were assured that their responses would be solely used to improve the questionnaire. Each pair was instructed about the interview procedure and the concepts investigated by the questionnaires. The questionnaire items were administered in printed form. Apprentices were asked to read each question and response option aloud, verbally express their thoughts, feelings, and any difficulties they experienced, and highlight any issues such as unclear wording, confusing instructions, or inappropriate response options.

Concurrent and retrospective think-aloud and probing techniques were implemented. The interviewees were asked to verbalize their thoughts while they answered the questions, with minimal intervention from the interviewer. However, if respondents paused or stopped verbalizing, the interviewer provided gentle reminders to continue thinking aloud. At the same time, concurrent probing questions were utilized to elicit respondents' thoughts on particular issues, such as suggesting alternative wording or commenting on the relevance of the questions. Scripted probes were utilized that aimed to guide apprentices in expressing their thoughts on specific issues, such as whether certain terms were understandable and if particular ones were preferable. At the end of the interview, retrospective probes allowed apprentices to reflect on the overall difficulty and comprehensibility of the questionnaire, as well as to provide additional feedback on any items they found problematic. The combination of think-aloud and verbal probing techniques allowed for a comprehensive evaluation of the survey items. The think-aloud method provided insights into respondents' real-time cognitive processes as they interpreted and answered questions, while verbal probing facilitated deeper exploration of specific issues. The interviewer audio-recorded the interviews and noted spontaneous utterances and reactions to cognitive probes during the whole procedure. The interviews lasted between 25 to 40 minutes.

Due to constraints in time and resources, a practical approach was followed to evaluate the interviews. The feedback gathered through cognitive interviewing provided valuable insights into the comprehensibility and usability of the survey items. During the interviews, apprentices' comments and reactions in real-time were documented. Their utterances were recorded, thereby facilitating the identification and improvement of problematic items. Apprentices identified instances of unclear wording and confusing response options, which informed suggestions for alternative phrasing to improve clarity. Specific issues raised regarding the questions' clarity, phrasing, or structure were noted. Additionally, several items were confirmed to be well-understood and required no changes. A detailed description of the necessary changes in each questionnaire is provided in Sect. 4.4. Following the cognitive interviews, the research team reviewed the collective feedback, addressed key issues by indicating problematic items, and discussed potential improvements. The questionnaires were then revised iteratively, focusing on improving clarity, reducing ambiguity, and ensuring that the questions were aligned with the intended constructs. This iterative process played a crucial role in refining the survey instruments, thereby rendering them well-suited to accurately capture vocational and continuing education learners' perceptions.

4.4 Instruments

Standardized online questionnaires in German were developed based on a literature search and existing instruments to measure learners' perceptions and learning outcomes. In the t_0-survey, which served as a pre-test, learners were asked to provide sociodemographic information (see Sect. 4.2), along with a subjective assessment of their prior knowledge in AI-related thematic areas, their experience with digital learning applications, and their learning styles. In the mid-course t_1-survey, the perceived individualization through the learning software and of the learning environment were measured. Adaptivity and cognitive learning outcomes were assessed in the t_2-survey, which was administered as a post-test. A systematic literature review was conducted to find out existing instruments in the field. Complete or partial scales and items were adapted and further developed. To investigate certain constructs, items or complete scales were developed from scratch. Closed-ended questions were formed, and unless otherwise stated, the response format was based on a Likert rating scale to allow for more granularity in the responses. An odd number of response options (3 or 5) was deliberately chosen for most scales to allow learners to select a neutral middle category. While a neutral mid-point response option increases the risk of distortion due to the ambiguity-indifference problem, where respondents might choose the neutral option out of uncertainty or indifference, omitting a middle category could lead to artificial variance by forcing respondents to choose a direction (Kankaraš & Capecchi, 2024). Hence, the potential distortions from lacking a neutral option were considered more problematic, making its inclusion more preferable, a choice further supported by the potential of better psychometric characteristics of scales including a neutral response option (Kankaraš & Capecchi, 2024). The instruments can be found in Appendix E in the electronic supplementary material. A detailed description of each instrument is provided below.

4.4.1 Prior Knowledge in AI

Learners' prior knowledge in AI was assessed in the pretest through the subjective assessment of their prior knowledge across various thematic areas of AI. A scale was developed from scratch (see Pretest in Appendix E in the electronic supplementary material), as no similar scale was available in previous research. Learners were asked how familiar they were with different thematic areas of AI, such as Basic Concepts of AI, ML, or Data Analysis. A 4-point Likert scale was utilized, ranging from *not at all* to *very well*. To ensure that the items of the scale effectively capture prior knowledge in AI as a single underlying factor, an exploratory factor analysis (EFA) was conducted on the nine items with oblique rotation (oblimin). Oblique rotation was selected as it was assumed that the different thematic areas of AI were interrelated. The Kaiser–Meyer–Olkin (KMO) measure verified the sampling adequacy for the analysis, KMO = .87. Further, all KMO values for individual items ranged from .79 to .93, namely well above the acceptable limit of .5 (Field, 2012). Bartlett's test of sphericity yielded a significant result, $\chi^2(36) = 904.78$, $p < .001$, indicating that the variables are sufficiently correlated for factor analysis. The results of the EFA supported a single-factor structure, with all items loading above 0.59 (see Table 4.3) on the single factor and accounting for 46% of the variance, suggesting that prior knowledge in AI can be effectively represented by the developed scale. Subsequently, the internal consistency of the scale was evaluated by calculating Cronbach's alpha (Cronbach, 1951), indicating good reliability ($a = .88$).

Table 4.3 Summary of EFA Results for the Prior Knowledge Scale

Topic	Oblimin rotated factor loading
	Prior knowledge
Basic concepts of AI	**.74**
Data management	**.73**
Fundamentals of data analysis	**.74**
Machine learning	**.69**
Opportunities, challenges, and ethical issues of AI	**.61**
Practical examples	**.63**
Programming	**.59**
(Potential) areas of application	**.69**
Other topics	**.67**

Note. $N = 217$. EFA = exploratory factor analysis. Factor loadings greater than .30 are shown in bold. The eigenvalue of the factor is 4.13, accounting for 46% of the explained variance. The items are translated into English. The original scale is in the Pretest in Appendix E in the electronic supplementary material

A knowledge test using the same items before and after the intervention to measure changes in the learners' knowledge in AI was not implemented for two reasons. First, AI as a topic of an additional qualification is relatively new. It was anticipated that learners would have difficulty answering specific questions about certain thematic areas of AI, given their limited familiarity with the topic and its broad, interdisciplinary nature. Second, due to the expected low prior knowledge in AI among learners, pretest effects could not be eliminated by the implementation of a knowledge test. The pretest itself can exert a treatment effect and change the learning outcomes, introducing bias (Bortz & Döring, 2006). Although the Solomon four-group design could have been used to mitigate pretest effects, it was not feasible to be implemented due to the limited number of study participants in each collection round.

4.4.2 Experience with Digital Learning Applications

To assess learners' prior experience with digital learning applications, the subjective assessment of their experience was measured in the pretest. The scale was developed by adapting the instrument *Monitor Digitale Bildung* (Schmid et al., 2016). Learners were asked to indicate how much experience they have with various digital learning applications. These included both overarching categories, such as online courses, LMSs (i.e., Moodle), learning software, as well as more specific learning tools, such as chat services, educational videos, and forums. Learners could indicate their level of experience in a 4-point response format, including options *no experience*, *some experience*, and *much experience*, as well as an option *I do not know* (see Pretest in Appendix E in the electronic supplementary material). An EFA, aimed at assessing whether the single-factor structure of the scale can be supported, was conducted on the 12 items of the scale with oblique rotation (oblimin), as the items were assumed to be interrelated. The KMO measure of sampling adequacy was .83, indicating that the data is suitable for factor analysis, with individual items' KMO values ranging from .74 to .89, which are well above the acceptable limit of .5 (Field, 2012). Additionally, Bartlett's test of sphericity was significant, $\chi^2(66) = 255.66$, $p < .001$, indicating that the variables are sufficiently correlated for factor analysis. The results of the EFA supported a single-factor structure, with item loadings ranging from .41 to .72 (see Table 4.4). The variance explained by the factor amounted to 28%, further indicating that the broader construct of experience with digital learning applications can effectively represent the items related to various digital learning applications. While the results suggested potential for a more complex factor structure that could better represent the individual applications, this was not further investigated, as the single-factor structure was deemed acceptable. The scale showed good reliability, as indicated by calculating Cronbach's alpha (a = .81).

Table 4.4 Summary of EFA Results for the Experience with Digital Learning Applications Scale

Digital learning application	Oblimin rotated factor loading
	Prior experience
Online courses	**.59**
Blended learning course	**.46**
Learning management systems (e.g., Moodle)	**.41**
Learning software and learning applications (e.g., Quizlet)	**.44**
Chat services	**.46**
Images, diagrams, graphs, and maps	**.49**
Learning videos (e.g., YouTube)	**.45**
Digital learning and simulation games	**.55**
Digital texts (e.g., eBooks, PDF documents)	**.55**
Subscription-based media files (e.g., audio or video podcasts)	**.58**
Digital tests or exercises	**.72**
Forums, communities, blogs, wikis	**.60**

Note. $N = 214$. EFA = exploratory factor analysis. Factor loadings greater than .30 are shown in bold. The eigenvalue of the factor is 3.38, accounting for 28% of the explained variance. The items are translated into English. The original scale is in the Pretest in Appendix E in the electronic supplementary material

4.4.3 Learning Styles

Learners' learning styles were assessed in the pre-test with the self-report questionnaire ILS (Felder & Soloman, 1997). The ILS was administered before the start of the course to avoid any fluctuations in the learning preferences (Soflano et al., 2015). The original ILS questionnaire consists of 44 items, including 11 items for each of the four learning styles dimensions. Previous analyses have extensively investigated its implementation, validating its reliability and psychometric properties (see Sect. 2.5.3). In this thesis, a shorter version was adopted due to the practical constraints of the project in which the thesis was initiated. It consisted of 20 items, including five items per dimension. These were selected in accordance with the analysis of Graf et al. (2007), which was further validated by Ortigosa et al. (2008) and implemented by Akakpo (2019). The decision to shorten the questionnaire was further supported by its established psychometric properties, including the justification resulting from the reliability and factor analysis of the individual items (Litzinger et al., 2007). Table 4.5 presents the selected questions along with the corresponding dimensions and their semantic meanings.

In the original ILS questionnaire, separate scores are calculated for each of the four scales, corresponding to the four learning styles dimensions, based on the responses to the respective items of each scale. The scales are bipolar, meaning that the items offer two mutually exclusive response options representing opposite preferences. As each scale includes 11 questions, the total score of preference on each scale can range from –11 to + 11. By selecting an answer option in each question, a value of + 1 for answer "a" or –1 for answer "b" is counted for each dimension. As shown in Table 4.5, answer "a" corresponds to the category in the first pole of each dimension (active, sensing, visual, sequential) while answer "b" corresponds to the category in the second pole of each dimension (reflective, intuitive, verbal, global). For instance, in the active/reflective dimension, choosing option "a" adds a value of 1 to the score for that dimension, increasing the learner's score toward the active preference. Conversely, selecting option "b" subtracts a value of 1 from the score for that dimension, decreasing the learner's score and directing it toward the reflective preference.

Therefore, the resulting total score is always represented by an odd integer number, leaving no possibility for a total score resulting in 0, showing no preference. As Litzinger et al. (2007) emphatically state, "the number of items on each learning style scale and the scoring method were also chosen such that a score of zero, indicating no preference, was not possible"(p. 310). A score of 1 or 3 (in either direction) means that the learner is fairly well balanced on the two categories of the corresponding dimension (e.g., active/reflective), with only a mild preference for one or another. A score of 5 or 7 shows a moderate preference for one category of the corresponding dimension. That means that a person with a moderate preference may sometimes learn less easily in a learning environment that does not address that preference. A score of 9 or 11 shows a strong preference for one of the opposite categories. Thus, a person may, at least some of the time, encounter difficulties in learning in an environment that does not

Table 4.5 Shortened Learning Styles Questionnaire with Dimensions and Semantic Groups

Question	Response option	Dimension	Semantic group
1. I understand something better after I	(a) try it out. (b) think it through.	(a) Active (b) Reflective	(a) trying something out (b) think about material
2. I would rather be considered	(a) realistic. (b) innovative.	(a) Sensing (b) Intuitive	(a) existing ways (b) new ways
3. When I think about what I did yesterday, I am most likely to get	(a) a picture. (b) words.	(a) Visual (b) Verbal	(a) pictures (b) spoken or written words
4. I tend to	(a) understand details of a subject but may be fuzzy about its overall structure. (b) understand the overall structure but may be fuzzy about details.	(a) Sequential (b) Global	(a) detail oriented (b) overall picture
5. If I were a teacher, I would rather teach a course	(a) that deals with facts and real-life situations. (b) that deals with ideas and theories.	(a) Sensing (b) Intuitive	(a) concrete material (b) abstract material

(continued)

Table 4.5 (continued)

Question	Response option	Dimension	Semantic group
6. I prefer to get new information in	(a) pictures, diagrams, graphs, or maps. (b) written directions or verbal information.	(a) Visual (b) Verbal	(a) pictures (b) spoken or written words
7. Once I understand	(a) all the parts, I understand the whole thing. (b) the whole thing, I see how the parts fit.	(a) Sequential (b) Global	(a) from parts to the whole (b) overall picture
8. I find it easier	(a) to learn facts. (b) to learn concepts.	(a) Sensing (b) Intuitive	(a) concrete material (b) abstract material
9. In a book with lots of pictures and charts, I am likely to	(a) look over the pictures and charts carefully. (b) focus on the written text.	(a) Visual (b) Verbal	(a) pictures (b) written words
10. In classes I have taken	(a) I have usually got to know many of the students. (b) I have rarely got to know many of the students.	(a) Active (b) Reflective	(a) social-oriented (b) impersonal oriented
11. I prefer the idea of	(a) certainty. (b) theory.	(a) Sensing (b) Intuitive	(a) concrete material (b) abstract material
12. I remember best	(a) what I see. (b) what I hear.	(a) Visual (b) Verbal	(a) pictures (b) spoken words
13. It is more important to me that an instructor	(a) lay out the material in clear sequential steps. (b) give me an overall picture and relate the material to other subjects.	(a) Sequential (b) Global	(a) sequential progress (b) relations/ connections

(continued)

Table 4.5 (continued)

Question	Response option	Dimension	Semantic group
14. I prefer to study	(a) in a study group. (b) alone.	(a) Active (b) Reflective	(a) social oriented (b) impersonal oriented
15. I would rather first	(a) try things out. (b) think about how I'm going to do it.	(a) Active (b) Reflective	(a) trying something out (b) think about material
16. When someone is showing me data, I prefer	(a) charts or graphs. (b) text summarizing the results.	(a) Visual (b) Verbal	(a) pictures (b) written words
17. When I am learning a new subject, I prefer to	(a) stay focused on that subject, learning as much about it as I can. (b) try to make connections between that subject and related subjects.	(a) Sequential (b) Global	(a) sequential progress (b) relations/ connections
18. I am more likely to be considered	(a) outgoing. (b) reserved.	(a) Active (b) Reflective	(a) social oriented (b) impersonal oriented
19. I prefer courses that emphasize	(a) concrete material (facts, data) (b) abstract material (concepts, theories).	(a) Sensing (b) Intuitive	(a) concrete material (b) abstract material
20. When solving problems in a group, I would be more likely to	(a) think of the steps in the solution process. (b) think of possible consequences or applications of the solution in a wide range of areas.	(a) Sequential (b) Global	(a)sequential progress (b) relations/ connections

Note. The items are translated into English. The original scale is in the Pretest in Appendix E in the electronic supplementary material address that preference (Felder & Soloman, 2000). For the short questionnaire implemented in this thesis, the total score for each scale ranges from –5 to +5, since each scale consists of 5 questions. In accordance with the original questionnaire, an odd integer represents the resulting total score of each scale, forcing the results only towards one direction of the scale and disabling any possibility for no preference. While this scoring method aligns with the original questionnaire, the shortened version restricts the ability to distinguish between balanced, moderate, and strong preferences. The narrower score range, compared to the broader range of the original questionnaire, reduces interpretive depth, limiting the ability to accurately capture and differentiate the degree of a learner's preference.

The original learning styles questionnaire was translated from English to German, as the course was delivered in German and the majority of learners were native German speakers (see Pretest in Appendix E in the electronic supplementary material for the implemented questionnaire). To ensure the translated items of the shortened version of the questionnaire were well-suited to the target group of vocational and continuing education learners, selected items were pretested through cognitive interviews (for details on the cognitive interview procedure see Sect. 4.3). Seven items were selected to be tested, including at least one item from each of the four dimensions to represent the full range of learning preferences (see items 2,5,8,12,15,19, and 20 in Table 4.5 for the questionnaire in English and in the Pretest in Appendix E in the electronic supplementary material for the implemented questionnaire in German). The aim was to assess the comprehensibility of the German translations relative to the original English items as well as the alignment with the theoretical framework of learning styles. For instance, in item 2, the translation of the original answer options ("realistic" and "innovative") was meant to be both understandable for the target group and aligned with the learning styles theory. Based on the interviewees' suggestions, examples introduced in this item by the research team were modified to enhance clarity for learners with a migration background or who had difficulties with the German language. At the same time, as no literal translation was adopted, it was important to verify whether the revised structure of the newly formed question in German was also comprehensible. In items 5 and 8, the answer options were simplified, and relevant examples were added to be more understandable for vocational and continuing education learners. Similarly, in item 12, additional clarification was included in the first answer option to denote that it referred to both spoken and written words, aligning with the theoretical framework. Lastly, items 15, 19, and 20 were evaluated and adapted to ensure that learners clearly understood the distinction between the two dimensions.

In order to test the psychometric properties of the shortened questionnaire, its construct validity and internal consistency were examined. Preliminary analyses were conducted to assess whether the learning styles data from the shortened questionnaire were suitable for factor analysis. First, a correlation matrix was calculated to ensure that the items of the scale correlate fairly well. Since the items had dichotomous answer options, a tetrachoric correlation matrix was calculated for all items, since no specific factors were initially assumed (see Appendix B, Table B1 in the electronic supplementary material). The results revealed that several items (2,3,4,7,13,14,17,20) had correlations below .30. Despite these findings, these items were retained for the factor analysis, due to the already limited number of items in the scale. Then, the Bartlett's test was performed to determine whether the correlation matrix differed significantly from an identity matrix. The test yielded a significant result, $\chi^2(190) = 510.55$, $p < .001$, indicating sufficient inter-item correlations to proceed with the factor analysis. To further evaluate the suitability of the data for factor analysis, the KMO test of sampling adequacy was computed. The value of the overall Mean Square of Averages (MSA) was .61, exceeding the minimum acceptable threshold of 0.5 (Field, 2012), confirming the adequacy of the sample size and data. However, individual MSA values of certain items (3,4,7,14) were relatively low, suggesting that these items may not strongly contribute to the factor structure. Despite this, these items were not eliminated, given the acceptable overall MSA value. Finally, the determinant of the correlation matrix was calculated to detect if there is any multicollinearity among the items. The determinant was sufficiently low at .08, remaining above the minimum threshold of .00001 (Field, 2012), suggesting no significant multicollinearity among the items, thereby further supporting the feasibility of conducting factor analysis.

Since the shortened version of the learning styles questionnaire has not been extensively tested, particularly in VET and CVET contexts, a principal component analysis (PCA) was conducted to explore its underlying structure. This approach aligns with previous studies utilizing the ILS, which recommended conducting a PCA in cases where there is uncertainty about the ILS's factor structure in a new context or population (Zwyno, 2003; Platsidou & Metallidou, 2009; van Zwanenberg et al., 2000). Initially, a PCA was conducted on all 20 items without rotation and assuming 20 factors, corresponding to the number of items (see Appendix B, Table B2 in the electronic supplementary material). This aimed to explore all possible patterns, capture the maximum amount of variance in the data, and determine the number of components to retain based on the eigenvalues. According to Kaiser's (1960) criterion, seven factors could be extracted, as they had eigenvalues greater than 1. However, further inspection of the scree plot suggested retaining either two or four components (see Fig. 4.1). The scree plot indicated an inflection point after three components, followed by another drop after four components, before a stable plateau is reached. Retaining two factors would prioritize those accounting for the most variance, while retaining four components aligns more closely with the theoretical framework of learning styles, suggesting these additional components may represent meaningful constructs. To determine the number of components to retain, the validity of Kaiser's criterion was evaluated in the context of this dataset. The learning styles dataset included 20 variables with a sample size of 211 learners, which rendered the criterion less reliable. Kaiser's criterion is known to overestimate the number of components in such cases (Field, 2012). Thus, the scree plot, combined with theoretical assumptions, provided stronger justification for a four-component solution. However, given the ambiguity of the scree plot and the need to validate the theoretically expected four-factor structure, two PCAs were subsequently conducted: one specifying four factors and the other two factors (see Appendix B, Tables B3 and B4 accordingly in the electronic supplementary material). The results indicated that the four-factor model provided a better fit compared to the two-factor model, as it explained more variance, had higher communalities, lower residuals, lower chi-square values, and better fit indices.

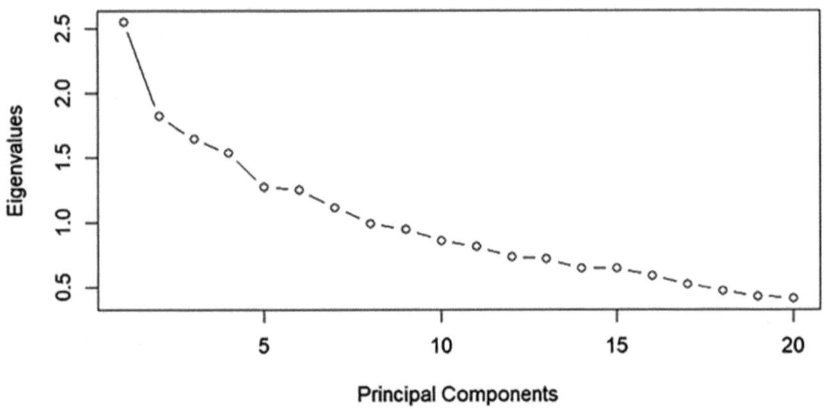

Fig. 4.1 Scree Plot Following PCA of the Shortened Learning Styles Scale. (*Note. N*= 211. PCA = principal component analysis)

To improve the interpretability of the factors, a PCA with factor rotation was performed, assuming a four-factor solution. Initially, an oblique rotation was conducted based on the theoretical expectation of correlations between factors, as suggested by prior research (Zwyno, 2003; Felder & Spurlin, 2005; Felder et al., 2005; Viola et al., 2006). Furthermore, 12 items in the initially examined four-factor PCA exhibited moderate loadings on more than one factor, suggesting that an oblique rotation may help clarify these loadings. In addition, the shortened scale has not been extensively tested, further supporting the use of an oblique approach that allows factors to correlate if they naturally do. The results of the oblique rotation (see Table 4.6) showed that most items load at least moderately on one factor (loadings above ± 0.30) except for items 4 and 7, which showed insufficient loadings, and item 1, which loaded on two factors. The pattern of item loadings facilitated the identification and the distinction between factors. For instance, items 5,8,11, and 19 loaded only on factor 1, revealing that this factor corresponds to the sensing/intuitive scale. Most loadings aligned with theoretical expectations, allowing the factors to be labeled accordingly (for the labels of each factor see Table 4.6). However, item 1, which theoretically belongs to the active/reflective scale, displayed cross-loadings on both the sequential/global scale and the active/reflective scale. This cross-loading suggests that the item may not serve as a pure indicator of a learner's preference for active engagement or reflective processing, potentially relating to broader learning traits encompassing characteristics from both scales. Additionally, item 14 loaded on the sequential/global scale, although theoretical expectations place it on the active/reflective scale.

Very low correlations were revealed among factors, with the highest but still particularly weak correlation between the sensing/intuitive and sequential/global scales (see Table 4.7). This relationship was also reported in previous studies, where the degree of association was found to be higher and moderate (Felder & Spurlin, 2005; Livesay et al., 2002; van Zwanenberg et al., 2000; Zwyno, 2003). Given the marginal strength of the correlation observed in this analysis, it was assumed that all the measured constructs are largely independent, representing distinct constructs.

Thus, an orthogonal rotation, which assumes no correlation between factors, was conducted to help clarify which items load most distinctly onto each factor (see Table 4.8). In this rotation, most items loaded at least moderately on one factor. Items 4 and 7 showed again insufficient loadings, and item 1 exhibited the same pattern as in the oblique rotation, it cross-loaded on the sequential/global and active/reflective scales. In addition, items 15 and 18, theoretically associated with the active/reflective scale, also showed moderate loadings on the sequential/global scale. These items might measure aspects that overlap between the

Table 4.6 Summary of PCA Results with Oblique Rotation

Item	Oblimin rotated factor loading			
	Factor 1 (Sensing/Intuitive)	Factor 2 (Sequential/Global)	Factor 3 (Visual/Verbal)	Factor 4 (Active/Reflective)
1	.07	**–.44**	.19	**.40**
2	.22	**.46**	.07	–.15
3	.00	.00	.17	**.39**
4	.11	–.06	–.26	-.03
5	**.78**	–.12	.02	–.11
6	.02	.18	**.71**	.04
7	.18	–.11	–.26	.08
8	**.58**	.18	.04	.13
9	−.01	–.16	**.71**	–.06
10	.02	–.09	–.05	**.76**
11	**.78**	.03	–.02	–.01
12	.03	**.56**	.15	.17
13	.09	**.54**	–.09	.22
14	.13	**-.31**	.14	.26
15	.12	**-.43**	.13	.30
16	–.09	.05	**.65**	–.07
17	.15	**.34**	.03	.10
18	–.13	.18	–.10	**.71**
19	**.69**	.11	–.10	.04
20	.11	**.51**	.18	–.04

Note. PCA = principal component analysis. Factor loadings greater than .30 are shown in bold. The four factors have eigenvalues of 2.25, 1.85, 1.75, and 1.70, accounting for 11%, 9%, 9%, and 9% of the explained variance, respectively

active/reflective scale and sequential/global scales, indicating that they could be inherently multidimensional or reflect shared concepts between the two scales. However, in the oblique rotation, item 15 loaded moderately on the sequential/ global scale and marginally moderately on the active/reflective scale, while item 18 loaded strongly only on the active/reflective scale. Furthermore, in oblique

Table 4.7 Interscale Correlations Following PCA with Oblique Rotation

Variable	1	2	3	4
Factor 1	–	.11	–.02	–.03
Factor 2	.11	–	–.08	.02
Factor 3	–.02	–.08	–	–.07
Factor 4	–.03	.02	–.07	–

Note. PCA = principal component analysis. Factor 1 refers to the sensing/intuitive scale; factor 2 to the sequential/global scale; factor 3 to the visual/verbal scale; and factor 4 to the active/reflective scale

rotation, item 14 loaded only on the sequential/global scale, while in the orthogonal it loaded higher on the active/reflective scale than on the sequential/global scale, aligning more closely with theoretical expectations.

The results from both rotation methods were similar, indicating some overlap between the sequential/global and active/reflective scales and suggesting that the overall factor structure was stable across rotation techniques. Previous research suggests that the sequential/global and active/reflective scales are expected to be correlated. The weak inter-factor correlation between these two scales found in the shortened questionnaire (0.11) is consistent with findings from earlier studies (Felder & Spurlin, 2005; Zwyno, 2003; van Zwanenberg et al., 2000; Viola et al., 2006). While this correlation is lower than previously reported, it may be attributed to differences in sampling, the questionnaire length, or variations among the study populations. The oblique approach allowed for modest inter-factor relationships, which are theoretically expected by the implementation of the original questionnaire. Therefore, considering the theoretically expected inter-factor relationships, retaining the oblique rotation ensures consistency with theoretical expectations while also allowing for an interpretation that aligns with both the observed data and the established literature. Subsequently, the factor solution derived from the oblique rotation was retained, and a reliability analysis was conducted to assess internal consistency and determine whether item retention or removal should be considered.

Following the extended previous research on ILS's reliability analysis (Felder & Spurlin, 2005; Graf, 2007; Litzinger et al., 2007; Livesay et al., 2002; van Zwanenberg et al., 2000; Viola et al., 2006; Zywno, 2003), Cronbach's coefficient alpha was calculated for each scale individually (see Appendix C, Table C1 in the electronic supplementary material), utilizing the five items on each scale as theoretically expected (for the five items corresponding to each dimension see

Table 4.8 Summary of PCA Results with Orthogonal Rotation

Item	Varimax rotated factor loading			
	Factor 1 (Sensing/Intuitive)	Factor 2 (Sequential/Global)	Factor 3 (Visual/Verbal)	Factor 4 (Active/Reflective)
1	.05	**–.36**	.12	**.48**
2	.23	**.44**	.07	–.22
3	–.01	.06	.11	**.39**
4	.09	–.04	–.26	–.04
5	**.79**	–.06	–.03	–.08
6	.06	.15	**.69**	.07
7	.15	–.06	–.29	.07
8	**.57**	.26	-.03	.09
9	.05	–.22	**.71**	.03
10	–.03	.06	–.16	**.75**
11	**.77**	.11	–.09	–.02
12	.03	**.58**	.12	.09
13	.07	**.59**	–.13	.12
14	.12	–.25	.09	**.32**
15	.11	**–.36**	.07	**.37**
16	–.04	–.01	**.66**	–.02
17	.14	**.37**	.00	.04
18	–.18	**.31**	–.19	**.65**
19	**.67**	.20	–.16	.01
20	.12	**.50**	.17	–.11

Note. PCA = principal component analysis. Factor loadings greater than .30 are shown in bold. The four factors have eigenvalues of 2.18, 1.88, 1.79, and 1.71, accounting for 11%, 9%, 9%, and 9% of the explained variance, respectively

Table 4.5). The active/reflective scale showed low internal consistency ($a = .46$). Even though this value is generally regarded as low, considering the generally accepted threshold of .8 for cognitive tests and the cut-off point of .7 for intelligence tests, Kline (1999) argues that psychological constructs can yield values lower than .7, particularly due to the diversity of constructs being measured. The alpha test reliability value of the active/reflective scale is, therefore, marginally acceptable, further considering Tuckman and Harper's suggestion of accepting values of .5 or greater for attitude assessments (Tuckman & Harper, 2012). The possibility of dropping items to enhance reliability was examined. As an uneven number of items is needed so that learners can be clearly assigned to one or the other dimension of the corresponding scale (Goldhammer & Hartig, 2020), two items needed to be dropped, resulting in a minimally enhanced reliability of .47 by removing items 14 and 15. The sensing/intuitive scale demonstrated a more acceptable reliability (*a* = .67), exceeding the acceptable value of .5 for attitude assessments (Tuckman & Harper, 2012) and aligning with Kline's (1999) expectation of values below .7 for social science data. Removing items 2 and 8 resulted to a slight increase in the reliability value (*a* = .72). The reliability of the visual/verbal scale was found low (*a* = .42). Removing items 3 and 12 resulted in an acceptable reliability value (*a* = .59). Finally, the reliability of the sequential/global scale was found quite low (*a* = .32), indicating poor internal consistency of the scale. Removing items 4 and 7 resulted in the reliability value of .41, which approaches an acceptable threshold (see Table 4.9).

Table 4.9 Reliability Values for 5-Item and 3-Item Learning Styles Scales

Scale	Cronbach's alpha	
	5-Item scale	3-Item scale
Active/Reflective	.46	.47
Sensing/Intuitive	.67	.72
Visual/Verbal	.42	.59
Sequential/Global	.32	.41

In conjunction with the factor analysis, the reliability analysis further contributed to determining whether items in each scale could be removed. In factor analysis, items with low or cross-loadings, as well as items that did not align with the theoretical constructs, were flagged for potential removal. In reliability analysis, in the active/reflective scale, the increase in internal consistency after removing two items was minimal, not necessarily justifying such removal. However, items 14 and 15, which could be removed but only slightly increase reliability, have been found problematic in the PCA. Both items were found to load on the sequential/global scale. This issue suggested that the items may not contribute to a cohesive measure of the construct, justifying their removal and ensuring that the remaining items better align with the scale's theoretical framework. Even though the Cronbach's alpha for the three items remains quite low (*a* = .47), the use of the 3-item scale is justifiable. The items capture partly different but conceptually related aspects of active and reflective tendencies.

Item 1 assesses cognitive processing style, measuring whether comprehension happens through practical experience or internal reflection. Item 10 focuses on social interaction in learning environments, indicating whether learners actively engage with peers or remain more detached. Item 18 measures broader personality traits, specifically extraversion against introversion, which extend beyond learning contexts to general social interactions. Given the diverse focus on cognitive processing, social interaction, and personality traits, weaker correlations between the items are unsurprising. Nevertheless, it is theoretically assumed that these items capture complementary aspects of the active/reflective preference. Thus, their sum serves as an aggregate measure of active/reflective preferences and is theoretically justified as a meaningful indicator of the broader active/reflective learning preference. Rather than reflecting a single underlying trait, the scale captures multiple facets of this dimension, further supporting its use in subsequent analyses.

Regarding the sensing/intuitive scale, there is a more meaningful, even slight improvement in internal consistency after removing items 2 and 8, since the alpha value exceeds the generally accepted cut-off point of .7. Such removal is further supported by the PCA, in which item 2 loaded on the sequential/global scale. Since two items need to be removed so that participants can be clearly assigned to one dimension, the removal of item 2 needed to be combined with the removal of item 8, as informed by the reliability analysis. In the visual/verbal scale, the increase in reliability was significant after removing items 3 and 12, rendering the scale reliable (Kline, 1999; Tuckman & Harper, 2012). This was further justified by the PCA, as both items loaded on different scales.

Finally, after removing items 4 and 7 from the sequential/global scale, the increase in reliability was slight, but it could be considered marginally acceptable. In the PCA, these items did not load even moderately on any scale, further justifying their exclusion. Despite the quite low reliability, the sequential/global scale can be used for further analyses with caution. Cortina (1993) underlined that the value of Cronbach's alpha depends on the number of items on the scale. Achieving high reliability for a test with a limited number of items is inherently challenging (Wang et al., 2006). In the shortened learning styles scale, the reduced reliability may be dramatically affected by the low number of items compared to the original scale. In addition, the items of the sequential/global scale cover quite diverse themes, such as how information is presented (item 13), how the learner approaches content (item 17), and how problem-solving is approached in social settings (item 20), which may explain the relative lack of consistency. The diverse contexts mean that responses may vary considerably based on individual preferences in these different situations, leading to weak item correlations. This lack of strong overlap in what the items measure could explain the low alpha value, suggesting that the items do not reflect a single latent construct. Nevertheless, the different aspects of sequential/global tendencies are theoretically relevant, and their sum constitutes a theoretically justifiable aggregate measure and indicator of the broader sequential/global learning preference. The decision to utilize the scale, even with low reliability, is further corroborated by previous studies that have found similar reliability results (Al-Azawei et al., 2015; Felder & Spurlin, 2005; Platsidou & Metallidou, 2009; van Zwanenberg et al., 2000) and also by the strong theoretical framework of the scale that has been extensively investigated, as explained in Sect. 2.5.2, and regards the sequential/global scale as a complementary aspect of learning styles. Consistent with Nunnally (1978), it is reasonable to accept an instrument with lower reliability values during the initial phases of research, as is the case with the shortened scale employed in this thesis. Therefore, the reliability analysis was performed again with only three items included per scale (see Appendix C, Table C2 in the electronic supplementary material). However, it is important to acknowledge the limited reliability of the learning styles scale and take this into account when interpreting the research findings.

Further reliability measures were calculated with three items per scale. Interscale correlations based on Pearson's correlation coefficient (Field et al., 2012) were found close to zero, indicating very weak linear relationships between the scales, ensuring that they measure independent constructs (see Table 4.10). The sensing/intuitive and sequential/global scales demonstrated a weak positive correlation, indicating that as scores in the sensing/intuitive scale increase, there is a tendency for scores in the sequential/global scale to increase as well. Previous studies found similar and even a stronger positive relationship between the sensing/intuitive and sequential/global preferences (Felder & Spurlin, 2005; van Zwanenberg et al., 2000). This is theoretically expected, as "sequential learners, who acquire understanding in logical connected steps, could be either sensors or intuitors, but global learners, whose thinking processes tend to be nonlinear and who acquire understanding holistically, would seem much more likely to be intuitive than sensing" (Felder & Spurlin, 2005, p. 2). Therefore, the slight relationship between these scales does not compromise the construct validity of the shortened ILS, suggesting that it captures distinct learning style dimensions. In addition, the average item-total correlations of the scales (see Appendix C, Table C2 in the electronic supplementary material) showed that the item-total relationships are strong, indicating that the respective items contribute well to measuring the respective constructs.

Table 4.10 Interscale Correlations with Three Items per Scale

Variable	1	2	3	4
Factor 1	–	–.06	–.06	–.00
Factor 2	–.06	–	–.06	.15
Factor 3	–.06	–.07	–	–.02
Factor 4	–.00	.15	–.02	–

Note. Factor 1 refers to the active/reflective scale; factor 2 to the sensing/intuitive scale; factor 3 to the visual/verbal scale; and factor 4 to the sequential/global scale

Finally, a PCA was conducted, assuming four factors, utilizing an oblique rotation and only three items per scale (see Table 4.11), as determined by the analysis so far. All items aligned moderately to strongly with one primary component. Item 1 demonstrated a marginally moderate cross-loading on the active/reflective and the sequential/global scales. The same overlap was found in previous studies (Litzinger et al., 2007; Van Zwanenberg et al., 2000; Viola et al., 2006; Zwyno, 2003). Collectively, the four components explain 55% of the total variance, compared to 38% of variance explained by the initially examined 5-item model, indicating that the 3-item model captures a more meaningful proportion of data. In addition, the loadings are stronger and the model fit is slightly better than the 5-item model, improving interpretability. Problematic items with cross-loadings from the 5-item model, except item 1, are removed. All in all, the moderate variance explained and fit indices suggest that the 3-item model captures key patterns, aligning more closely with the theoretical framework, even though all underlying variance is not explained. As further improvements were not feasible to be implemented in the shortened questionnaire, the 3-item model was considered adequate for further analyses. A confirmatory factor analysis (CFA) was planned to be conducted in order to more rigorously validate the shortened version of the ILS and its alignment with the theoretical 4-factor structure proposed by its developers (Felder & Soloman, 1997). However, CFA was not possible to conduct due to convergence issues. These issues likely arose from a combination of factors, including the limited number of items per factor, the presence of missing data, and the complexity introduced by modifications in the original ILS scale (Brown, 2015; Byrne, 2010; Kline, 2023). Finally, due to the performed reduction of three items in each scale, a distinction between balanced, moderate, and strong learning style preference was not possible to be formed.

Table 4.11 Summary of PCA Results with Oblique Rotation and Three Items per Scale

Item	Oblimin rotated factor loading			
	Factor 1 (Sensing/Intuitive)	Factor 2 (Visual/Verbal)	Factor 3 (Active/Reflective)	Factor 4 (Sequential/Global)
1	−.02	.14	**.34**	−.30
5	**.81**	.03	−.06	−.09
6	.04	**.72**	.04	.17
9	.00	**.71**	−.07	−.16
10	.06	.04	**.86**	−.11
11	**.82**	−.02	−.01	.03
13	.02	−.11	.11	**.66**
16	−.05	**.77**	.04	.02
17	.01	.05	−.03	**.70**
18	−.08	−.05	**.79**	.15
19	**.75**	−.02	.10	.09
20	.04	.15	−.11	**.59**

Note. PCA = principal component analysis. Factor loadings greater than .30 are shown in bold. The four factors have eigenvalues of 1.93, 1.68, 1.52, and 1.46, accounting for 16%, 14%, 13%, and 12% of the explained variance, respectively

4.4.4 Individualization

A questionnaire on individualization, consisting of two scales, was developed by the author of the thesis to measure during the delivery of the course the extent to which individualized support was provided through features that allow autonomy, individualized learning paths, and alignment with learners' competences, unique needs, preferences, and prior knowledge (see Midtest in Appendix E in the electronic supplementary material). The first scale, *Individualization Through the Learning Software,* included self-developed items and individual items adapted from existing instruments (Bürgermeister et al., 2012; Institut für Qualitätsentwicklung Hessen, 2013). Learners were asked to what extent they agreed with certain statements. These aimed to measure whether the individualization features, which were specifically developed for the course and embedded in the learning software, supported personalized learning by aligning with learners' specific needs and preferences (see items 1 to 7 in Midtest in Appendix E in the electronic supplementary material, and for the translated version in Table 4.12).

These features included enabling independent work, assessing learning progress, and the ability to select preferred learning materials. Additionally, it was evaluated whether the software provided tasks suited to learners' competences, facilitated individualized learning paths, assessed prior knowledge, and considered learning difficulties. Overall, this first scale, capturing individualization, evaluated how the software itself facilitated learner autonomy and personalization in the learning process. The second scale, *Individualization of the Learning Environment*, was developed based on the adaptation of an existing instrument measuring the individualization of the learning environment (Lehmann, 2010) and individual items (Schwinger et al., 2020). This scale extended the focus to the broader context of the learning experience, aiming to capture whether learners perceived the overall learning environment as individualized to their needs. Learners were asked to what extent they agreed with statements, which focused on assessing whether the learning materials, as presented in the most recent learning unit, aligned with learners' individual characteristics. It further measured the degree of learner autonomy, including learners' ability to control their learning process and pace (see items 8 to 13 in Midtest in Appendix E in the electronic supplementary material, and for the translated version in Table 4.12). This scale focused on the perceived personalization and customization of the entire learning environment, tapping into various facets of individualization and offering a more holistic view of individualization beyond the developed learning software.

Before administering the questionnaire of individualization to learners, nine questions measuring individualization were included in the cognitive interview (for details on the cognitive interview procedure see Sect. 4.3). This step was deemed necessary since the scales were partially developed from scratch and adapted from previous questionnaires. The aim was to ensure the questions were understandable and suitable for vocational and continuing education learners. During the interviews, three of the nine questions had to be read twice, indicating they were overly complex. These questions were subsequently simplified. Apprentices also suggested replacing certain terms and adding explanations to make the questions more comprehensible. The feedback received was reviewed with the research team, and questions were revised based on apprentices' suggestions. Additionally, three questions were identified as redundant and were removed from the questionnaire. The response options were initially designed as a 4-point Likert scale. However, after the review by the research team, it was decided to include a middle response option to improve the questionnaire's psychometric properties (Kankaraš & Capecchi, 2024) and allow learners to express varying levels of perceived individualization. Consequently, the response format was changed to a 5-point Likert scale with a middle category. The response options of the scale *Individualization Through the Learning Software* ranged from *completely disagree* to *completely agree*, while those from the scale *Individualization of the Learning Environment* ranged from *does not apply at all* to *fully applies*. This slight differentiation in the response options was chosen to adhere to the original scales. In addition, after a thorough review of the theoretical framework, two further questions initially developed for the questionnaire on individualization were excluded from the analysis to ensure the conceptual clarity and validity of the scale.

To assess the psychometric properties of the questionnaire on individualization, the two scales were merged, assuming they both capture the broader construct of individualization. An EFA was performed to examine the questionnaire's construct validity, hypothesizing a single factor that reflects the overarching concept of individualization. An oblique rotation was selected, as the different components of the questionnaire, such as alignment with learners' needs, competences, and preferences, reflect the various aspects of individualization in both the learning software features and the overall learning environment, making them conceptually interrelated. The adequacy of the data for factor analysis was assessed using the KMO measure and Bartlett's test of sphericity. The overall KMO value was .86, indicating good sampling adequacy. However, the KMO values of individual items varied, with most items showing high adequacy, except for item 9, which marginally exceeded the acceptable limit of .5 (Field, 2012), and item 10, which fell below it, suggesting limited shared variance for these items. Bartlett's test of sphericity was significant, $\chi^2(78) = 757.47, p < .001$, confirming that the correlation matrix was suitable for factor analysis. The results of the factor analysis demonstrated that most items load either highly or moderately on the single factor, with the exception of two items. Items 9 and 10 showed very low loadings, indicating that they did not meaningfully contribute to the single factor (see Table 4.12). Further inspecting their communalities (h^2) and uniqueness (u^2) values, it was plausible that the factor explained almost none of their variance. Therefore, these items were excluded from the analysis.

The EFA was conducted again without these items (see Table 4.13). The amount of variance explained was 42%, indicating that the factor captures a substantial amount of the underlying variance. All items showed moderate to high loadings, suggesting they are well-represented by the single factor. The fit of the model, based upon off-diagonal values, was 0.97, further confirming the model's adequacy in capturing the underlying structure. Despite some indications of potential improvements, demonstrated by the values of the Tucker Lewis Index (TLI) and Root Mean Square Error of Approximation index (RMSEA), the model showed reasonable fit and was considered adequate for explaining the

Table 4.12 Summary of EFA Results for the Individualization Scale

Item	Oblimin rotated factor loading
	Individualization
1. The learning software enables me to work on the learning units independently.	**.65**
2. The learning software supports me in reviewing my learning progress.	**.74**
3. The different learning materials (written learning material, explanatory videos, etc.) are supportive.	**.71**
4. It is helpful that the learning software provides tasks that correspond to my competences.	**.74**
5. The option provided by the learning software to choose the order of content to be studied is helpful.	**.65**
6. The option provided by the learning software to assess my prior knowledge by checking a box is helpful.	**.68**
7. I feel that the learning software understands my difficulties in completing the tasks.	**.44**
8. The last learning unit exactly matches my individual learning needs.	**.58**
9. I could have learned better if this learning unit had considered my individual preferences.	–.14
10. The last learning unit gives me the impression that it was not designed for learners like me.	.04
11. During this learning unit, I was able to control my own learning process.	**.67**
12. In the last learning unit, I was able to decide on my own how quickly I wanted to learn.	**.65**
13. The last learning unit built on my prior knowledge and prior experiences.	**.57**

Note. $N = 156$. EFA = exploratory factor analysis. Factor loadings greater than .30 are shown in bold. The eigenvalue of the factor is 4.64, accounting for 36% of the explained variance. The items are translated into English. The original scale is in the Midtest in Appendix E in the electronic supplementary material

factor structure. Regarding the internal consistency of the scale (see Appendix C in the electronic supplementary material, Table C3), it showed good reliability ($a = .88$). Inspecting the changes in the reliability values if certain items were dropped, none of the items would increase Cronbach's alpha by being deleted. Item statistics further demonstrated that all items positively contribute to the overall reliability of the scale.

Table 4.13 Summary of Final EFA Results for the Individualization Scale

Item	Oblimin rotated factor loading
	Individualization
1. The learning software enables me to work on the learning units independently.	**.64**
2. The learning software supports me in reviewing my learning progress.	**.74**
3. The different learning materials (written learning material, explanatory videos, etc.) are supportive.	**.72**
4. It is helpful that the learning software provides tasks that correspond to my competences.	**.74**
5. The option provided by the learning software to choose the order of content to be studied is helpful.	**.65**
6. The option provided by the learning software to assess my prior knowledge by checking a box is helpful.	**.68**
7. I feel that the learning software understands my difficulties in completing the tasks.	**.44**
8. The last learning unit exactly matches my individual learning needs.	**.58**
9. During this learning unit, I was able to control my own learning process.	**.67**
10. In the last learning unit, I was able to decide on my own how quickly I wanted to learn.	**.65**
11. The last learning unit built on my prior knowledge and prior experiences.	**.57**

Note. $N = 156$. EFA = exploratory factor analysis. Factor loadings greater than .30 are shown in bold. The eigenvalue of the factor is 4.62, accounting for 42% of the explained variance. The items are translated into English. The original scale is in the Midtest in Appendix E in the electronic supplementary material (items 1–8 and 11–13)

4.4.5 Adaptivity

A scale to measure the construct of adaptivity was developed by the author of the thesis, incorporating items referring to the adaptive features of the learning software, as well as individual items adapted from existing instruments (Schwinger et al., 2020; Szogs et al., 2021). The scale aimed to measure at the end of the course the extent to which the learning software dynamically adjusted its content and support to learners' needs and progress. Learners were requested to indicate to what extent they agree with certain statements. These assessed whether the software dynamically provided content appropriate to the learner's knowledge level, simplified or tailored content based on learning habits and prerequisites, supported learners in overcoming comprehension difficulties, encouraged active engagement with the material, and enabled continuous assessment of learning progress (see Posttest in Appendix E in the electronic supplementary material for the implemented scale and Table 4.14 for the translated scale).

Five out of the 14 questions on adaptivity were selected to be examined in the cognitive interviews (for details on the cognitive interview procedure see Sect. 4.3). Three of these items were adapted from existing scales, while two were newly developed. Most of the questions were deemed understandable by the apprentices, though suggestions were made to rephrase two items to improve clarity for their peers. The questions were modified accordingly. One item was excluded from the scale, as it referred to a feature that was ultimately not incorporated into the learning software. Based on the questions' review by the research team, the initially developed 4-point Likert scale response format was changed to a 5-point response format to include a middle category, ranging from *completely disagree* to *completely agree*, aiming to enhance the questionnaire's psychometric properties (Kankaraš & Capecchi, 2024). Following an in-depth review of the theoretical framework, seven questions, initially developed to measure adaptivity, were excluded from the analysis. These items were found to lack a clear connection to the construct of adaptivity, and their removal was deemed necessary to maintain the scale's conceptual precision and validity.

To examine the scale's psychometric properties, its construct validity and reliability were assessed. An EFA was conducted with the assumption of a single factor, representing the underlying construct of adaptivity. An oblique rotation was selected, as the questions developed aimed to capture distinct yet related aspects of adaptivity based on theoretical considerations, such as content adjustment, progress tracking, and learner support. The KMO measure verified the sampling adequacy for the analysis (KMO = .89), with all KMO values in individual items ranging from .86 to .95, indicating all items are well-suited for factor analysis. Bartlett's test of sphericity was significant, $\chi^2(21) = 383.76$, $p < .001$, supporting the suitability of the data for factor analysis. The results of the EFA revealed that all items loaded highly on the single factor (see Table 4.14). The variance explained amounted to 50%, indicating that the single factor captures a substantial portion of the variability in the data. Further measures of the goodness of fit, such as the TLI at 0.94 and the RMSEA at 0.09 with 90% confidence intervals (CIs) [0.06, 0.12], demonstrated a good fit of the one-factor model overall, suggesting that the single factor is a good representation of the underlying construct. Regarding the internal consistency of the scale (see Appendix C in the electronic supplementary material, Table C4), it showed good reliability ($a = .87$). None of the items would improve Cronbach's alpha further if they were removed. According to item statistics, all items were found to positively contribute to the overall reliability.

Table 4.14 Summary of EFA Results for the Adaptivity Scale

Item	Oblimin rotated factor loading
	Adaptivity
1. The difficulty level of the contents provided by the learning software was appropriate for my level of knowledge.	**.57**
2. The learning software supported me by simplifying the content.	**.75**
3. The learning software adapted the learning contents to my learning habits.	**.74**
4. The learning software adapted the learning contents to my learning requirements.	**.82**
5. The learning software helped me with comprehension difficulties.	**.70**
6. The learning software encouraged active engagement with the contents.	**.69**
7. With the help of the learning software, I was constantly able to assess my learning progress.	**.67**

Note. $N = 130$. EFA = exploratory factor analysis. Factor loadings greater than .30 are shown in bold. The eigenvalue of the factor is 3.52, accounting for 50% of the explained variance. The items are translated into English. The original scale is in the Posttest in Appendix E in the electronic supplementary material

4.4.6 Learning Outcomes in AI

An 18-item scale was developed by the research team to assess cognitive learning outcomes at the end of the course. It measured the extent to which learners acquired knowledge and skills related to AI concepts and applications (see Posttest in Appendix E in the electronic supplementary material for the implemented scale and Table 4.15 for the translated scale). It consisted of four subscales, corresponding to the thematic areas taught in the course on AI and ML: (a) Basic Concepts of AI (items 1 to 5), (b) Opportunities, Challenges, and Ethical Issues of AI (items 6 to 8), (c) Data Management (items 9 to 12), and (d) Basic Concepts of Data Analysis and ML (items 13 to 18). Designed to capture learners' subjective self-assessment, the response format was a 5-point Likert scale ranging from *completely disagree* to *completely agree*. Learners were requested to state to what extent they agree with certain statements. A broad spectrum of cognitive skills was addressed as outlined in the taxonomy of educational objectives (Bloom et al., 1956). The items primarily focused on assessing the abilities to remember (items 6,12,17) and comprehend key AI principles (items 8,11,18), while a few items assessed the abilities to apply knowledge in practical AI tasks (items 4,5) and analyze relationships between variables, by drawing connections and interpreting data (item 14). Higher-order thinking skills, including the abilities to synthesize and evaluate new work in the context of AI, were less explicitly addressed (items 10 and 9, respectively).

The construct validity and reliability of the scale were assessed by an EFA and the calculation of Cronbach's alpha. The EFA was conducted assuming a single underlying factor, representing the construct of cognitive learning outcomes on AI, and using an oblique rotation to account for potential interrelations among subscales. This approach aligns with the scale's theoretical framework, which suggests that thematic areas of AI, such as applying AI concepts and understanding fundamental AI concepts, build upon each other, and that dimensions of learning outcomes, such as comprehension and application, may be interdependent and contribute to a shared overarching construct. The KMO measure of sampling adequacy was high (KMO = 0.91), indicating that the data is suitable for factor analysis. Individual items' KMO values ranged between .89 and .95, further supporting the adequacy of the scale. Bartlett's test of sphericity was significant, $\chi^2(153) = 1228.24$, $p < .001$, suggesting that factor analysis is appropriate for this dataset. The results of the EFA showed that all items loaded moderately to strongly on the single factor (see Table 4.15). The single factor explained 42% of the variance, indicating that the factor captures a substantial amount of variability in the data. The model demonstrated a good fit, as indicated

Table 4.15 Summary of EFA Results for the Learning Outcomes Scale

Item	Oblimin rotated factor loading
	Learning outcomes
1. I can assess well what role data play in the context of AI.	**.67**
2. I can describe in detail how machine learning works.	**.74**
3. I can describe well what an AI model is.	**.71**
4. I find it easy to train an AI model with Teachable Machines.	**.69**
5. I have many ideas on how AI can or could be applied in my training company.	**.46**
6. I know methods and ways to avoid algorithmic biases.	**.66**
7. I can describe exactly how personal data can be protected.	**.63**
8. I understand exactly why model parameters of artificial neural networks cannot be easily interpreted.	**.57**
9. It is easy for me to describe the purpose and function of databases.	**.65**
10. I can merge data from various sources into a table and prepare them for use as training data.	**.63**
11. I can explain exactly what an algorithm is.	**.63**
12. I know different measures to protect data, e.g., from unauthorized access.	**.66**
13. I am usually successful when I need to read the slope of a linear function in a coordinate system.	**.60**
14. I can explain what it means when there is a correlation between factors or variables.	**.66**
15. I can explain in detail how data can be modeled through linear regression.	**.69**
16. I can describe how to train and apply a decision tree.	**.72**
17. I know exactly why training data are important for machine learning.	**.72**
18. I can explain well how artificial neural networks work.	**.59**

Note. $N = 156$. EFA = exploratory factor analysis. Factor loadings greater than .30 are shown in bold. The eigenvalue of the factor is 7.65, accounting for 42% of the explained variance. The items are translated into English. The original scale is in the Posttest in Appendix E in the electronic supplementary material by an off-diagonal value of 0.97, which supports its adequacy in representing the underlying structure. The TLI and RMSEA values suggest a moderate but acceptable fit, further supporting that the single factor is a good representation of the underlying construct. The results of the scale's reliability analysis (see Appendix C in the electronic supplementary material, Table C5) demonstrated an excellent internal consistency ($a = .93$), indicating that the items consistently measure the underlying construct of cognitive learning outcomes on AI. The item statistics indicated that removing any items would not lead to an improvement in Cronbach's alpha, suggesting that all items make a positive contribution to the overall reliability of the scale.

4.5 Data Analysis

To investigate the research questions, the statistical analysis was performed with the statistical computing and programming language R using version 4.3.1 (R Core Team, 2023). Six datasets in total, collected at t_0, t_1, and t_2 during the two data collection rounds, as described in Sect. 4.1, were downloaded from Unipark. These datasets were cleaned and merged into a single comprehensive dataset using basic R functions and the dplyr package (Wickham, François, et al., 2023). The dplyr package was further used to describe the sociodemographic variables and perform data manipulation. Frequency distributions and percentages were calculated to summarize participants' sociodemographic characteristics. For the description of the sociodemographic data, the psych package was also employed (Revelle, 2024).

A priori power analyses were conducted utilizing the pwr package (Champely, 2020) to determine the required sample size for the planned analyses concerning the research questions RQ2.1, RQ2.2, RQ2.3, and RQ2.4. As these questions aimed to investigate differences in learning outcomes between learners with different learning styles, a moderate effect size of $d = 0.5$ (Cohen, 1988) for independent t-tests was assumed based on theoretical considerations detailed in Chap. 3 and a significance level of .05. The power analysis determined that a minimum sample size of 50 participants per group would be necessary to achieve 80% power.

The psych package was further utilized along with the dplyr package to evaluate the validity and reliability of the scales. The polycor package (Fox, 2022) was used for preliminary analysis of the validity of the ILS through polychoric correlations. CFA of the ILS was assessed using the lavaan package (Rosseel, 2012). To assess the reliability of the ILS, along with the psych package, the

Hmisc package was utilized (Harrell, 2023) to conduct interscale correlations. Descriptive statistics were computed with the aid of the psych package, while the results were exported utilizing the writexl package (Ooms, 2024). For contingency tables requiring transformations from wide to long formats, the package tidyr was necessary (Wickham, Vaughan, et al., 2023).

To answer RQ1, a multiple linear regression analysis was performed to test for the effect of adaptivity, individualization, prior knowledge, and experience with digital learning applications on learning outcomes, utilizing the stats package of base R (R Core Team, 2023). To conduct further analyses regarding the calculation of standardized coefficients and checking assumptions, the packages psych (Revelle, 2024), QuantPsych (Fletcher, 2022), car (Fox & Weisberg, 2019), lmtest (Zeileis & Hothorn, 2002), and ggplot2 for visualizations (Wickham, 2016) were used. Inferential statistics were further calculated for RQ2.1, RQ2.2, RQ2.3, and RQ2.4 to test whether learners with particular learning styles achieved better learning outcomes. One-tailed independent samples t-tests were performed utilizing the stats package of base R (R Core Team, 2023), the packages dplyr (Wickham et al., François, 2023) and car (Fox & Weisberg, 2019), the package ggplot2 for checking assumptions via visualizations (Wickham, 2016), and the package effsize for calculating effect sizes (Torchiano, 2020).

Results of the Surveys

5

This chapter examines whether the hypotheses outlined in Chap. 3 are supported by the survey responses of learners who participated in the AI course. Due to the small sample size in the first round of data collection (see Sect. 4.2), responses from both data collections were combined and analyzed together, as separate statistical analyses for the planned investigations were not methodologically feasible.

The AI course was designed for learners from VET and CVET institutions and incorporated adaptive and individualized features to accommodate their individual learning needs and thereby enhance their learning outcomes. Furthermore, given that prior knowledge is widely recognized as a key predictor of learning outcomes, prior knowledge was assessed by the system to ensure the delivery of appropriately tailored learning content. In addition, since the course was delivered via a digital learning platform requiring experience with various digital learning applications, learners' familiarity with these tools was also expected to play a crucial role in improving their learning outcomes. Therefore, the first research question (RQ1) examined whether prior knowledge, experience with digital learning applications, individualization, and adaptivity influenced learning outcomes. It was hypothesized that these factors would have a positive effect. To test this hypothesis, a multiple linear regression (MLR) analysis was conducted to determine whether a significant effect could be supported. The model's assumptions were assessed to evaluate its robustness and generalizability to the broader population of learners in VET and CVET institutions. Before addressing whether this hypothesis was supported in Sect. 5.2, descriptive results of the investigated

---

Supplementary Information The online version contains supplementary material available at https://doi.org/10.1007/978-3-658-51517-1_5.

E. Petridou, *Personalized Learning in Vocational and Continuing Education*, https://doi.org/10.1007/978-3-658-51517-1_5

variables are initially presented in Sects. 5.1.1 to 5.1.5. These results include frequency distributions illustrated through histograms, percentage distributions visualized with bar charts, and key descriptive statistics, i.e., means and standard deviations, presented in tables.

The second research question (RQ2) examined whether learners with certain learning styles achieved higher learning outcomes in the AI course. The construct of learning styles is considered a key characteristic that can differentiate learning outcomes in an adaptive learning environment. Given the inconclusive results of prior research regarding the impact of certain learning styles on learning outcomes, RQ2.1 focused on investigating whether learners with active learning styles achieved higher learning outcomes than learners with reflective learning styles. RQ2.2 aimed to investigate whether learners with sensing learning styles outperformed those with intuitive learning styles. RQ2.3 focused on examining whether learners with visual learning styles achieved higher learning outcomes than learners with verbal learning styles, while RQ2.4 aimed to assess whether learners with sequential learning styles achieved higher learning outcomes than those with global learning styles. Descriptive results of the learning styles construct are first presented in Sect. 5.3, utilizing a bipolar plot and a bar graph. In Sect. 5.4, it is assessed whether any significant difference exists in the learning outcomes of the learning styles' groups. Independent t-tests were conducted, and their assumptions were tested to ensure the validity of the analysis. Key results from the inferential analysis of the research questions are presented using plots and tables.

5.1 Descriptive Results of Constructs in the First Research Question

5.1.1 Prior Knowledge in AI

Prior knowledge in AI was considered a key predictor of learning outcomes in the AI course. Assessing learners' prior knowledge levels was essential to gain an overview of the sample's foundational understanding of AI. Prior knowledge was assessed with a scale that included items covering various AI-related thematic areas. The scale ranged from a theoretical minimum of 1 (*no prior knowledge at all*) to a theoretical maximum of 4 (*very good prior knowledge*). Learners ($N = 218$) reported on average limited prior knowledge in AI ($M = 2.07$, $SD = 0.57$), rating their knowledge across various AI thematic areas as relatively low. As illustrated in Table 5.1, the highest amount of prior knowledge was reported in the thematic area of practical examples, followed by AI areas of application, AI opportunities, challenges, and ethical considerations, as well as fundamental AI concepts. In these areas, learners demonstrated foundational understanding. In contrast, they reported less prior knowledge in basic data analysis concepts and other AI-related topics, with the least amount of knowledge in programming.

Table 5.1 Means and Standard Deviations of Prior Knowledge in Thematic Areas of AI

Topic	*M*	*SD*
Practical examples	2.43	0.78
(Potential) areas of application	2.34	0.81
Opportunities, challenges, and ethical issues of AI	2.26	0.83
Basic concepts of AI	2.16	0.78
Data management	2.11	0.79
Machine learning	2.02	0.77
Basic concepts of data analysis	1.88	0.80
Other thematic areas [a]	1.81	0.72
Programming	1.68	0.78

Note. $N = 218$. Response options ranged from 1 (*not at all*) to 4 (*very well*). M = Mean, SD = Standard Deviation
[a] $N = 217$. One value was regarded as missing

A histogram was plotted to illustrate the distribution of prior knowledge scores among learners (see Fig. 5.1). The distribution appeared to be somewhat skewed, with the majority of participants having lower scores, indicating limited prior knowledge in AI. Very few participants had scores above 3, suggesting that high knowledge levels were less common. As the inspection of the histogram suggested a deviation of normality, a Shapiro-Wilk test was conducted (Shapiro & Wilk, 1965), which indicated a significant deviation from normality ($W = 0.97$, $p < .001$). However, the assessment of skewness (–0.03) and kurtosis (–0.05) suggested that the distribution was approximately symmetric. Given the large sample size ($N = 218$), it was assumed that the Central Limit Theorem (CLT) applies (Howell, 2010), ensuring that the sampling distribution of prior knowledge was normally distributed regardless of the shape of the observed data. According to the CLT, even when the sample data are not approximately normal, the sampling distribution of the mean tends to approximate a normal distribution when the sample size is large, typically greater than 30.

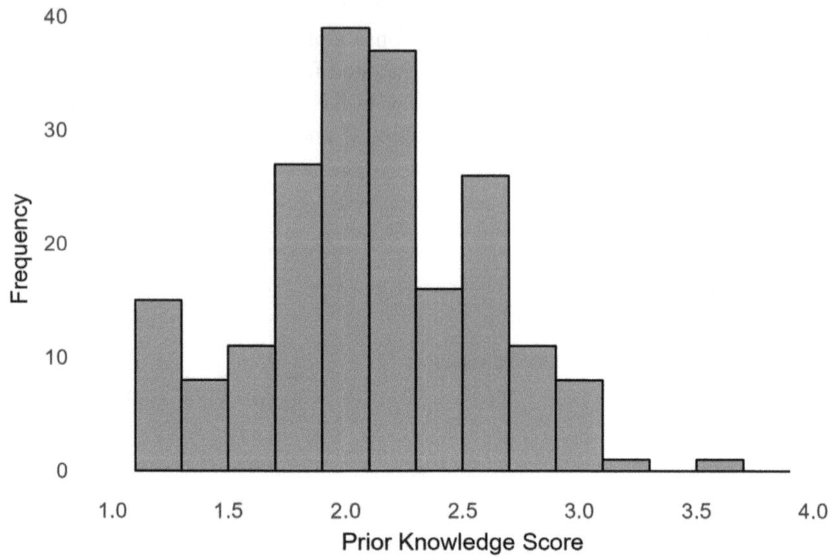

Fig. 5.1 Frequency Distribution of Prior Knowledge. (*Note.* N = 218. Response options ranged from 1 (*not at all*) to 4 (*very well*))

5.1.2 Experience with Digital Learning Applications

Learners' experience with digital learning applications was considered an important factor in achieving high learning outcomes in AI. Their experience was measured with a scale that included items covering different learning applications. A 4-point response scale was utilized, ranging from 1 (*much experience*) to 3 (*no experience*), and a fourth response option (*I do not know*). To calculate the descriptive statistics, the response options were reversed, and the fourth response option was excluded. On average, learners ($N = 212$) reported having a moderate level of prior experience ($M = 2.18$, $SD = 0.39$), indicating some familiarity with certain applications but not extensive experience. This could be further confirmed by the histogram in Fig. 5.2, which demonstrates that the majority of learners reported moderate experience. The histogram further showed an approximately symmetrical distribution of the variable with no strong skewness (–0.15) and a slight negative kurtosis (–0.22), indicating approximate normality. The normality of the variable was also supported by the Shapiro-Wilk test (Shapiro &

Wilk, 1965), which indicated that its distribution was not significantly different from normal ($W = 0.99$, $p = .067$).

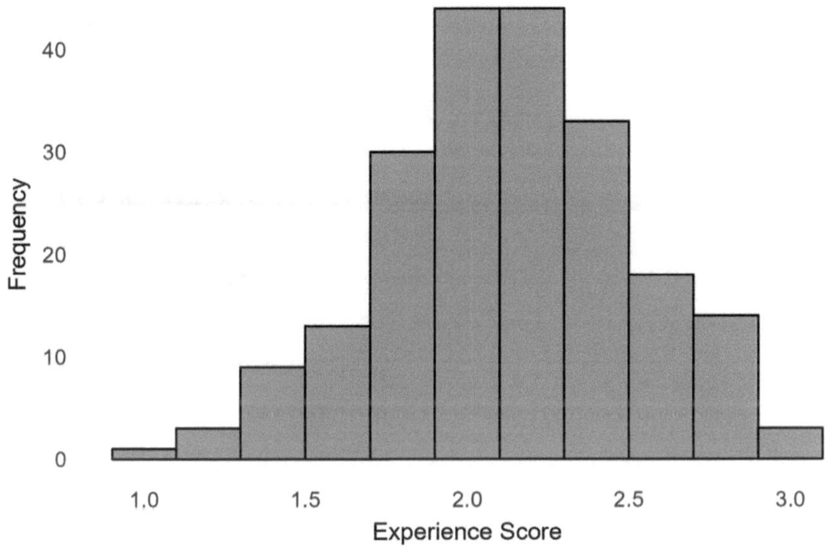

Fig. 5.2 Frequency Distribution of Experience with Digital Learning Applications. (*Note. N* = 212. Response options ranged from 1 (*no experience*) to 3 (*much experience*))

As shown in Fig. 5.3, learners reported using most frequently learning videos. Half of the participants indicated a high level of familiarity with digital texts, such as e-books and PDF documents. In addition, 43.5% of learners reported substantial experience with chat services, while 39.7% were particularly familiar with visual learning materials, including pictures, diagrams, graphs, and maps. More than half of the participants reported having some familiarity with online courses, LMSs, learning software and applications, digital learning and planning games, simulations, and digital tests or exercises. However, forums, communities, blogs, wikis, and subscription-based media files were less commonly used, with over 20% of learners reporting no experience with these applications. The least familiar format was the blended learning course, with nearly half of the participants (48.6%) indicating no familiarity with the concept.

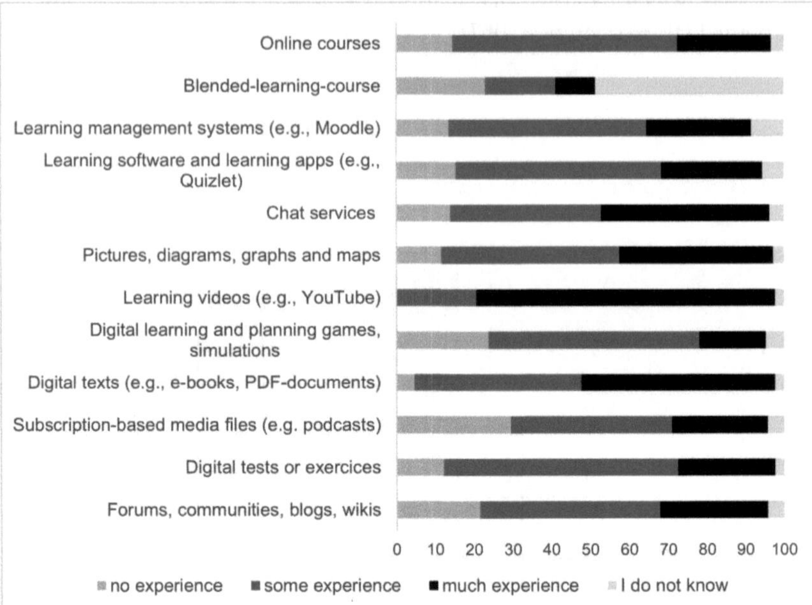

Fig. 5.3 Distribution of Responses about Experience with Digital Learning Applications in Percentages. (*Note.* $N = 214$. Adapted from "Evaluationsbericht: Ergebnisse und Schlussfolgerungen der Evaluation der Zusatzqualifikation „KI und maschinelles Lernen" im Rahmen des Projekts „Künstliche Intelligenz in die berufliche Bildung bringen (KI B^3)," by Lao et al., 2024, p. 21 (https://www.ki-fortbildung.de/downloadbereich). In the public domain)

5.1.3 Individualization

A key feature integrated into the learning environment to enhance learning outcomes in the AI course was individualization. Individualization was measured using the scales of *Individualization Through the Learning Software* and *Individualization of the Learning Environment*. These scales were combined into a single scale with 11 items in total, capturing the broader construct of individualization. The scale had a theoretical minimum of 1 (*completely disagree/does not apply at all*) and a theoretical maximum of 5 (*completely agree/fully applies*). The individualized support provided to learners ($N = 156$) was on average perceived as slightly above moderate ($M = 3.48$, $SD = 0.63$). The distribution of the individualization scores, depicted in the histogram in Fig. 5.4, confirmed that most participants perceived individualized support as moderate to high, with the majority of responses clustering around the middle to upper values. The distribution was slightly left-skewed, indicating that higher ratings were more frequent than lower ones. However, the overall shape was still reasonably close to normal. This interpretation was supported by the skewness value (–0.33), indicating a slight left skew, and the kurtosis value (1.29), suggesting a somewhat flatter distribution compared to a normal curve. The Shapiro-Wilk test (Shapiro & Wilk, 1965) indicated a statistically significant deviation from normality ($W = 0.97$, $p = .005$), suggesting that the data did not perfectly follow a normal distribution. However, given the sufficiently large sample size ($N = 156$), based on the CLT, it was regarded that the sampling distribution of individualization scores was approximately normal (Howell, 2010), even if the observed data were not perfectly normal.

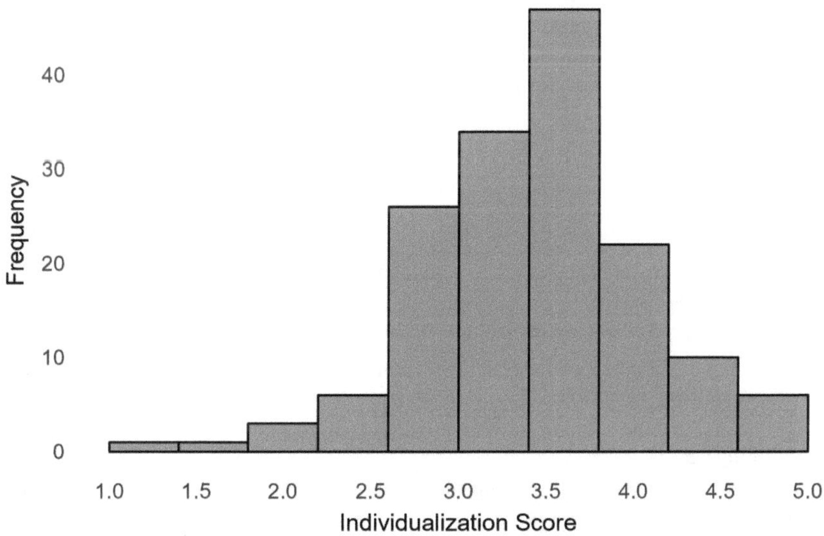

Fig. 5.4 Frequency Distribution of Individualization. (*Note.* $N = 156$. Response options ranged from 1 (*completely disagree/does not apply at all*) to 5 (*completely agree/fully applies*))

The descriptive results of the scale measuring individualization through the learning software revealed that learners agreed on average that the individualization features integrated into the learning software supported personalized learning by addressing their specific needs and preferences ($M = 3.58$, $SD = 0.67$). More specifically, as shown in Table 5.2, the results from the individual items indicated that learners strongly agreed that the learning software facilitated independent work, suggesting that the software was effective in supporting independent learning. Learners further reported being strongly supported by the different learning materials provided, highlighting the value of diverse instructional formats. In addition, a high level of agreement was observed regarding the possibility of reviewing their learning progress, suggesting that learners found the software's progress-tracking features particularly supportive. Learners also perceived as helpful the competence-based tasks provided by the software, the flexibility to choose the learning sequence, as well as the prior knowledge assessment. However, learners were not particularly satisfied with the software's ability to understand their learning difficulties while completing tasks. This suggests that the software's ability to recognize and respond to individual challenges may require further improvement. Overall, learners perceived the learning software as supportive of individualized learning, especially in fostering independence and providing diverse materials. Nonetheless, a potential area for the software's improvement could be its ability to adapt to learners' difficulties.

Table 5.2 Means and Standard Deviations of the Scale Individualization Through the Learning Software

Item	*M*	*SD*
1. The learning software enables me to work on the learning units independently.	3.92	0.89
2. The learning software supports me in reviewing my learning progress.	3.72	0.99
3. The different learning materials (written learning material, explanatory videos, etc.) are supportive.	3.88	0.92
4. It is helpful that the learning software provides tasks that correspond to my competences.	3.69	0.87
5. The option provided by the learning software to choose the order of content to be studied is helpful.	3.49	0.99
6. The option provided by the learning software to assess my prior knowledge by checking a box is helpful.	3.51	0.93
7. I feel that the learning software understands my difficulties in completing the tasks.	2.81	0.90

Note. $N = 156$. Response options ranged from 1 (*completely disagree*) to 5 (*completely agree*). M = Mean, SD = Standard Deviation

Furthermore, the descriptive results of the scale measuring individualization of the learning environment demonstrated that, on average, learners ($N = 156$) moderately agreed that the overall learning environment was tailored to their needs ($M = 3.34$, $SD = 0.69$). As presented in Table 5.3, while learners perceived the features to regulate their learning process and particularly their learning pace as supportive, they reported somewhat lower agreement regarding the consideration of their prior knowledge and experiences. In addition, they expressed only moderate agreement that the most recent learning unit fully aligned with their individual learning needs. Overall, even though learners felt a greater sense of autonomy in managing their own learning process and pace, their responses suggested that the content could be more closely aligned with their existing knowledge and past learning experiences and accommodate their individual learning needs.

Table 5.3 Means and Standard Deviations of the Scale Individualization of the Learning Environment

Item	*M*	*SD*
1. The last learning unit exactly matches my individual learning needs.	3.08	0.89
2. During this learning unit, I was able to control my own learning process.	3.42	0.80
3. In the last learning unit, I was able to decide on my own how quickly I wanted to learn.	3.60	0.96
4. The last learning unit built on my prior knowledge and prior experiences.	3.25	0.97

Note. $N = 156$. Response options ranged from 1 (*does not apply at all*) to 5 (*fully applies*). M = Mean, SD = Standard Deviation

5.1.4 Adaptivity

Adaptivity was another key feature of the learning environment designed to improve learning outcomes in the AI course. Adaptivity was measured with a scale consisting of seven items, which aimed to assess the support provided by the adaptive features of the software. The scale ranged from 1 (*completely disagree*) to 5 (*completely agree*). Learners ($N = 131$) perceived on average the learning software's adaptivity to their needs and progress as slightly below moderate by the end of the course ($M = 2.93$, $SD = 0.79$). The inspection of adaptivity's histogram revealed an approximately symmetrical distribution of adaptivity scores with a slight right skew (see Fig. 5.5). This finding was further supported by the skewness (0.20) and kurtosis (–0.18) values, indicating approximate normality, as well as the results of the Shapiro-Wilk test (Shapiro & Wilk, 1965), which suggested that the data of adaptivity are normally distributed ($W = 0.98$, $p = .143$).

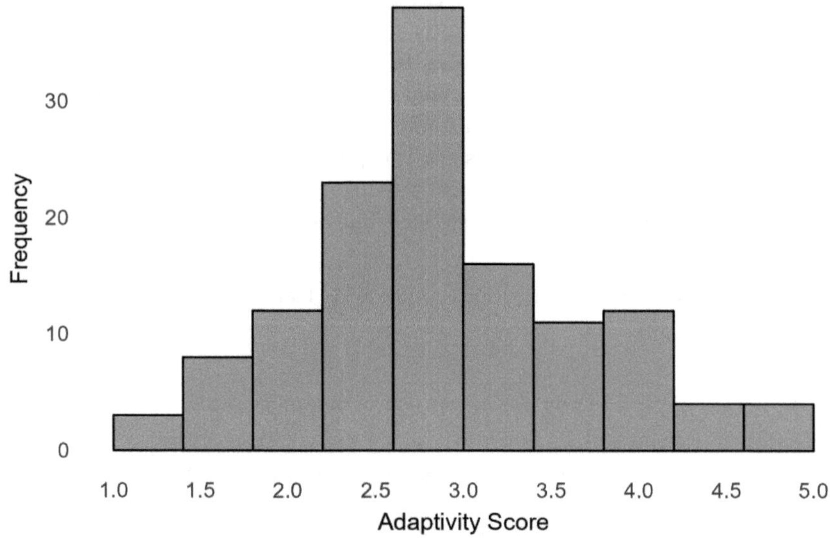

Fig. 5.5 Frequency Distribution of Adaptivity. (*Note.* $N = 131$. Response options ranged from 1 (*completely disagree*) to 5 (*completely agree*))

The descriptive analysis of the individual items of the scale further confirmed the mixed learners' perceptions regarding the extent to which the software dynamically adjusted to their needs (see Table 5.4). The highest-rated statement was that the difficulty level of the content was appropriate for their level of knowledge, followed by the perception that the software simplified content and helped learners to constantly assess their learning progress. The learning software's ability to encourage proactive involvement with the learning content was rated slightly lower. The comparatively lowest-rated aspects were the software's capability to address comprehension difficulties as well as its ability to tailor learning content to individual learning habits and requirements. Overall, learners' responses indicated that while the learning environment provided a foundational degree of dynamic adjustment to individual learning needs and preferences, there was still potential in its ability to be more responsive to learners' difficulties and fully tailor the learning content and its support to individual learning trajectories.

Table 5.4 Means and Standard Deviations of the Adaptivity Scale

Item	*M*	*SD*
1. The difficulty level of the contents provided by the learning software was appropriate for my level of knowledge.	3.18	1.03
2. The learning software supported me by simplifying the content.	3.11	1.00
3. The learning software adapted the learning contents to my learning habits. [a]	2.62	1.04
4. The learning software adapted the learning contents to my learning requirements.	2.78	1.13
5. The learning software helped me with comprehension difficulties.	2.79	1.00
6. The learning software encouraged active engagement with the contents.	2.96	1.07
7. With the help of the learning software, I was constantly able to assess my learning progress.	3.09	1.04

Note. $N = 131$. Response options ranged from 1 (*completely disagree*) to 5 (*completely agree*). M = Mean, SD = Standard Deviation
[a] $N = 130$. One value was regarded as missing

5.1.5 Learning Outcomes in AI

Cognitive learning outcomes were considered a significant indicator of learners' success in the AI course. They were measured with an 18-item scale aimed at assessing whether learners acquired knowledge and skills in the thematic areas of AI introduced in the course. The scale had a theoretical minimum of 1 (*completely disagree*) and a theoretical maximum of 5 (*completely agree*). The descriptive results of learners' cognitive learning outcomes ($N = 134$) indicated that learners assessed on average their learning outcomes as slightly above moderate ($M = 3.46$, $SD = 0.69$), reflecting a competent level of cognitive learning achievement. A similar pattern emerged in learners' self-assessment of their learning outcomes across various thematic areas of AI, indicating a largely consistent perception of their cognitive achievements. Learners reported having achieved high learning outcomes in Data Management ($M = 3.64$, $SD = 0.75$). They also evaluated their learning outcomes as above moderate in Basic Concepts of Data Analysis and Machine Learning ($M = 3.50$, $SD = 0.79$) and Basic Concepts of AI ($M = 3.45$, $SD = 0.76$). Their ratings were somewhat lower but still moderate regarding Opportunities, Challenges, and Ethical Issues of AI ($M = 3.13$, $SD = 0.85$), suggesting that they felt less competent in this thematic area. Table 5.5 demonstrates how strong learners' evaluations were with respect to each of the different aspects of the individual AI topics. Learners rated the importance of training data

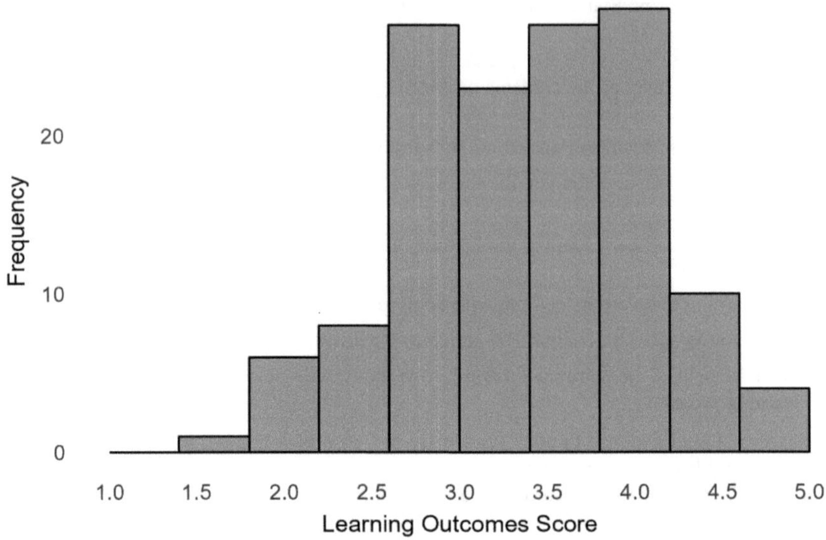

Fig. 5.6 Frequency Distribution of Learning Outcomes. (*Note.* $N = 134$. Response options ranged from 1 (*completely disagree*) to 5 (*completely agree*))

for machine learning, as well as their understanding of the scope and function of databases, as particularly high. Similarly, they expressed confidence in identifying the slope of a linear function in a coordinate system. In contrast, they expressed the lowest confidence in comprehending the interpretation difficulties of model parameters of artificial neural networks and in identifying strategies to mitigate algorithmic bias, topics related to challenging issues of AI applications. Overall, learners demonstrated a solid understanding of the fundamental concepts of AI, data management, and basic aspects of data analysis and machine learning. However, their self-assessments regarding opportunities, challenges, and ethical issues of AI indicated a need for more profound instructional emphasis on ethical considerations and the interpretability of AI models.

To assess the distribution of learning outcomes scores, a histogram was plotted (see Fig. 5.6). The histogram showed that the scores' distribution was roughly symmetrical, with most values clustering around the middle and slightly higher values, suggesting no substantial deviation from a normal distribution. The Shapiro-Wilk test (Shapiro & Wilk, 1965) further supported the assumption of normality ($W = 0.98$, $p = .136$). The skewness value of –0.20 confirmed that

Table 5.5 Means and Standard Deviations of the Learning Outcomes Scale

Item	*M*	*SD*
Basic Concepts of AI		
1. I can assess well what role data play in the context of AI.	3.83	0.94
2. I can describe in detail how machine learning works.	3.22	0.86
3. I can describe well what an AI model is.	3.51	0.96
4. I find it easy to train an AI model with Teachable Machines.	3.37	1.17
5. I have many ideas on how AI can or could be applied in my training company.	3.32	1.18
Opportunities, Challenges, and Ethical Issues of AI		
6. I know methods and ways to avoid algorithmic biases.	3.00	1.06
7. I can describe exactly how personal data can be protected.	3.42	1.02
8. I understand exactly why model parameters of artificial neural networks cannot be easily interpreted.	2.96	1.13
Data Management		
9. It is easy for me to describe the purpose and function of databases.	3.91	0.95
10. I can merge data from various sources into a table and prepare them for use as training data.	3.41	0.95
11. I can explain exactly what an algorithm is.	3.66	0.97
12. I know different measures to protect data, e.g., from unauthorized access.	3.58	1.01
Basic Concepts of Data Analysis and Machine Learning		
13. I am usually successful when I need to read the slope of a linear function in a coordinate system.	3.91	1.10
14. I can explain what it means when there is a correlation between factors or variables.	3.35	1.15
15. I can explain in detail how data can be modeled through linear regression.	3.13	0.99
16. I can describe how to train and apply a decision tree.	3.63	0.97
17. I know exactly why training data are important for machine learning.	3.96	0.96
18. I can explain well how artificial neural networks work.	3.05	1.04

Note. $N = 134$. Response options ranged from 1 (*completely disagree*) to 5 (*completely agree*). M = Mean, SD = Standard Deviation the distribution was nearly symmetric, while the kurtosis value of –0.61 indicated a slightly flatter shape compared to a normal distribution. Although this minor deviation from normality was observed, the sample size was sufficiently large for the CLT to apply (Howell, 2010), ensuring that the sampling distribution of learning outcomes scores could be treated as approximately normal.

5.2 Results of the Inferential Analysis for the First Research Question

Based on RQ1 and the corresponding theoretical expectations detailed in Chap. 3, the following hypothesis was investigated:

H1: Adaptivity, individualization, prior knowledge, and experience with digital learning applications have a positive effect on learning outcomes.

This hypothesis was derived from previous research and the design of the learning environment developed for the AI course. Adaptive and individualized features were central in the software's development to facilitate AI knowledge and skills' acquisition, thereby expecting to enhance learning outcomes. Learners' prior knowledge was further expected to improve learning outcomes, as previously acquired knowledge and skills transfer to new learning and facilitate knowledge construction. In addition, it was hypothesized that experience with digital learning applications would positively affect learning outcomes, as familiarity with digital learning applications was assumed to facilitate navigation in the course, thereby directly contributing to better learning outcomes.

To test this hypothesis, an MLR analysis was conducted. Prior to the analysis, individual scatterplots were created to visually inspect the relationship between each predictor variable and learning outcomes (see Fig. 5.7). Adaptivity, individualization, and prior knowledge appeared to have a clear positive relationship with learning outcomes. Their regression lines had noticeably steeper slopes, indicating that higher scores on these variables were associated with higher learning outcomes. The spread of data points around each line varied, reflecting differences in variability across the predictors. However, experience with digital learning applications displayed a nearly flat regression line and a more dispersed distribution of points, suggesting a very weak or negligible relationship with learning outcomes. Overall, the visual inspection of the scatterplots suggested that while three predictors were positively related to learning outcomes, experience with digital learning applications showed no meaningful relationship.

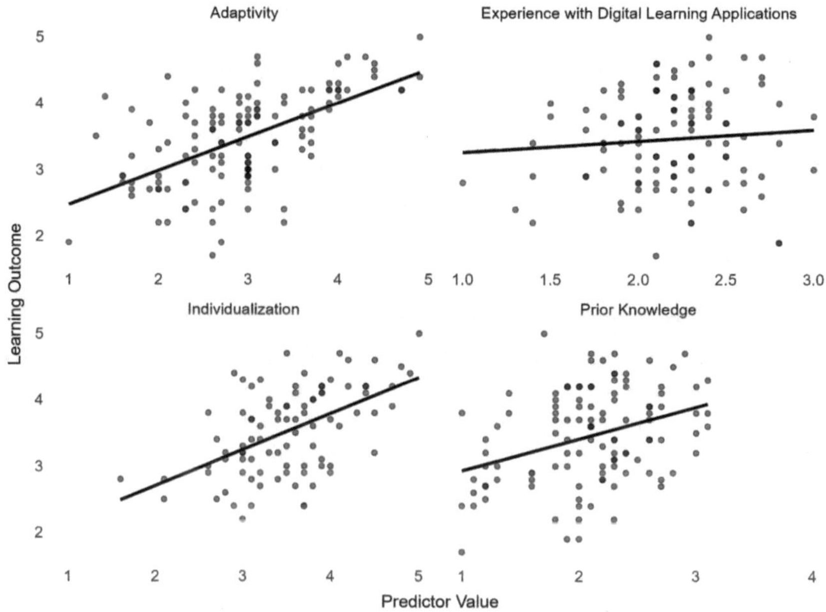

Fig. 5.7 Relationships Between Key Predictors and Learning Outcomes. (*Note.* $N = 79$)

The forced entry method was selected for the MLR analysis, as no theoretical rationale justified a certain predictor order (Field, 2012). As demonstrated in Table 5.6, the overall model was significant. All predictors, except experience with digital learning applications, which indicated a nearly zero relationship, showed a positive relationship with learning outcomes. Therefore, the research hypothesis H1 was partially supported. More specifically, it was found that adaptivity, individualization, and prior knowledge were significant predictors of learning outcomes. Their relatively small standard errors indicated precise estimates, and their confidence intervals did not include zero, supporting their significant positive effect. However, experience with digital learning applications did not significantly predict learning outcomes. Its p-value indicated that this estimate can be explained by mere sampling variability. Its standard error was relatively large compared to its coefficient, suggesting a highly uncertain and nonsignificant effect. Its confidence interval included zero, further supporting its lack of significance.

To examine the individual contribution of each predictor regardless of the predictors' different units of measurement, the standardized beta coefficients (β) were calculated, which are further presented in Table 5.6. Adaptivity had the strongest impact on learning outcomes, followed by prior knowledge and individualization. Experience with digital learning applications did not contribute significantly to explaining learning outcomes. As suggested by the value of multiple R^2, which assesses the overall fit of the model, approximately 54% of the variability in learning outcomes was explained by the MLR model. This suggested a moderate to strong relationship between the predictors and the outcome, underscoring that these predictors explained a substantial proportion of the variance in learning outcomes. The adjusted R^2, which adjusts for the number of predictors in the model, was very close to the multiple R^2, indicating that 51% of the variance in learning outcomes would be explained by these predictors, if the model were derived from the population. This small difference between the two values indicated that most predictors contributed meaningfully to the model and that the model's explanatory power was still relatively strong. In addition, the highly significant F-statistic ($p < .001$) denoted that the predictors collectively had a significant effect on learning outcomes, rendering the overall model statistically significant. The model's residual error of 0.47, given the 5-point Likert scale of the outcome variable, suggested that, on average, the model's predictions deviated by approximately half a point from the actual learning outcomes. This relatively small error indicated that the MLR model produced fairly accurate predictions within the context of a Likert-scale measurement.

Table 5.6 Results of the Multiple Linear Regression Analysis Predicting Learning Outcomes

Predictor	*B*	*SE*	β	*t*	*p*	95% CI
Intercept	0.51	0.51		1.00	.320	[–0.51,1.54]
Adaptivity	0.38	0.09	0.45	4.37	<.001	[0.20,0.55]
Individualization	0.26	0.10	0.26	2.63	.010	[0.06,0.46]
Prior Knowledge	0.46	0.11	0.33	4.19	<.001	[0.24,0.67]
Experience with Digital Learning Applications	0.00	0.18	0.00	0.02	.983	[–0.35,0.36]

Note. $N = 79$. $R^2 = .54$, Adjusted $R^2 = .51$, $F(4,74) = 21.35$, $p < .001$. B = unstandardized regression coefficient; SE = standard error; β = standardized regression coefficient; CI = confidence interval

To assess the accuracy of the regression model, standardized residuals were calculated to identify potential outliers. The residuals observed in the model were converted into z-scores in order to be comparable across models. In a normally distributed sample, approximately 95% of z-scores should lie between –1.96 and +1.96, 99% between –2.58 and +2.58, and 99.9% between –3.29 and +3.29. Given the total sample size of 79 in the MLR model, it was expected that approximately four cases (5%) could have large standardized residuals exceeding ±1.96 and approximately one case (1%) could lie outside of the limits ±2.58. The analysis revealed that only two cases had large standardized residuals exceeding ±1.96, and only one case out of these two was found to exceed the limits of ±2.58, which aligned with expectations. Thus, no extreme outlier was detected, suggesting that the MLR model was fairly accurate.

To determine whether these cases could have an undue influence on the model, additional casewise diagnostics were performed (Field, 2012). Cook's distance values were examined, showing that none exceeded the threshold of 1 (Cook & Weisberg, 1982), indicating no influential cases. In addition, hat values were computed to assess leverage, suggesting how much influence these cases had on the regression model's predictions. No high-leverage points were identified following the recommendations of Hoaglin and Welsch (1978) as well as Stevens (2002), further supporting that these cases were not influential. Finally, covariance ratios were calculated to measure the impact of each observation on the covariance matrix of the regression coefficients. One case had a covariance ratio slightly below the acceptable range (Belsey et al.,1980), but given the Cook's distance results, it was not considered influential. In summary, these diagnostic tests ensured that the model was fairly robust and was not influenced by any particular case.

Furthermore, the model's generalizability beyond the sample used in this analysis was assessed (Field, 2012). The assumption of all predictor variables being quantitative was met, as they were measured using Likert scales, which are commonly treated as interval data. While Likert data are inherently ordinal variables, in social sciences, they are commonly treated as continuous when averaged across multiple items (Carifio & Perla, 2008; Norman, 2010). This is based on the assumption that creating a composite score by aggregating multiple items helps approximate an underlying continuous construct. The use of Likert scale data as interval data is a well-established practice in research and is commonly accepted in methodological literature (Bortz & Döring, 2006; Field, 2012; Sullivan & Artino, 2013). In addition, the outcome variable needed to be quantitative, continuous, and unbounded. As the variable of learning outcomes was measured on a Likert scale, it was assumed to be quantitative and approximately continuous. Even though the observed values of the outcome variable ranged from 1.7 to 5, not fully covering the 5-point Likert scale, this range was considered sufficiently wide to be treated as unbounded. Normality assessments further confirmed that the outcome variable was approximately normally distributed and displayed adequate variability. In addition, all predictors needed to show some variation in their values. Variance calculations confirmed that all four predictors had non-zero variance, meeting this assumption.

Another key assumption in an MLR analysis is the absence of perfect multicollinearity among the predictors (Fox, 2016). To ensure that the predictors were not highly correlated with each other, a heatmap correlation matrix was generated to visualize relationships between predictors. As illustrated in Fig. 5.8, the strongest positive correlation was observed between adaptivity and individualization, while adaptivity and experience with digital learning applications showed a weak-to-moderate positive relationship. The remaining correlations were weaker or near-zero. Since no values exceeded .70, multicollinearity was deemed unlikely. Given that the correlation analysis alone does not fully account for collinearity effects across multiple predictors, collinearity diagnostics were conducted (Field, 2012). The variance inflation factor (VIF) values, which indicate whether a predictor has a strong linear relationship with the other predictors, remained below the recommended threshold of 10 (Myers, 1990), with an average VIF value very close to 1 (Bowerman & O'Connell, 1990). In addition, the tolerance statistics were well above 0.2 (Menard, 1995), further confirming that the predictors were sufficiently independent of each other.

Furthermore, it was important to ensure that no external variables, namely factors that were not included in the model and may influence the outcome, correlated with any of the predictors (Field, 2012). If such correlations exist, the conclusions drawn from the model may become unreliable, as other variables could also explain AI learning outcomes. Given the sample size, a maximum of two sociodemographic variables could have been included as control variables to account for potential confounding effects. To explore this, an additional MLR analysis was conducted, incorporating age and gender as control variables. The results indicated that their inclusion did not lead to any substantial changes and did not yield a significant result (see Table D1 in Appendix D in the electronic supplementary material). The variables showed nearly zero relationship with learning outcomes. Neither variable significantly predicted learning outcomes nor influenced the overall model fit, thereby confirming their lack of significance in predicting learning outcomes. Providing that the primary focus of this thesis was to examine the effects of adaptivity, individualization, prior knowledge, and

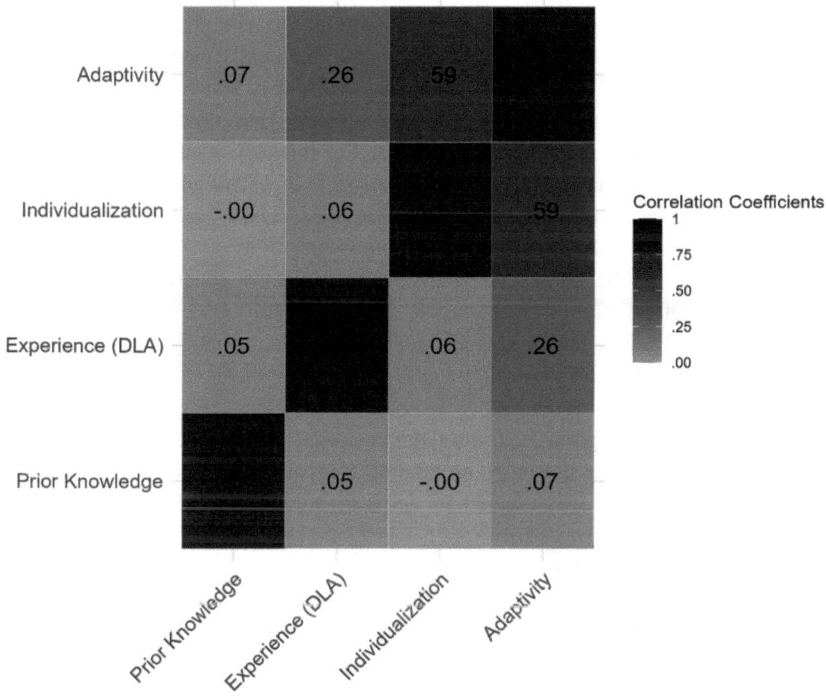

Fig. 5.8 Correlation Heatmap of Predictor Variables. (*Note.* DLA = Digital Learning Applications. The values represent Pearson correlation coefficients denoted as r (Pearson, 1896). Sample sizes vary due to missing data: Adaptivity ($N = 131$), Individualization ($N = 156$), Experience with Digital Learning Applications ($N = 212$), and Prior Knowledge ($N = 218$))

experience with digital learning applications on learning outcomes, these sociodemographic variables were not included in the subsequent MLR analyses, as they would not contribute any meaningful insights to the model.

Moreover, the assumptions related to the residuals of the MLR model were primarily visually assessed (Fox, 2016). The plot of the standardized residuals (y-axis) against the predicted values (x-axis) was created to determine whether the assumptions of random errors, linearity, and homoscedasticity have been met (see Fig. 5.9). The residuals appeared randomly scattered around the zero-residual reference line without a systematic pattern, suggesting no major violations of the random errors' assumption. Additionally, the relationship between the predictors and the outcome variable needed to be linear. The plotted graph of the standardized residuals against the fitted values indicated that the data points are somewhat evenly scattered across the range of fitted values. The locally estimated scatterplot smoothing (LOESS) fit remained close to zero with only some slight curvatures, suggesting merely a minor violation of the linearity assumption. These slight deviations didn't look severe, indicating that the linearity assumption was met. Furthermore, the residual spread seemed relatively consistent across fitted values, suggesting that the residuals had constant variance. There was no clear funnel shape, indicating that the assumption of homoscedasticity was largely satisfied. Slight violations of the homoscedasticity assumption are generally not a major issue, as simulation studies have shown (Hayes, 1996). This was further confirmed by the Breusch-Pagan test (Breusch & Pagan, 1979), which yielded a nonsignificant result ($BP(4) = 2.19$, $p = .701$), supporting the assumption of constant variance.

Another key assumption regarding the residuals of an MLR model is that the residuals need to be normally distributed (Hayes, 2018). To this end, a q-q (quantile-quantile) plot was created to demonstrate if there are any deviations from normality. As illustrated in Fig. 5.10, most residuals closely followed the diagonal reference line, indicating that the residuals approximately follow a normal distribution. There were slight deviations from the line at the lower left and upper right, suggesting minor departures from normality in the tails. However, these deviations were not substantial, indicating that the normality assumption was largely satisfied.

The normality assumption was further tested with a histogram displaying the distribution of the standardized residuals. In Fig. 5.11, the residuals appear roughly symmetric, forming a roughly symmetrical bell-shaped curve. Residuals were centered around 0 and showed a relatively balanced spread on either side. Most values fell between –2 and +2, with a few extending slightly beyond these limits. Overall, the histogram's shape suggested that the normality assumption for residuals was reasonably met.

The independence of errors was evaluated by assessing whether they were uncorrelated. This assumption was tested using the Durbin-Watson test, which examines serial correlations among residuals in regression models (Durbin & Watson, 1951). The test results indicated no significant autocorrelation ($DW = 1.80$, $p = .184$), suggesting that the residuals were approximately uncorrelated. Finally, the independence assumption for the outcome variable, which requires all values to be independent, was considered met since each participant provided only one learning outcome score.

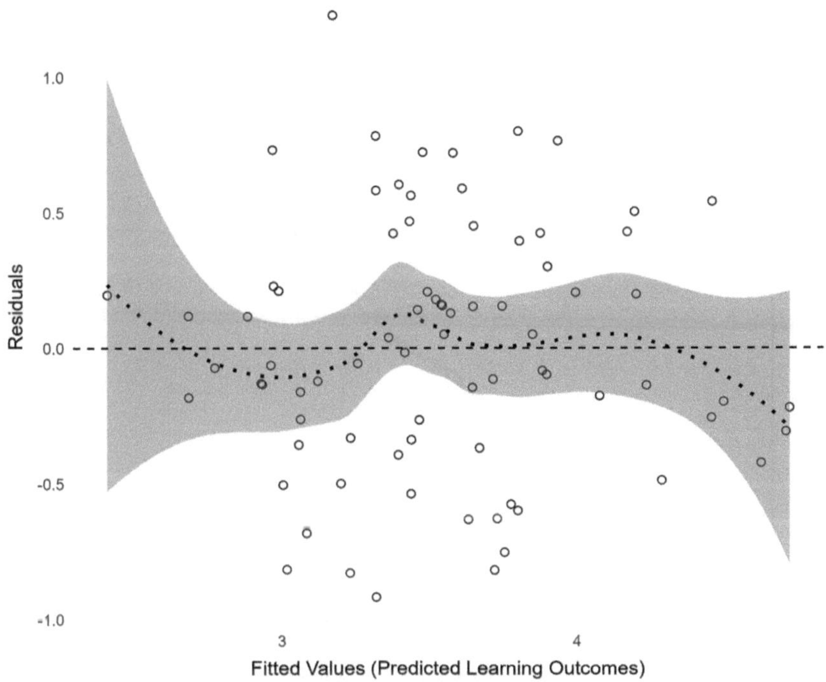

Fig. 5.9 Standardized Residuals Across Fitted Values of Learning Outcomes. (*Note.* N = 79. The dashed line represents the zero-residual reference line. The dotted line represents a locally estimated scatterplot smoothing (LOESS) fit, illustrating the trend in residuals. The shaded area represents the confidence interval for the LOESS fit)

In summary, the MLR model demonstrated both accuracy for this study's sample of learners and generalizability to the broader population of learners from VET and CVET institutions, as all key assumptions were met. While adaptivity, prior knowledge, and individualization were indicated as significant predictors of learning outcomes, experience with digital learning applications did not show a significant effect. This MLR model accounted for a substantial portion of the variance in learning outcomes (R^2 = .54), indicating a reasonably good fit for the data. However, a considerable share of variability remained unexplained, suggesting that additional factors may also influence learning outcomes.

To further assess the model's generalizability, cross-validation was conducted by testing whether the same predictors could accurately predict learning outcomes

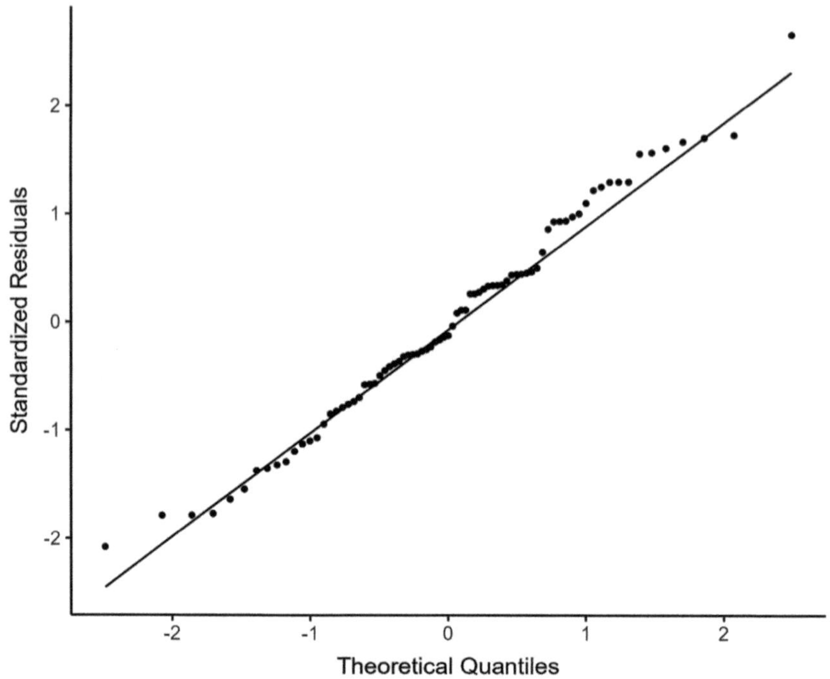

Fig. 5.10 Q-Q Plot of Standardized Residuals. (*Note.* $N = 79$. Q-Q stands for quantile-quantile plot. Theoretical quantiles on the x-axis represent the expected values of standardized residuals under a normal distribution assumption)

in a different sample (Field, 2012). The adjusted R^2 value ($R^2 = .51$), which shows the amount of variance explained by the predictors if the model were derived from the population, as detailed above, showed only a slight decrease from the multiple R^2 value ($R^2 = .54$), suggesting minimal loss of predictive power. Given critiques of adjusted R^2 as a cross-validation measure (Field, 2012), Stein's formula was also applied (Stevens, 2002), yielding an adjusted R^2 of .47, reflecting only a minor reduction. These results suggested that the model generalizes well to the population of learners in vocational and continuing education.

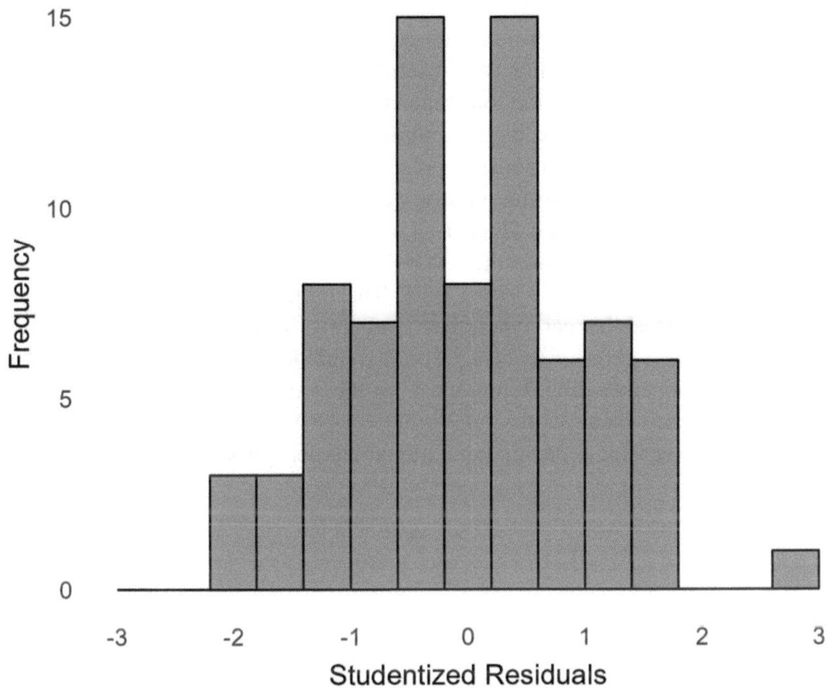

Fig. 5.11 Distribution of Standardized Residuals. (*Note. N* = 79. Studentized residuals on the x-axis follow a t-distribution representing the standardized residuals)

5.3 Descriptive Results of the Construct of Learning Styles

As a significant parameter according to which learners can be differentiated and achieve different learning outcomes, learning styles were initially descriptively analyzed to gain an overview of the participants' learning preferences. Learning styles were measured using a scale consisting of 12 items (see Sect. 4.4.3 for details on the scale items). Each of the four learning style dimensions, namely processing, perception, input, and understanding, was assessed using three items. The response options were bipolar, with option "a" corresponding to the left pole of each dimension and option "b" corresponding to the right pole. Option "a" was scored as 1 and option "b" was scored as 2. To determine learning styles, the three items for each dimension were combined to create the scales for each learning style dimension. Subsequently, the mean scores and standard deviations for each dimension were calculated. The bipolar plot in Fig. 5.12 presents the mean scores of the four bipolar learning style dimensions. Learners' scores were relatively balanced across dimensions, with most mean scores close to the midpoint. The dimensions of processing and perception, represented by the active/reflective and sensing/intuitive learner types, respectively, both had a mean of 4.05 ($SD = 0.97$ and $SD = 1.14$, respectively). This mean score showed only a slight tendency towards the left pole of the scales, suggesting that there was no strong preference for either pole. The dimension of input, represented by the visual/verbal learner types, had a slightly lower mean of 3.73 ($SD = 0.96$), suggesting a stronger tendency toward visual learning among learners. The dimension of understanding, represented by the sequential/global learner types, showed the highest mean score of 4.34 ($SD = 0.96$), indicating a fairly balanced preference between the sequential and global learner types.

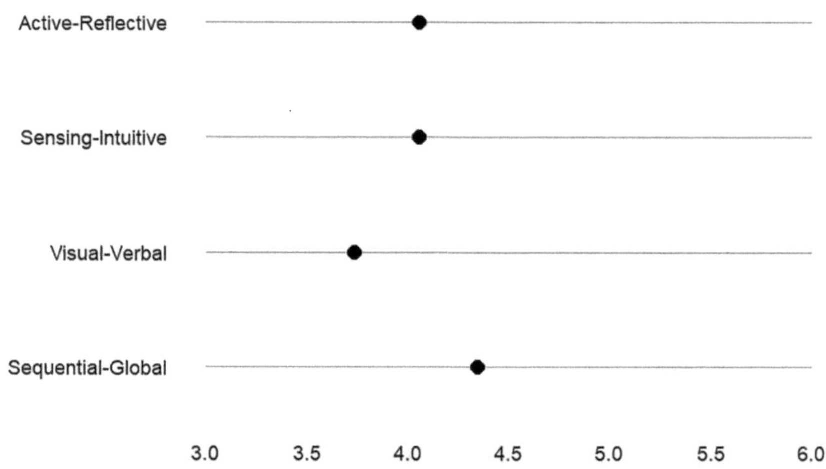

Fig. 5.12 Mean Scores of Learning Styles Scales. (*Note.* $N = 211$. Sample sizes for each learning style group differ. Active: $n = 137$, Reflective: $n = 74$, Sensing: $n = 142$, Intuitive: $n = 69$, Visual: $n = 168$, Verbal: $n = 43$, Sequential: $n = 122$, and Global: $n = 89$. Learning styles scores range from 3 to 6, due to the three items per scale. The black dots represent the mean scores of each learning style dimension, with values lower than the midpoint of 4.5 indicating a preference toward the first pole of each dimension)

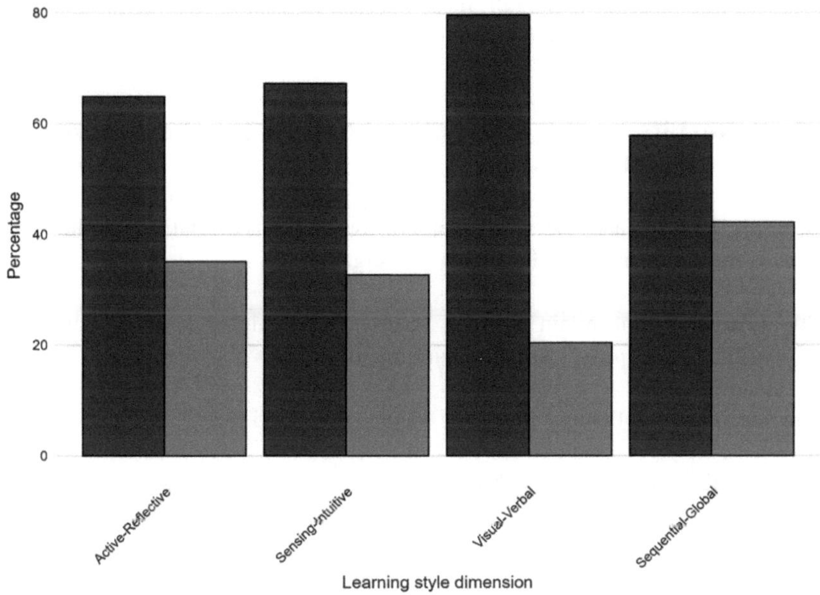

Fig. 5.13 Distribution of Learning Style Preferences. (*Note.* $N = 211$. Sample sizes for each learning style group differ. Active: $n = 137$, Reflective: $n = 74$, Sensing: $n = 142$, Intuitive: $n = 69$, Visual: $n = 168$, Verbal: $n = 43$, Sequential: $n = 122$, and Global: $n = 89$. Dark-shaded columns represent the left poles of the learning style dimensions, while light gray columns represent the corresponding right poles. Percentages indicate the proportion of participants favoring each pole within each dimension)

A clearer picture of the distribution of learning styles was provided by the percentage calculations for each pole of the learning style dimensions. Figure 5.13 depicts the distribution of learning style preferences among learners across the four bipolar dimensions. Regarding the processing dimension, the majority of learners were identified as active (64.9%), while 35.1% preferred a reflective learning approach. A similar pattern was observed in the dimension of perception, whereby most learners (67.3%) were classified as sensing learners, whereas 32.7% were classified as intuitive learners. With respect to the dimension of input, a notable proportion of participants favored a visual learning style (79.6%), compared to 20.4% who preferred a verbal approach. Concerning the dimension of understanding, more than half of the learners (57.8%) exhibited a sequential learning preference, while the rest of them (42.2%) showed a preference for a global learning approach. Overall, these insights suggested clear preferences for specific learning styles among learners.

5.4 Results of the Inferential Analysis for the Second Research Question

According to RQ2 and the corresponding theoretical expectations outlined in Chap. 3, the following hypothesis was investigated:

H2: Learners with certain learning styles achieve higher learning outcomes within an adaptive learning environment.

More specifically, following RQ2.1, it was hypothesized that:

H2.1: Active learners achieve higher learning outcomes than reflective learners.

This hypothesis was based on the premise that an adaptive learning environment developed for an AI course is grounded in CAI and is further designed as an action-oriented learning setting, which incorporates activities requiring active engagement, thereby primarily benefiting learners with active learning styles.

In addition, to address RQ2.2, it was hypothesized that:

H2.2: Sensing learners achieve higher learning outcomes than intuitive learners.

Sensing learners are believed to benefit from CAI and achieve higher learning outcomes than intuitive learners, as the learning materials of an AI course delivered in a digital learning platform include practice-oriented exercises and collaborative activities, which predominantly facilitate sensing learners.

In addition, to answer RQ2.3, it was expected that:

H2.3: Visual learners achieve higher learning outcomes than verbal learners.

Visual learners are hypothesized to outperform verbal learners, as an AI course delivered primarily in a self-directed learning format offers more learning opportunities for learners with visual learning styles. This is attributed to the increased use of visual representations and the limited face-to-face instruction and spoken explanations.

Lastly, RQ2.4 was addressed by the hypothesis that:

H2.4: Sequential learners achieve higher learning outcomes than global learners.

This hypothesis draws on previous research as well as on the design of the adaptive learning environment, which predominantly supports sequential learners, as it favors a sequential learning order by restricting access to advanced or unfamiliar content.

To assess these hypotheses, one-tailed independent t-tests were conducted separately for each learning style pair in order to compare the mean learning outcomes of the two groups. Prior to these analyses, it was essential to verify that there were no outliers in the data and that the assumptions required for conducting independent t-tests were met.

First, boxplots were created for each learning style pair (see Fig. 5.14) to inspect the data for potential outliers that could distort the mean and variance, further contributing to violating assumptions and misleading results. The boxplots of learning outcome scores for active and reflective learners revealed differences in median values and score distributions between the two groups. Reflective learners had a higher median learning outcome than active learners, suggesting only a small potential effect. The interquartile range (IQR) of reflective learners' scores was wider, indicating a wider variability of the middle 50% of their scores. No extreme outliers were detected for both groups. The boxplots of the sensing/intuitive scale demonstrated that the intuitive group had a higher median learning outcome than the sensing group, suggesting that, on average, intuitive learners had slightly better learning outcomes. However, the difference did not seem large. Sensing learners' scores showed a slightly wider distribution, indicating a slightly wider variability in the central 50% of their scores. There were no outliers detected, supporting the robustness of both scales. The boxplots of the visual and verbal learning styles scales presented very similar median learning outcomes scores between the two groups, suggesting minimal difference in median learning outcomes between visual and verbal learners, with visual learners slightly outperforming verbal learners. Both groups had similar IQR, suggesting that the middle 50% of their scores were similarly spread out, with the visual group showing slightly higher values. No obvious extreme outliers were observed. The last boxplots comparing the median learning outcomes between sequential and global learners illustrated a higher median learning outcome score for global learners, with no extreme outliers displayed. Additionally, the IQRs slightly differed, indicating that the middle 50% of their values were distributed similarly, with sequential learners showing a slightly wider variability.

Overall, median learning outcome scores showed minimal variation across learning style groups, indicating no substantial differences. While some differences in score variability were observed, the distributions were generally comparable. No extreme outliers were detected, suggesting that assumption violations were less likely, which supported the robustness of subsequent analyses.

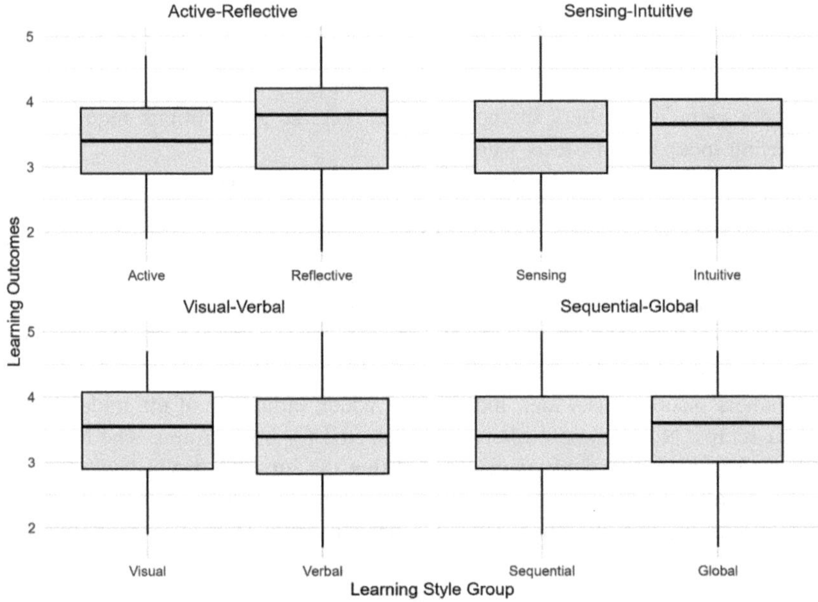

Fig. 5.14 Distribution of Learning Outcomes Across Learning Style Dimensions. (*Note. N* = 112. Sample sizes for learning outcomes across learning styles' groups differ. Active: n = 76, Reflective: n = 36, Sensing: n = 82, Intuitive: n = 30, Visual: n = 82, Verbal: n = 30, Sequential: n = 45, and Global: n = 67. Learning outcomes were measured on a 5-point Likert scale ranging from *completely disagree* to *completely agree*)

Concerning the assumptions of independent t-tests, the normality assumption needed to be initially tested. In statistical tests, such as the t-test, it is assumed that the sampling distribution is normally distributed. As the sample size largely exceeded the threshold of 30 participants, it was regarded that the CLT applied (Howell, 2010). Furthermore, the assumption of homogeneity of variance, requiring the variances to be the same throughout the data, was tested with Levene's test (Levene, 1960). The Levene's test was calculated for each learning styles scale individually (see Table 5.7). All Levene's tests were found to be nonsignificant, suggesting that the variances were not significantly different, rendering the homogeneity of variance assumption tenable.

Table 5.7 Levene's Test for Homogeneity of Variance for the Learning Styles Scales

Scale	*F* (1,110)	*p*
Active/Reflective	1.14	.289
Sensing/Intuitive	0.01	.917
Visual/Verbal	1.01	.317
Sequential/Global	0.20	.653

Note. $N = 112$. F = F-statistic

In addition, the assumption of measuring the dependent variable at least at the interval level was assumed to be met. Even though learning outcomes were measured with a Likert scale and individual Likert items are inherently ordinal, the dependent variable representing learning outcomes was derived by calculating the mean scores per participant across multiple items. This approach is widely considered to approximate an interval scale, as multiple Likert-scale items are aggregated, allowing for the application of parametric statistical analyses (Carifio & Perla, 2008; Norman, 2010). Finally, the assumption of independence was met. Each participant was assigned to only one learning style group and contributed one score on the learning outcomes scale, ensuring that no individual appeared in multiple groups and no participant's score influenced another participant's score.

As the focus of RQ2 was to examine whether learners with certain learning styles achieved higher learning outcomes, a directional independent t-test for RQ2.1, RQ2.2, RQ2.3, and RQ2.4 was conducted for each question separately. Table 5.8 summarizes the results of the t-tests. On average, participants in the reflective group had slightly higher learning outcomes than those in the active group. However, this difference was not statistically significant, the effect size was small, and the confidence interval was wide and included zero, indicating uncertainty. A similar trend was observed for the sensing/intuitive scale. Participants in the intuitive group scored slightly higher than participants in the sensing group, though the difference was not statistically significant, with a negligible effect size and a confidence interval being quite large and crossing zero. With regard to the visual/verbal scale, both groups demonstrated similar mean scores, with the visual group showing a slightly higher average. However, this difference was not statistically significant, the effect size was minimal, and the confidence interval was large and included zero. Likewise, in the sequential/global scale, the global group only marginally outperformed the sequential group, but this difference was not statistically significant with a negligible effect size and large confidence interval, which crossed zero. Overall, no statistically significant differences were observed between learning style groups, the effect sizes were small or negligible, and the confidence intervals included zero, indicating that the impact of learning style preference on learning outcomes could not be supported in this study. Hence, the research hypotheses H2, H2.1, H2.2, H2.3, and H2.4 were not supported.

Table 5.8 Independent T-Tests Results for Learning Outcomes Across Learning Styles Scales

Scale	Group 1		Group 2		*t* (110)	*p*	95% CI	Cohen's *d*
	M	*SD*	*M*	*SD*				
Active/ Reflective	3.40	.68	3.59	.78	−1.332	.907	[−0.43, Inf]	−0.270
Sensing/ Intuitive	3.44	.72	3.50	.71	0.425	.336	[−0.17, Inf]	−0.084
Visual/ Verbal	3.47	.68	3.42	.81	−0.318	.625	[−0.30, Inf]	0.070
Sequential/ Global	3.45	.73	3.47	.70	0.189	.425	[−0.20, Inf]	−0.036

Note. $N = 112$. CI = confidence interval. Group 1 represents the left pole of each learning styles scale, while Group 2 represents the right pole. For instance, in the Active/Reflective scale, Group 1 corresponds to Active learners, whereas Group 2 corresponds to Reflective learners

5.5 Summary of the Results

The results from the descriptive and inferential statistical analyses detailed in the previous sections shed light on critical perceptions and key characteristics of learners from VET and CVET institutions, as well as on effective features of the adaptive learning software developed for the delivery of the AI course. The adaptive learning software was embedded into a blended learning setting requiring familiarity with digital learning applications. It was specifically designed to account for learners' prior knowledge and integrated individualized and adaptive elements in order to enhance AI learning outcomes.

The descriptive results revealed that while learners were moderately familiar with various digital learning applications, their experience with blended learning settings was particularly low, reflecting the scarcity of such instructional formats in vocational and continuing education contexts. Learners' prior knowledge in AI was limited, indicating a restricted understanding of AI and its thematic areas. This suggested that despite having some exposure to AI-related topics, they lacked a deeper understanding of its core concepts. The evaluation of the software's individualized and adaptive features showed that learners perceived the system's support as moderately tailored to their needs. This indicated that while the system offered some degree of personalization, it did not fully meet their expectations in terms of adapting to individual learning progress. Learners further rated their cognitive learning outcomes as above moderate, suggesting they felt competent in the AI knowledge and skills they had acquired by the end of the course. The inferential analysis clarified which learner characteristics and software functions were effective in enhancing AI learning outcomes. It highlighted a statistically significant and positive impact of learners' prior knowledge and the software's individualized and adaptive support on their learning outcomes. However, learners' experience with different digital learning applications showed no statistically significant impact, underscoring that this study could not support its contribution to shaping AI learning achievements.

Furthermore, the analysis of learning outcomes across learning style groups could not yield any insights into the role of learning preferences in cognitive achievements. The majority of learners were identified as active, sensing, visual, and sequential learners, while a small proportion were classified as reflective, intuitive, verbal, and global learners. Thus, most learners preferred active, learner-centered, and practice-oriented learning, further favoring visually rich materials and a sequential, step-by-step learning approach. No statistically significant differences in learning outcomes were found between the learning style groups. Contrary to theoretical expectations, reflective learners performed better than active learners, while sensing learners exhibited slightly lower learning outcomes than their intuitive counterparts. Visual learners achieved marginally better outcomes than verbal learners, which was consistent with theoretical assumptions. Although prior theoretical assumptions suggested otherwise, global learners slightly outperformed sequential learners. However, as these differences were not statistically significant, these findings concern only this study, and a generalization beyond the current context is hardly possible.

In conclusion, the results provide valuable insights into the significance of crucial learner characteristics and the effectiveness of specific software features in enhancing learning outcomes in an AI course offered in VET and CVET institutions. While the results on the influence of certain learning styles on learning outcomes were inconclusive, and learners' experience with digital learning applications has not been found to affect AI learning outcomes, learners' prior knowledge, along with the individualized and adaptive support provided by the learning software, play a crucial role in fostering AI learning achievements. The interpretation of these results is presented in the following chapter.

Discussion of the Results

6

The key insights derived from the results presented in Chap. 5 are discussed in Sects. 6.1 and 6.2 in light of the hypotheses formulated in Chap. 3 and prior research findings. As described in this chapter, the results of this thesis could only partly corroborate previous research findings. While some results aligned with theoretical expectations, others were contradictory or inconclusive. The implications for VET and CVET learning settings and the instructional design of adaptive learning environments are addressed in Sects. 6.3 and 6.4, respectively. Subsequently, the study's limitations and directions for future educational research and practice are discussed in Sect. 6.5. The thesis concludes in Chap. 7 by highlighting the study's contributions and the relevance of its conclusions for future research, as well as VET and CVET practice.

6.1 Key Predictors of Learning Outcomes

As detailed in Chap. 2, despite the growing significance of AI technologies across various fields, their integration into VET and CVET learning environments remains limited. Both specialists and emerging professionals often lack the necessary competences to effectively apply AI in their work. To address this gap, an additional AI qualification was delivered with the aid of an adaptive learning software to offer AI-related knowledge and skills among young adults with diverse characteristics.

At the core of this thesis was the investigation of learner characteristics and software features that contributed to enhanced AI learning outcomes. The results responding to the first research question empirically supported that learners' AI prior knowledge, along with the adaptive and individualized support provided by

E. Petridou, *Personalized Learning in Vocational and Continuing Education*,
https://doi.org/10.1007/978-3-658-51517-1_6

the learning software, positively affected AI learning outcomes. However, learners' experience with digital learning applications did not show a significant effect. Consequently, hypothesis H1 was only partially supported. Among the examined factors, adaptivity showed the strongest impact on learning outcomes, emphasizing the value of adaptive learning systems that dynamically adjust to learners' needs. This aligns with theoretical endeavors highlighting the potential of adaptive learning systems in improving learning outcomes (Jonassen & Grabowski, 2012; Kinshuk, 2016; Taylor et al., 2021) as well as studies demonstrating their positive effects (Chiu et al., 2023; Chrysafiadi et al., 2023; Gomede et al., 2021; Karakostas & Demetriadis, 2011). Adaptive learning systems are designed to improve individual learning experiences by tailoring various system components and learning pathways to each learner's specific needs and progress (Hwang, Xie, et al., 2020). Therefore, adaptivity was a critical feature integrated into the learning software to ensure a personalized learning experience. Yet, as the descriptive findings revealed, the perceived adaptivity of the software received somewhat moderate endorsement. While learners generally found the difficulty level of the content appropriate and appreciated the software's role in simplifying content and constantly tracking progress, the lower ratings concerning adaptation to individual learning habits and needs suggest that the software may not have fully aligned with learners' specific preferences and requirements. This finding highlights that the system lacked strong diagnostic and responsive mechanisms, suggesting that learners who faced challenges may not have received adequate support, potentially leading to frustration or gaps in understanding. Moreover, the slightly below moderate ratings for engagement and comprehension support underscore that further improvements in interactive and scaffolding features could strengthen the software's effectiveness in facilitating deep learning.

The results further demonstrated the significant impact of individualization on AI learning achievements, reinforcing the importance of personalized learning approaches in promoting comprehension and knowledge construction, in line with prior research (Manea et al., 2023; Wang et al., 2020; Zhang et al., 2019). As the descriptive findings revealed, learners felt that the learning software moderately supported personalized learning. While this suggests that the learning environment was generally successful in addressing individual learning needs, there were notable variations in how learners experienced different aspects of individualization. One of the strongest aspects of the learning software was its support for independent learning, suggesting that learners were particularly satisfied with the flexibility to independently engage in the learning process. Additionally, the support provided by the diverse instructional materials was highly valued, reinforcing the importance of offering multiple learning formats to accommodate different learning preferences. Another key strength was the ability to track their learning progress, which enabled learners to take control of their learning pathways. Furthermore, learners appreciated features such as competence-based tasks, flexible learning sequences, and assessments of prior knowledge. Nevertheless, they were less satisfied with the software's ability to recognize their learning difficulties during task completion. This suggests that while the learning software offered an adequate degree of personalized support, it lacked sufficient responsiveness to individual learning challenges. The broader digital learning environment, beyond the software itself, was further perceived as moderately tailored to learners' needs. While learners felt empowered to regulate their learning pace and process, they indicated that the instructional content could have been better aligned with their prior knowledge, existing experiences, and individual learning needs. These findings highlight a need for refining instructional design to ensure that the learning environment addresses learning difficulties and that learning materials build more explicitly on learners' needs and existing competences. Overall, the study's findings underscore the value of embedding features of individualization and adaptivity into digital learning environments but also highlight areas for improvement. While the AI course successfully supported self-directed learning and progress tracking, further refinements are needed to enhance the system's responsiveness to learning difficulties, individual competences, and needs.

The results also revealed the significant role of prior knowledge in enhancing AI learning outcomes. The strong effect observed suggests that learners with profound knowledge in AI-related concepts are better equipped to comprehend AI learning content and achieve higher learning outcomes than learners with limited AI knowledge. This finding corroborates existing research findings that shed light on the positive impact of prior knowledge on learning outcomes (Li, 2019; Mampadi et al., 2009). From a cognitivist perspective, previously acquired knowledge serves as a critical foundation for constructing new knowledge (Schunk, 2012). Learners integrate new information more effectively when they can connect it to prior experiences and conceptual frameworks, facilitating deeper understanding and retention. Therefore, the findings suggest that prior knowledge needs to be actively assessed and leveraged in adaptive learning environments utilized for AI training programs that aim to foster knowledge construction and acquisition. Consistent with previous research (Chao et al., 2021; Stamenković et al., 2023), young adults in this study exhibited only limited prior knowledge in AI. While they were somewhat familiar with its practical applications, chances, challenges, and ethical considerations, as well as its basic concepts, their understanding was particularly low in data analysis, especially in programming. These findings highlight the necessity for comprehensive AI training, which includes foundational

AI knowledge with a strong emphasis on data-analytic scenarios, to better equip learners for the demands of AI-driven work environments.

Based on teachers' unanimous agreement, a blended learning format was considered the most appropriate learning setting for delivering the additional AI qualification, given learners' limited self-regulation skills (Rott et al., 2022). Learners received direct input and support from knowledgeable instructors during in-person or online sessions while utilizing an adaptive learning platform that allowed them to engage with AI training at their own pace and convenience. Effectively using such a platform requires familiarity with digital learning applications. However, learners in this study reported on average moderate prior experience, with greater exposure to learning videos, digital texts, chat-based services, and visual learning materials. Their familiarity with online courses, LMSs, learning software, and learning applications was not particularly high, indicating that the use of digital learning tools has not yet become widespread among vocational and continuing education learners. Notably, nearly half were unfamiliar with the blended learning format, suggesting that this instructional approach is only scarcely implemented in vocational and continuing education settings. This lack of experience with digital and blended learning formats could have influenced how effectively learners engaged with self-directed digital components, underscoring the need for structured guidance in digital and blended AI training programs.

Interestingly, the inferential analysis revealed that learners' experience with digital learning applications did not significantly affect AI learning outcomes, indicating that digital experience is insufficient to enhance learning. This finding implies that merely being familiar with digital learning tools does not necessarily translate into more effective learning, and it contradicts previous research findings linking digital experience to improved learning performance (Brinkerhoff et al., 2001; Hasan & Ali, 2004; Pagani et al., 2016). This might be attributed to other factors influencing this relationship, which were not examined in this study, or to the measurement approach. Previous research has emphasized that merely knowing how to navigate digital learning applications does not guarantee effective learning. Instead, active engagement might be necessary for effective use of digital technology and comprehension of the learning content (Henrie et al., 2015; Wekerle et al., 2022). Learners with high digital experience may not necessarily engage deeply with these tools, which could limit their ability to construct knowledge and develop skills. In addition, research has shown that when students use digital tools independently, without active guidance from teachers, learning tends to be less effective or even negatively impacted (Bergdahl et al., 2020; Goldhammer et al., 2016; Hietajärvi et al., 2019). Especially in the vocational learning context, whereby learners prefer a teacher-centered approach (Rott et al., 2022), the role of teacher support in facilitating the effective use of digital technologies becomes even more apparent. Although the blended learning format in this study allowed teachers to offer support, it may not have been adequate to fully promote active engagement and ensure the effective use of digital tools. This suggests that additional teacher-led sessions might be necessary to help learners become familiar and confidently utilize digital technologies as part of the learning process. Furthermore, how experience with digital learning applications is measured might be critical in capturing its relationship with learning outcomes. The scale implemented in this study assessed learners' self-reported familiarity with digital learning applications. The nonsignificant results might indicate that measuring experience solely based on general familiarity may fail to capture the depth of interaction or the quality of engagement with these tools. Alternative measurement approaches, such as assessing the frequency and quality of use, could provide a more comprehensive understanding of digital fluency. Furthermore, recent methodological advancements, including log data analysis and eye-tracking measures, can offer objective assessments of learners' interaction with digital learning applications (Lakshmi et al., 2013; Punde et al., 2017), providing more in-depth insights. Overall, these findings suggest that learners' digital experience, as measured by self-reported familiarity, may not be a key predictor of achieving high learning outcomes in VET and CVET learning settings. This indicates that digital experience alone does not play a central role in AI learning achievements, underscoring the need for a more holistic approach that incorporates comprehensive measurements and considers both the depth of engagement with digital tools and the instructional support provided to fully understand the impact of digital experience on learning outcomes.

To evaluate learning achievements in the AI course, learners' cognitive learning outcomes were examined. The descriptive findings revealed that learners generally perceived their achievements in AI as competent. The highest self-reported learning gains were observed in data management, followed by fundamental aspects of data analysis, ML, and basic AI concepts. These results suggest that the course effectively conveyed foundational and technical knowledge, particularly equipping learners with data-driven skills for data handling and analysis. However, learners felt less confident in understanding AI's potential, challenges, and ethical implications. This suggests that while the course strengthened their technical and foundational AI knowledge, it placed less emphasis on evaluating AI's broader societal and ethical implications. This gap underscores the need to expand the curriculum beyond basic and technical skills to include learning opportunities for critical reflection on AI's societal and ethical dimensions, relevant for AI-driven workplaces.

6.2 Variations in Learning Outcomes Across Learning Styles

Given the key role of learning styles in differentiating how learners perceive and process information (Lehmann, 2010), thereby facilitating personalization (Kinshuk, 2016; Tseng et al., 2008) and contributing to enhanced learning outcomes (Chang et al., 2016; El-Bishouty et al., 2019; Karagiannis & Satratzemi, 2018), the second research question examined whether learners possessing certain learning styles, as defined by the FSLSM, achieved higher learning outcomes in the AI course. The inferential analysis revealed no statistically significant differences in the learning outcomes of learning style pairs. Therefore, hypothesis H2 was not supported. In light of the nonsignificant results, two possibilities exist. Either there might be no effect of learning styles on learning outcomes, or learning styles may indeed affect learning outcomes, but there was no empirical support in this study to support this hypothesis. Consequently, the findings of this study remain inconclusive and should be interpreted as preliminary. No definitive conclusions can be drawn about the role of learning styles in shaping learning outcomes, limiting the generalizability of the results and highlighting the need for further research to investigate this relationship in greater depth.

More specifically, the results regarding RQ2.1 showed that reflective learners had higher learning outcomes than active learners, a finding that contradicts the study's hypothesis but aligns with prior research identifying active learners among the lowest performers (Chang et al., 2016). Thus, hypothesis H2.1, which predicted that active learners would outperform reflective learners, was not supported. This finding could reflect mere random variation in the learning outcomes of the learning style groups or be partly attributable to characteristics of the learning environment. While the learning environment was designed to promote active, learner-centered learning, thereby predominantly supporting active learners, the results suggest that the preferences of reflective learners may have been better accommodated. Active learning and social interaction may not have been sufficiently fostered, both of which are crucial elements for active learners to excel. Several explanations could support such an interpretation. First, the adaptive learning environment, primarily supporting personalized learning, may have emphasized independent learning tasks that demanded self-directed learning and encouraged learners to spend extensive time reflecting on the material. Even though activities involving hands-on engagement and peer collaboration were included, they may not have been adequate to support the application of learned concepts. Since active learners benefit from practice-oriented tasks, incorporating additional problem-solving assignments, opportunities for knowledge application, and peer-driven knowledge construction could enhance their learning achievements. Second, the variability in how the blended learning format was implemented across participating schools may have affected the extent to which learners received instructional support and engaged in collaborative learning activities. While some instructors may have facilitated active engagement and promoted group-based interactive discussions, others may have relied more on self-paced, independent learning components. This inconsistency might have limited the potential benefits of social interaction for active learners who typically thrive in collaborative settings and rely on sufficient instructional support to actively engage in the learning process.

Furthermore, contrary to hypothesis H2.2, intuitive learners demonstrated slightly higher learning outcomes than sensing learners. According to the theory of FSLSM, sensing learners typically benefit more from CAI and, therefore, are expected to demonstrate higher learning outcomes within an adaptive learning environment. Their learning is facilitated by concrete materials and practical information rather than abstract learning content. The findings suggest that the results may either be due to random variation or a lack of adequate support for sensing learners to fully leverage their learning preferences and outperform intuitive learners. As highlighted by the above-mentioned results, the course content might not have included adequate practice-oriented activities, primarily focusing on theoretical and conceptual frameworks that predominantly support intuitive learners. The limited delivery of case studies, profession-specific examples, and real-world applications may have restricted sensing learners' ability to fully engage with the course material and achieve higher learning outcomes.

In addition, while visual learners showed higher learning outcomes than verbal learners as expected, the difference was both marginal and not statistically significant, aligning with previous research (Brown et al., 2006). Hence, hypothesis H2.3 was not supported. This finding illustrates either random variation or deficiencies in the design of the learning environment. Although the learning environment incorporated various visual elements, they may not have been adequate to support visual learners in significantly enhancing their learning outcomes compared to verbal learners. The design of the AI course emphasized visual representations, including images, explanatory videos, and visually-rich programming activities, while relying less on extensive textual explanations or instructors' spoken explanations. These elements align well with the preferences of visual learners, who tend to process information more effectively through graphical representations. Nevertheless, verbal learners also demonstrated their ability to effectively acquire AI knowledge and skills, as reflected in their above-moderate performance. This finding might be attributed to the following reasons. First, verbal learners might have compensated for the lack of extensive textual explanations by using additional text-based learning materials, discussing concepts with peers, or taking detailed notes to structure their understanding. Second, the explanatory videos, even being primarily visual, also included verbal explanations, which may have helped bridge the gap between visual and verbal learning preferences, enabling verbal learners to sufficiently benefit from the content.

Finally, global learners exhibited only marginally higher learning outcomes than sequential learners. Thus, hypothesis H2.4 was not supported. This finding may be due to variation in learning outcomes stemming from mere chance, or it might be attributed to the design of the learning environment. Although the learning environment promoted a sequential learning order by restricting access to advanced, unfamiliar topics until prior material was completed, sequential learners did not benefit adequately to outperform global learners. This result is inconsistent with previous studies, which found that sequential learners were among the highest performers and the most supported in adaptive learning environments (Chang et al. 2016; El-Bishouty et al., 2019). One possible explanation is that while the structured, linear approach aligns with sequential learners' preferences for gradually building knowledge in logical steps, it might not have been optimized enough to provide them with a substantial advantage. At the same time, global learners, who prefer learning through a holistic perspective or interdisciplinary connections, may have compensated for the lack of explicitly designed global learning approaches in the AI course. Global learners may have benefited from instructional explanations provided by teachers, who may have helped set learning goals, elaborated on broader applications, linked concepts to other related fields, or discussed interdisciplinary implications, thereby facilitating global learners' knowledge integration.

On the descriptive level, the analysis of learning styles provided valuable insights into how learners in the AI course preferred to engage with instructional content. The results indicate a strong preference for active learning, with most learners favoring hands-on engagement and social interactions over reflective, solitary learning. Similarly, the majority expressed a preference for a practical, facts-based approach, favoring concrete information and real-world applications rather than abstract concepts. The findings also highlight a clear visual preference, with most learners favoring diagrams, images, and graphical representations over text-based or verbal explanations. Additionally, a sequential, step-by-step learning approach focusing on the current topic was preferred by the majority of learners, indicating their inclination toward sequential instruction rather than a more holistic method that emphasizes cross-subject connections. Overall, learning preferences underscore the importance of designing AI learning environments that incorporate interactive exercises, practice-oriented tasks, visually-rich materials, and structured instructional sequences.

6.3 Implications for VET and CVET Practice

Critical implications are drawn from the study's findings for instructors and stakeholders in VET and CVET learning settings, emphasizing the need to employ highly adaptive learning systems, deliver comprehensive AI training, and adopt blended learning formats.

Vocational and continuing education learners constitute a highly diverse group, characterized by a wide range of educational backgrounds, occupations, age groups, and individual learning goals. This diversity necessitates instructional approaches that are responsive to their varying characteristics and needs. To address this heterogeneity, the implementation of adaptive learning software emerges as a valuable strategy. Adaptive learning systems can personalize instructional content and adapt to the specific needs and preferences of individual learners (Kabudi et al., 2021). As demonstrated by the study's findings, integrating features of adaptivity and individualization within adaptive learning software is crucial, as these foster knowledge construction and contribute to enhanced learning outcomes. To this end, adaptive learning systems need to offer tailored support through prior knowledge assessments and competence-based tasks that respond to individual skill levels and learning progress. Equally critical are features of progress tracking and flexible selection of learning sequences, which empower learners to shape their learning trajectories according to their personal preferences and needs. These approaches can foster independent learning, enabling learners to assume responsibility for their learning progress. Moreover, offering support through a variety of learning materials, such as explanatory videos, image-based books, and PDF documents, ensures learner engagement and alignment with diverse learning preferences. While these features constitute core elements necessary to be embedded into adaptive learning systems employed in vocational and continuing education contexts, the results further underscore the need for more dynamic and fully responsive adaptive mechanisms. Such systems are capable of accommodating evolving competences and engagement levels by providing real-time, tailored support, offering highly personalized learning experiences and sustained learning outcomes. Ultimately, adaptive learning systems can support learners in mastering complex training topics, thereby promoting sustainable lifelong learning in an AI-driven society (Petridou & Lao, 2024). By enabling individuals to engage in personalized training that is closely aligned with their competences and professional goals, these systems support continuous upskilling and enhance learners' ability to remain responsive to the ongoing advancements of AI.

Given the growing integration of AI across diverse industries and the corresponding demand for an AI-ready workforce, alongside the limited inclusion of AI courses within vocational and continuing education curricula (Petridou & Lao, 2024), supplementary AI courses need to be systematically incorporated into the curricula of VET and CVET programs. In this context, the implementation of additional AI qualifications, even comparatively new to the vocational and continuing education landscape, represents a promising avenue for AI knowledge acquisition (Petridou & Lao, 2024; Rott et al., 2022). In this respect, a teaching workforce that is both knowledgeable and proficient in AI is required (Chao et al., 2021; Stamenković et al., 2023). Continuous professional development in emerging AI technologies is essential to enable educators to effectively integrate AI into their instructional practices (Kim et al., 2022; Lindner et al., 2019). Nonetheless, structured guidance from instructors alone may not suffice. Adaptive learning technologies, as detailed above, offer an important complement by addressing learners' diverse levels of prior knowledge and providing tailored support. Introductory training opportunities can assist learners with limited experience in AI, while more advanced learning approaches can challenge those with existing competences. This individualized approach supports the development of an inclusive and differentiated AI education framework. By fostering AI literacy and competence with an additional AI qualification tailored to diverse learners' needs, vocational and continuing education institutions can play a crucial role in conveying profound AI knowledge and skills and adequately train the next generation of professionals for the evolving demands of the job market.

Provided that vocational and continuing education learners possess only limited prior knowledge in AI (Chao et al., 2021; Rott et al., 2022; Stamenković et al., 2023) and prior knowledge constitutes a significant predictor of learning outcomes, as this study showed, comprehensive AI-related content needs to be imparted in the framework of VET and CVET curricula. As per this study's findings, young adults demonstrate familiarity with practical applications and basic concepts of AI. However, their prior experience with data analysis and programming is particularly low. Since data-driven decision-making and algorithmic processes constitute the backbone of AI technologies, this gap highlights a critical area for improvement in AI education. In this regard, data-analytic problem-solving tasks and industry-specific applications must be conveyed along with foundational AI principles. This approach ensures that learners gain both theoretical knowledge and practical experience in data analysis, coding, and model development. In addition, the study findings underlined learners' lower confidence in comprehending AI's broader implications, including its potential, challenges, and ethical dimensions. To this end, curricula and stakeholders should raise awareness for the growing significance of AI-related skills and AI's ethical and societal dimensions as a response to societal and professional demands of emerging AI-driven workplaces. Future instructional improvements need to follow a more holistic instructional approach and emphasize discussions on fairness, accountability, transparency, and the social consequences of AI to deepen learners' engagement with ethical and interpretability issues. By reinforcing these aspects, a thorough understanding of AI's impact beyond technical implementation can be achieved, equipping learners with both technical expertise and the ability to critically assess AI's broader implications. Strengthening these aspects can ensure a more comprehensive learning experience, preparing learners not only as proficient AI users but also as informed and responsible professionals within their respective fields.

Following this study's findings, blended learning settings offer a flexible solution for imparting AI knowledge to young professionals from different disciplines and with diverse learning needs. By combining teacher-led sessions with self-directed learning, these settings provide opportunities for both structured instructional support and autonomous learning trajectories (Steib & Stoffers, 2022). Blended learning environments allow experienced instructors to share their expertise, provide targeted support, and facilitate interactive discussions, ensuring that learners receive the necessary guidance to navigate complex AI concepts. At the same time, blended learning empowers learners to take an active role in the learning process by engaging in self-directed learning, thereby regulating their learning experience in accordance with their individual needs. This dual approach is particularly beneficial for VET and CVET learning settings, where learners often benefit from opportunities for independent learning combined with personalized guidance. Empirical support for this approach is also found in previous research, where all participating instructors expressed a clear preference for blended learning formats over purely online courses, due to apprentices' underdeveloped self-regulated learning skills and their extensive need for direct guidance, feedback, and motivation from instructors (Rott et al., 2022). Nevertheless, a critical challenge identified in this study is that nearly half of the vocational and continuing education learners reported no prior experience with blended learning formats and only moderate familiarity with digital learning applications, revealing a considerable gap in their digital readiness. This underscores that many learners may not yet possess the required skills for effective engagement in technology-enhanced learning environments. Consequently, there is a pressing need for targeted instructional guidance to help them effectively navigate digital learning technologies and engage in the learning process, thereby developing essential digital learning competences. Furthermore, more blended learning formats need to be integrated into VET and CVET curricula to ensure that learners gain exposure to these flexible learning settings, sustain motivation, and cultivate key self-regulation skills to plan, monitor, and reflect on their learning progress. Given the flexibility to engage in learning at their own pace and convenience (Wright, 2017) while receiving instructional support (Steib & Stoffers, 2022), blended learning formats may offer greater accessibility and enhance learners' participation and interest in AI training, thereby fostering sustainable lifelong learning.

6.4 Implications for the Instructional Design of Adaptive Learning Environments

The study's findings further yield valuable implications for the instructional design of adaptive learning environments. To foster meaningful knowledge construction, adaptive learning systems should incorporate several key elements. In addition to features of adaptivity and individualization that personalize the learning experience, these systems must assess and adapt to learners' prior knowledge to enhance learning outcomes. The importance of ensuring seamless navigation within adaptive learning environments is further underscored to enable efficient learning regardless of learners' prior digital experience or familiarity with blended learning formats. Furthermore, the results shed light on the necessity of accommodating diverse learning preferences and adhering to established pedagogical principles when designing adaptive learning environments to effectively address learners' diverse needs and cultivate profound and transferable AI-related competences.

To enhance learning outcomes, adaptive learning systems should be designed to accurately assess learners' prior knowledge, activate relevant preexisting understanding, and strategically utilize it to guide the learning process. As emphasized in cognitive learning theories, prior knowledge plays a crucial role in knowledge construction and acquisition (Schunk, 2012), serving as a key determinant for assimilating novel information. Prior knowledge needs to be activated to enable learners to retrieve information from memory and establish meaningful connections with the new content (Brod, 2021). Given the diverse educational and professional backgrounds of learners, adaptive instruction is essential to accommodate varying prior knowledge levels in AI-related topics. When instructional support is adapted to learners' current knowledge levels, it aids in the formation of robust mental representations, allowing new information to be more seamlessly incorporated into existing cognitive structures. This approach is promising to facilitate cognitive processing and reduce cognitive load. It further enables learners to progress at a pace aligned with their abilities, fostering more personalized and efficient learning trajectories. To this end, cognitivist principles can guide the development of effective adaptive learning environments. As learners are seen as active processors of information, integrating prior knowledge assessments and AI support tailored to existing knowledge and skills is critical for fostering engagement and activating the cognitive processes necessary for effective knowledge acquisition, thereby maximizing overall learning outcomes.

Individualization embedded into adaptive learning systems also plays a vital role in improving learning outcomes. While learners valued the system's support for independent learning, allowing them to regulate their learning pace and process, instructional designers should further refine personalization features by ensuring that learning content is explicitly aligned with learners' existing competences and experiences and is responsive to individual learning difficulties. This indicates a pressing need for more sophisticated diagnostic and responsive mechanisms that identify learning difficulties in real-time and provide immediate targeted interventions to guide struggling learners through difficulties. By optimizing learning within each learner's ZPD, the system can ensure that challenges are appropriately tailored to the learner's current level of understanding, promoting gradual skill development without inducing cognitive overload. Additionally, embedding diverse and interactive learning materials, including videos, simulations, and hands-on activities, can accommodate varying learning preferences and enhance engagement. Following constructivism, multiple learning media enable learners to engage with the content from multiple perspectives, thereby fostering autonomy. Moreover, learners highly valued the feature of progress tracking, as it enables learners to monitor their learning and assume greater control over their individual learning trajectories. They further underscored the importance of integrating competence-based tasks and flexible learning pathways. Future systems should build on these learning approaches by leveraging principles of behaviorism. Concepts can be introduced based on readiness and following programmed instruction, logically and incrementally, but without adhering to a strict learning path. Learners need to be able to co-define with the AI-based learning system their learning trajectories by creating customized learning paths. In addition, learners need to receive tailored insights into their achievements and opportunities for growth. Personalized badges displaying learning milestones grounded in Skinner's notion of reinforcement, along with recommended next steps and targeted practice exercises, can further enhance active engagement and motivation.

Furthermore, robust adaptive features should be incorporated into adaptive learning systems to maximize learning outcomes (Gligorea et al., 2023; Kochmar et al., 2020). While learners generally considered the difficulty level of the provided content appropriate and valued the features of content simplification and progress tracking, the system's adaptive features did not fully respond to learners' individual learning habits and needs. Future adaptive learning systems should integrate dynamic, real-time adjustments that personalize learning paths based on learners' evolving competences and engagement levels (Baradari et al., 2025; Song et al., 2024). Personalized hints, scaffolded feedback, and automated recommendations for supplementary materials can help ensure that learners receive the support they need at critical moments (Kochmar et al., 2020; Ueno & Miyazawa, 2018). Dynamically adjusted learning pathways to individual learning progress can prevent frustration and learning gaps (Kumar et al., 2024). Reducing cognitive load following cognitivist principles is also critical to avoid overwhelming learners with tasks beyond their current capabilities (Mayer & Moreno, 2003). In this sense, adaptive learning systems should enable step-by-step progression and adjust task complexity based on learners' individual competences. Additionally, as learners rated the engagement and comprehension support they received from the system moderately, future adaptive learning systems should employ more sophisticated interactive and scaffolded learning experiences to support deeper learning and active engagement. These systems should actively guide learners in navigating complex concepts through diverse instructional strategies. Engaging, collaborative activities can promote interaction and facilitate comprehension, gamification elements can maintain motivation, and real-time feedback can support their learning progress more effectively. By refining the aforementioned features, the adaptive learning environments can advance beyond static personalization and more effectively address individual learning requirements, thereby fostering a more responsive and supportive learning experience. Overall, to maximize their educational impact, adaptive learning environments should not rely solely on foundational adaptive elements. They should incorporate robust, real-time personalization strategies that not only accommodate diverse learning needs but also dynamically support learners in overcoming challenges as they arise. By embedding stronger diagnostic and responsive strategies, instructional designers can create more effective and inclusive AI-driven learning environments, ultimately supporting a broader range of learners in achieving optimal learning outcomes and preparing them to apply AI knowledge and skills confidently in their professional fields.

Moreover, drawing from the study's findings, the lack of extensive familiarity with digital learning technologies, particularly with LMSs, learning software, educational applications, online courses, and blended learning approaches, may pose challenges in effectively navigating adaptive learning environments. Limited digital experience may impede learners' ability to actively engage with digital and self-directed learning components and maximize their learning potential within adaptive learning environments. If learners are unfamiliar with core functionalities such as navigating content, using interactive elements and self-assessment tools, or understanding the structure of blended learning, they may be unable to fully leverage the system's adaptive features. Consequently, these challenges may prevent learners from leveraging personalized learning experiences and hinder their ability to effectively combine digital and face-to-face learning components. To address learners' limited familiarity with blended learning formats, instructional design needs to emphasize the added value of blended learning settings, clarifying how self-directed and instruction-led sessions complement each other. Limited familiarity with digital learning technologies may also contribute to disparities in engagement levels. Some learners may require additional time and effort to become accustomed to the learning environment before they can actively participate in meaningful learning activities. To overcome these challenges, developers of adaptive learning environments should incorporate comprehensive instructional guidance that ensures a seamless learning experience regardless of prior exposure to digital and blended learning approaches. Targeted instructions are critical to introduce learners to essential functionalities and assist them in navigating both adaptive and blended learning formats effectively. Ensuring that all learners can effectively engage with adaptive learning environments in blended learning settings is crucial for maximizing learning outcomes. By proactively addressing potential usability barriers and supporting learners with limited experience in digital learning applications, instructional designers can create inclusive, accessible, and engaging learning experiences that enable all learners to fully benefit from adaptive and blended learning settings.

In addition, the diverse learning preferences identified in this study, along with the adaptive learning system's foundation in established pedagogical principles, underscore the importance of adopting a flexible, learner-centered instructional approach to effectively impart AI knowledge and adequately support learners. Based on the descriptive results of learning styles, learners demonstrated a clear preference for active engagement in the learning process, favoring practical, fact-based learning content and opportunities for peer collaboration. In addition, most learners preferred visual representations over text-based materials and a sequential learning order that allows for structured, step-by-step progression. These findings suggest important, though not exhaustive, considerations for the instructional design of adaptive learning environments. Further grounding their design on established pedagogical principles is crucial to maximize learning results. Following constructivist principles, meaningful learning requires learners to actively engage with the content and take responsibility for their learning decisions. Instructional content should therefore provoke active participation through visually engaging and interactive materials. However, from a cognitivist perspective, particularly considering dual coding and the multimedia learning theory (Mayer, 2001; Paivio,1986), visual elements alone are insufficient for effective knowledge construction. To facilitate the integration of novel information with prior knowledge and support the formation of robust mental representations, visual materials should be paired with verbal information, ensuring a deeper understanding and retention. As such, instructional design should incorporate coherently structured visual elements alongside explanatory text or narration to optimize cognitive processing and learning outcomes. Opportunities for peer interaction and collaboration, whether through group discussions or problem-solving tasks, can further enhance engagement and knowledge retention. These approaches date back to the constructivist principle of situated cognition (Anderson et al., 1996; Cobb & Bowers, 1999; Greeno, 1998; Schunk, 2012), which emphasizes that learning is most effective when it occurs in meaningful, social, and contextually rich environments. Through active participation in collaborative learning settings, learners benefit from exposure to diverse perspectives, which challenge their thinking, promote critical reflection, and encourage deeper cognitive processing. In this context, emphasizing practice-oriented activities and real-world AI applications alongside theoretical foundations can facilitate deeper knowledge acquisition. By demonstrating how AI concepts are applied in authentic real-world scenarios, learners can develop a more concrete understanding of AI and enhance knowledge transfer by bridging theoretical knowledge with practical application. Furthermore, given that self-directed learning is a fundamental component of adaptive learning environments, it is also essential to equip learners with effective strategies for self-regulated learning, helping them develop skills to independently set, monitor, and achieve their learning goals. Self-regulated learning skills will enable them to navigate adaptive learning environments effectively and actively engage with personalized content, thereby enhancing learning outcomes. Finally, while a structured, step-by-step instructional approach may benefit learners by providing a clear learning sequence, it is equally important to incorporate holistic instructional methods that emphasize interdisciplinary connections. Since AI is applied across various domains, fostering an understanding of its broader applications can help learners contextualize their knowledge and better comprehend the diverse possibilities AI offers across different fields. Overall, to effectively foster AI knowledge construction and accommodate diverse learning preferences, it remains essential to design inclusive adaptive learning environments grounded in established pedagogical principles, thereby providing learners with the necessary support for sustainable learning success.

6.5 Limitations and Directions for Future Educational Research and Practice

Having illustrated the study's implications, it is important to acknowledge its limitations and consider avenues for further refinements in future endeavors within educational research and practice.

While the study emphasized the significant influence of learners' prior knowledge and the system's individualization and adaptivity features on AI learning outcomes, it also revealed a nonsignificant effect of learners' experience with digital learning applications. This finding suggests that digital proficiency may not be a prerequisite for achieving enhanced AI learning outcomes in adaptive learning environments, highlighting the potential prominence of other factors in shaping learners' success. To gain a more comprehensive understanding of the role of digital proficiency, future research should explore potential moderating factors such as the degree of learners' active engagement and the presence of teacher support, both of which may influence how digital experience relates to learning outcomes (Bergdahl et al., 2020; Goldhammer et al., 2016; Henrie et al., 2015; Hietajärvi et al., 2019; Wekerle et al., 2022). Moreover, this unexpected result may be partially attributed to the measurement approach employed in this study, which relied on self-reported familiarity with a broad range of digital learning applications. Future studies should refine the assessment of digital learning experience by incorporating more differentiated indicators that capture both the frequency and the qualitative aspects of digital tool usage. Instead of solely relying on subjective self-assessments, objective assessment methods, such as logfile analysis and eye-tracking techniques, can offer more precise insights into learners' interactions with digital learning applications and help clarify their relationship with learning outcomes. By advancing methodological approaches, future research can more thoroughly explore the interplay between digital experience and effective knowledge acquisition in adaptive learning settings.

Moreover, while the results identified significant predictors of learning outcomes in the AI course, they further suggested that additional factors, not examined in the current study, may also substantially influence learning success. Due to sample size constraints, only a limited range of additional variables could be examined in the current study, namely age and gender. However, neither of these sociodemographic factors exhibited a significant impact on learning outcomes. This underscores the necessity for future research to investigate a broader set of predictors that may shape learning outcomes within adaptive learning environments, such as learning motivation and self-efficacy (Hwang, Xie, et al., 2020), given their well-established roles in influencing learners' effort, goal orientation, and resilience. Besides, future endeavors may also benefit from exploring learners' behavioral patterns during the learning process, as these have been identified as promising predictors of learning outcomes (Akhuseyinoglu & Brusilovsky, 2022; Nguyen, 2017). Analyzing such patterns can elucidate how learners engage with adaptive learning systems and contribute to a better understanding of the learning processes underlying knowledge acquisition (Chen & Li, 2021; Hou, 2012).

Furthermore, while the current study identified key learner characteristics and software features that contribute to improved learning outcomes within an adaptive learning environment, it did not address the long-term effects of AI knowledge acquisition. Future studies are encouraged to employ longitudinal designs that include follow-up assessments, enabling a deeper understanding of knowledge transfer and sustained skill development. Given the current scarcity of empirical research evaluating the development and sustainment of AI competences, particularly within the contexts of VET and CVET, future studies integrating AI-focused courses into authentic lifelong learning educational settings are essential. To this end, future endeavors should prioritize investigating not only short-term AI learning outcomes within adaptive learning environments, which assess immediate effects, but also long-term learning outcomes, which explore lasting effects of AI-focused education and learners' ability to apply and transfer AI knowledge to real-world contexts. Such research would not only advance the field of AIEd but also reinforce the foundations of sustainable lifelong learning.

In addition, the lack of significant differences in learning outcomes among learners with different learning styles observed in this study fails to address the research gap concerning the impact of certain learning styles on learning outcomes (see Sect. 2.5.4). These inconclusive findings must be interpreted with caution, necessitating further research to clarify the significance of learning styles. One possible explanation is that no meaningful effect may exist within the specific sample or learning context, since this study could not demonstrate otherwise. Therefore, the observed mean differences would be attributable to mere random variation in learning outcomes scores. In this case, the absence of an effect would be consistent with critiques of learning styles, which argue that personal preference does not necessarily translate into better learning performance (Kirschner, 2017). Alternatively, an effect may exist, but the current study lacked sufficient empirical support to confirm it. This absence of empirical support could reflect a Type II error, which may arise for several reasons (Visentin et al., 2020). First, the 'true' effect size, specifically, the mean difference between learning styles groups, might be too small to detect. Second, the standard deviation, representing the variation within the learning styles groups, may be too large. Third, the sample size could be insufficient, leading to an underpowered study. While the first reason cannot be assessed, and the second is not supported by the results, the third can be partially confirmed, as the a priori power analysis has shown. The power analysis indicated that a minimum sample size of 50 participants per group would be required to achieve 80% statistical power. However, in all comparisons, one out of the two groups fell below this threshold. As a result, it is assumed that the study lacked adequate power to reliably reject the null hypothesis of no effect, thereby reducing its ability to detect 'true' effects (Cohen, 1988). As such, this study could not decrease uncertainty, suggesting that potential effects may have gone undetected.

Since the study's inconclusive findings on the impact of certain learning styles on learning outcomes did not allow for any definitive implications to be drawn, they necessitate further research to clarify whether certain learning styles lead to learning success in adaptive learning environments or whether learning styles are ultimately ineffective in enhancing learning achievements. Future research endeavors should aim to recruit an adequate number of participants to ensure sufficient statistical power to detect an effect, given that there is one in the learners' population, and particularly if small differences need to be detected. Even though the design of the current study was assumed to favor particular learning preferences, future adaptive learning systems may need to explicitly tailor the instructional content to different learning styles to determine whether such customization leads to measurable improvements in learning outcomes. As previous studies have demonstrated (Chang et al., 2016; El-Bishouty et al., 2019; Filippidis & Tsoukalas, 2009), by systematically integrating and evaluating adaptive features based on learning styles, such as tailored instructional format, content delivery, and interaction modes, future research can provide valuable insights into whether and how personalized approaches tailored to learning styles contribute to enhanced learning experiences and performance.

Besides, the inconclusive findings might be partly attributed to the measurement approach used in this study to assess learning styles. While the FSLSM conceptualizes learning styles as flexibly stable indicators, allowing for fluctuations in learning styles' preferences depending on the learning context, a static self-report measurement of learning styles may not fully capture these dynamic fluctuations. As a result, detecting statistically significant differences in learning outcomes becomes more challenging. In case learners adapted their learning approaches in response to the instructional design and to meet course objectives, the predefined classification of learning styles before engaging in the course based on the ILS may have been insufficient to explain variations in learning outcomes. Additionally, as detailed in Sect. 4.4.3, the low reliability values of the individual learning styles scales, though theoretically expected due to the diversity of learning preferences represented by the different items of the scales, suggest that the ILS might not be optimal to capture learning preferences, especially in an adaptive learning environment, where learners may dynamically adjust their learning approaches according to their learning needs.

To address these limitations, future research should explore alternative approaches to measure learning styles. For instance, based on the FSLSM, Schiaffino et al. (2008) designed an intelligent agent that utilized Bayesian networks to infer learning styles based on learners' interactions. Similarly, using the ILS framework, Gambo and Shakir (2021) created a learning agent that applied artificial neural networks to categorize students' learning styles. In this regard, logfile analysis appears particularly promising, as it enables an objective, real-time assessment of learning processes. Drawing on the FSLSM, Joseph et al. (2022) utilized learning analytics to examine learners' log data in online learning environments, recommending personalized learning paths tailored to individual learning styles, which subsequently resulted in improved learning outcomes. As noted in previous research, "since all the learning style models have been initially proposed for traditional learning settings, they need to be adapted for use in technology-enhanced environments." (Popescu, 2010, p. 244). Therefore, existing instruments should either be modified or entirely new assessment tools should be developed to more accurately capture learning preferences in adaptive learning contexts.

Given that this study exclusively relied on self-report measurements, there are certain limitations inherent to these measurements that need to be acknowledged. As self-report assessments represent subjective evaluations of survey questions, different respondents might interpret the same questionnaire items differently, leading to variability in responses. However, such variation might not reflect actual differences in the measured constructs, misleading the study's results. This measurement approach can thus introduce bias and affect the accuracy of participants' responses. Individuals may respond in ways they perceive as socially desirable rather than providing accurate answers (Krumpal, 2013). Responses may further be arbitrary, which can result in distorted findings that fail to accurately represent participants' actual preferences (Karagiannis & Satratzemi, 2018). Bias may also arise from response tendencies to agree with statements regardless of their content or a tendency to consistently choose extreme or midpoint options (Baumgartner & Steenkamp, 2001). Another issue is that individuals might misjudge their competences, leading to an overestimation of their real abilities (Kruger & Dunning, 1999). Nevertheless, despite these limitations, self-report instruments remain a valuable, practical, and well-established measurement of learners' attitudes and perceptions in educational research. While they do not provide a direct measure of mental abilities, they capture learners' self-perceptions, which are indirectly related to cognitive functioning. This is based on the assumption that individuals typically favor the mental processes and cognitive styles in which they feel more skilled and accustomed (Jonassen & Grabowski, 2012).

Future research may continue to employ self-report instruments in conjunction with complementary methods, when resources allow. A promising approach is the combination of self-report instruments with interview-based assessments. Interviews offer the opportunity to explore learners' perceptions in greater depth and to contextualize questionnaire responses. Employing a mixed-methods approach, which involves gathering and examining both qualitative and quantitative data, can yield comprehensive insights that would not emerge from either qualitative or quantitative data alone (Creswell & Creswell, 2018; Johnson et al., 2007). In this context, a promising avenue might also be the inclusion of instructors' perspectives on learners' preferences and performance within an adaptive learning environment. Interviews with instructors combined with learners' surveys can yield in-depth and holistic insights into the learning process and contextual factors influencing learning outcomes (Petridou & Lao, 2024), thereby contributing to a robust triangulation of findings. Additionally, self-report data may be enriched through the integration of log data, which serve as an objective means of capturing learning processes and behaviors. While self-reports reflect learners' subjective perspectives and intentions, log data enable a fine-grained, real-time analysis of their actual interactions within adaptive learning environments. The combination of these data sources can improve the validity of the findings by facilitating cross-validation between reported perceptions and empirically traceable behaviors.

Finally, the study is subject to methodological limitations related to its research design. As a quasi-experimental approach was employed, data collection relied on convenience sampling, without the inclusion of a control group or random assignment of participants. Due to practical constraints, it was not feasible to recruit an additional sample to engage in AI-focused learning within a non-adaptive learning environment. Consequently, participation bias cannot be ruled out, as learners who chose to participate in the study may have been particularly interested in the topic under investigation. The absence of random assignment further restricts the ability to draw causal inferences. As such, the findings of the current endeavor regarding the effectiveness of the adaptive learning environment are only speculative and do not permit definitive conclusions to be drawn. Future research should seek to address these limitations by incorporating randomized controlled designs with sufficiently large samples to more rigorously examine whether adaptive learning environments lead to improved learning outcomes compared to traditional instructional settings. As a final point, although the sample size was insufficient for conducting robust comparisons of learning outcomes across learning styles groups, it can nonetheless be considered representative of the broader population of learners that could have participated in the study, based on the observed response rates. Although the number of participants was reduced over time and across surveys, which might be attributed to several reasons that justify these variations (see Sect. 4.2), the response rates remained relatively high (between 43% and 97%), reflecting a high degree of participant engagement and perceived relevance of the topic.

Conclusion 7

In light of the growing demand for AI skills across diverse professional sectors (Rott et al., 2022) and the ongoing lack of consensus regarding the value of implementing adaptive learning technologies in authentic educational settings (Kabudi et al., 2021; Özyurt & Özyurt, 2015; Zhang & Aslan, 2021), the findings of this study highlight the significant potential of adaptive learning systems to enhance AI literacy among learners in VET and CVET settings. Accommodating learners' prior knowledge in AI and leveraging system features of individualization and adaptivity that enable one-to-one personalized instruction at scale significantly contribute to shaping AI learning outcomes. Given that learners engage in the learning process, initiating their individual characteristics and needs, personalized instructional support and learning pathways designed to dynamically adjust content delivery to learners' existing knowledge and unique requirements can more effectively recognize and address learners' needs, often overlooked in one-size-fits-all learning approaches. This underscores the broader potential of well-designed diagnostic and responsive adaptive learning environments that integrate prior knowledge assessments alongside individualization and adaptive mechanisms, positioning them as promising approaches for large-scale implementation in contemporary learning settings. Notably, these technologies represent a viable solution for delivering equitable and sustainable AI-related learning opportunities in the framework of VET and CVET institutions to prepare skilled workers for the digital transformation driven by AI.

Whether learners with particular learning styles can achieve significantly better outcomes within adaptive learning environments remains an open question for future research. Following the inconclusive findings from previous studies regarding the impact of certain learning styles on learning outcomes (Brown et al.,

E. Petridou, *Personalized Learning in Vocational and Continuing Education*, https://doi.org/10.1007/978-3-658-51517-1_7

2006; Beckmann et al., 2015), the current endeavor could not provide any further empirical support in this regard. As such, future research should explore whether any added value exists in differentiating instructional support based on learning styles to enhance learning outcomes. In this sense, despite the widespread use of established learning styles instruments within individualized adaptive learning environments that have long been employed in educational research (Özyurt & Özyurt, 2015), the present study's inconclusive results raise important questions about the suitability of the extensively used ILS questionnaire to capture learning preferences in the context of adaptive learning. This accentuates the need to either refine existing self-report learning styles inventories or to develop novel instruments that are better aligned with the demands of adaptive learning environments. In addition, integrating objective, data-driven measures, such as learning analytics and system log data, may provide a more valid and dynamic understanding of learners' preferences and their relationship with learning achievements within adaptive learning platforms.

Considering the limited self-regulation skills of vocational and continuing education learners, their reliance on teacher support, and the significant workload resulting from both vocational responsibilities and AI coursework (Petridou & Lao, 2024), the implementation of a blended learning approach emerges as a particularly well-suited solution for VET and CVET learning contexts. Given the combination of instruction-led sessions with self-directed digital learning, blended learning formats can afford learners greater flexibility in engaging with the learning process, addressing learners' dependence on instructional assistance, and helping compensate for the lack of tailored support in fully teacher-led sessions. By leveraging adaptive learning environments, individualized support can be delivered, offering personalized learning experiences that align with the diverse needs and backgrounds of learners. In this regard, these environments can effectively cater to a heterogeneous learner group, allowing for enhanced accessibility and inclusion. Importantly, familiarity with blended learning formats and digital learning applications is essential to effectively navigate adaptive learning platforms and engage with the provided personalized learning opportunities. This underscores the need for targeted instructional guidance to familiarize learners with critical functionalities, ensuring equitable access to learning and a seamless digital learning experience. Nevertheless, following the study's findings, familiarity with digital learning applications does not translate into enhanced learning outcomes. Thus, researchers and practitioners should explore more targeted ways to harness learners' digital competences to improve learning outcomes, either by accounting for moderating factors such as learners' active engagement with digital tools or the availability of teacher support, or by adopting more refined methodologies to assess digital experience.

A pedagogical framework rooted primarily in key principles of cognitivism and constructivism is considered well-suited for effectively conveying AI-related content within adaptive learning environments. Cognitivism's emphasis on the role of prior knowledge as the foundation for constructing new knowledge is of utmost importance for the development of effective adaptive learning environments. For learners to meaningfully integrate novel information about AI concepts, adaptive learning systems should first assess and activate their existing knowledge base. This process fosters deeper comprehension and retention by building on familiar cognitive structures. The use of visually engaging and interactive materials further supports cognitive processing, thereby promoting better knowledge acquisition. At the same time, constructivist principles that emphasize learner responsibility, active engagement, peer collaboration, and interaction with the learning system are crucial for creating a dynamic learning experience. Adaptive systems must go beyond merely delivering content. They should foster an environment where learners assume responsibility for their learning while interacting with the system and collaborating with peers. Additionally, the inclusion of core behavioral principles, involving personalized feedback and task readiness, further supports learners' motivation and reinforces their learning efforts. Essentially, fostering self-regulated learning is a prerequisite for navigating adaptive learning systems independently, ensuring that learners can maximize their potential and achieve optimal learning outcomes. By integrating these pedagogical principles into adaptive learning systems, it becomes possible to bridge the gap between the technological potential of AI-based learning tools and sound educational theory. This alignment ensures that adaptive learning systems do not merely deliver tailored content but actively support learners in building lasting knowledge and transferring acquired skills into real-world contexts.

As the field of AIEd advances and adaptive learning technologies continue to evolve, developing more sophisticated and theory-grounded customization of instructional content to address the diverse needs of learners contributes a vital step toward the creation of more equitable and sustainable educational opportunities. Future research, as well as VET and CVET practitioners, need to prioritize the integration of AI-related courses within authentic, robust adaptive learning systems. These systems should not only be responsive to individual learning needs but also be grounded in sound pedagogical frameworks, ensuring that learners' distinct requirements are addressed and their learning outcomes maximized. Such integration is essential to foster AI literacy and minimize the growing skills gap in the contemporary workforce. As AI's societal and economic impact gains prominence and the demand for AI competences increases across sectors (Cedefop, 2025), learning with and about AI is not only relevant but increasingly indispensable. Comprehensive and continuous AI training becomes crucial for equipping professionals with the skills necessary to apply AI knowledge meaningfully and effectively within their occupational roles. Personalized, adaptive learning solutions that acknowledge and accommodate a broad range of learner profiles hold considerable promise in empowering individuals to navigate and contribute to the increasingly AI-driven workplaces. By fostering sustainable lifelong learning, such learning approaches lay the foundation for more inclusive and impactful upskilling and reskilling initiatives, ensuring that learners with diverse backgrounds, needs, and competences are afforded the opportunity to thrive in a rapidly evolving technological landscape.

References

Akakpo, M. G. (2019). *The influence of learner characteristics on interactions to seek and share information in e-learning: A media psychology perspective* (Publication No. 27603595) [Doctoral dissertation, Bayerische Julius-Maximilians-Universität Würzburg]. PQDT Open. https://www.proquest.com/openview/5106a03d92531a15420978515f845521/1?cbl=2026366&diss=y&pq

Akbulut, Y., & Çardak, C. S. (2012). Adaptive educational hypermedia accommodating learning styles: A content analysis of publications from 2000 to 2011. *Computers & Education, 58*(2), 835–842. https://doi.org/10.1016/j.compedu.2011.10.008

Akçapinar, G., & Bayazit, A. (2019). Moodleminer: Data mining analysis tool for Moodle learning management system / MoodleMiner: Moodle öğrenme yönetim sistemi için veri madenciliği analiz aracı. *Elementary Education Online, 18*(1), 406–415. https://doi.org/10.17051/ilkonline.2019.527645

Akhuseyinoglu, K., & Brusilovsky, P. (2021). Data-driven modeling of learners' individual differences for predicting engagement and success in online learning. In J. Masthoff, E. Herder, N. Tintarev, & M. Tkalčič (Eds.), *UMAP' 21: Proceedings of the 29th ACM Conference on User Modeling, Adaptation and Personalization* (pp. 201–212). Association for Computing Machinery. https://doi.org/10.1145/3450613.3456834

Akhuseyinoglu, K., & Brusilovsky, P. (2022). Exploring behavioral patterns for data-driven modeling of learners' individual differences. *Frontiers in Artificial Intelligence, 5*, Article 807320. https://doi.org/10.3389/frai.2022.807320

Akkoyunlu, B., & Soylu, M. Y. (2008). A study of students' perceptions in a blended learning environment based on different learning styles. *Educational Technology & Society, 11*(1), 183–193. https://www.jstor.org/stable/jeductechsoci.11.1.183

Akuma, S., & Ndera, T. (2021). Adaptive educational hypermedia system for high school students based on learning styles. *International Journal of Educational and Pedagogical Sciences, 15*(2), 228–234.

Al-Ajlan, A., & Zedan, H. (2008). Why Moodle. *2008 12th IEEE International Workshop on Future Trends of Distributed Computing Systems* (pp. 58–64). IEEE. https://doi.org/10.1109/FTDCS.2008.22

Al-Azawei, A., Parslow, P., & Lundqvist, K. (2015). A psychometric analysis of reliability and validity of the index of learning styles (ILS). *International Journal of Psychological Studies, 7*(3), 46–57. https://doi.org/10.5539/ijps.v7n3p46

E. Petridou, *Personalized Learning in Vocational and Continuing Education*, https://doi.org/10.1007/978-3-658-51517-1

Aleksander, I., Vivet, M., Kerr, D., Gillingham, J., Fernandez de Castro, M. I., Diaz de Ilarraza Sanchez, A., Felisa Vordejo Maillo, M., & Lees, P. (1988). *Artificial intelligence and its potential as an aid to vocational training and education*. CEDEFOP. https://eric.ed.gov/?id=ED316734

Al-haimi, B., Hujainah, F., Nasir, D., & Alhroob, E. (2021). Higher education institutions with artificial intelligence: Roles, promises, and requirements. In A. Hamdan, A. E. Hassanien, R. Khamis, B. Alareeni, A. Razzaque, & B. Awwad (Eds.), *Applications of Artificial Intelligence in Business, Education and Healthcare* (pp. 221–238). Springer Cham. https://doi.org/10.1007/978-3-030-72080-3_13

Alshammari, M. T., & Qtaish, A. (2019). Effective adaptive e-learning systems according to learning style and knowledge level. *Journal of Information Technology Education: Research*, 18, 529–547. https://doi.org/10.28945/4459

Ameisen, E. (2020). *Building machine learning powered applications: Going from idea to product*. O'Reilly Media.

Anderson, J. R. (2015). *Cognitive psychology and its implications* (8th ed.). Worth Publishers.

Anderson, L. W., & Krathwohl, D. R. (2001). *A taxonomy for learning, teaching, and assessing: A revision of Bloom' s taxonomy of educational objectives: complete edition*. Addison Wesley Longman.

Anderson, J. R., Reder, L. M., & Simon, H. A. (1996). Situated learning and education. *Educational Researcher*, *25*(4), 5–11. https://doi.org/10.3102/0013189X025004005

Attwell, G., Bekiaridis, G., Deitmer, L., Perini, M., Roppertz, S., & Tütlys, V. (2020). *Artificial intelligence in policies, processes and practices of vocational education and training*. (Report No. 2019–1-DE02-KA202–006317). Institut Technik und Bildung (ITB). https://doi.org/10.26092/elib/307

Baddeley, A. D. (1990). *Human Memory*. Allyn and Bacon.

Baddeley, A. D., Eysenck, M. W., & Anderson, M. C. (2015). *Memory* (2nd ed.). Psychology Press. https://doi.org/10.4324/9781315749860

Badrus, B., & Arifin, Z. (2021). The effect of the blended learning model on the improvement of student learning outcomes. *Nazhruna: Jurnal Pendidikan Islam*, *4*(1), 108–116. https://doi.org/10.31538/nzh.v4i1.836

Bae, C. L., Therriault, D. J., & Redifer, J. L. (2019). Investigating the testing effect: Retrieval as a characteristic of effective study strategies. *Learning and Instruction*, *60*, 206–214. https://doi.org/10.1016/j.learninstruc.2017.12.008

Bajraktarevic, N., Hall, W., & Fullick, P. (2003). Incorporating learning styles in hypermedia environment: Empirical evaluation. *Proceedings of the workshop on adaptive hypermedia and adaptive web-based systems,* 41–52.

Bandler, R., & Grinder, J. (1979). *Frogs into princes: Neuro linguistic programming*. Real People Press.

Bandura, A. (1982). Self-efficacy mechanism in human agency. *American Psychologist*, *37*(2), 122–147. https://doi.org/10.1037/0003-066X.37.2.122

Bandura, A. (1986). *Social foundations of thought and action: A social cognitive theory*. Prentice Hall.

Bandura, A. (1997). *Self-efficacy: The exercise of control*. W. H. Freeman and Company.

Bandura, A. (2001). Social cognitive theory: An agentic perspective. *Annual Review of Psychology*, *52*(1), 1–26. https://doi.org/10.1146/annurev.psych.52.1.1

Bandura, A. (2006). Toward a psychology of human agency. *Perspectives on Psychological Science, 1*(2), 164–180. https://doi.org/10.1111/j.1745-6916.2006.00011

Baradari, D., Kosmyna, N., Petrov, O., Kaplun, R., & Maes, P. (2025). NeuroChat: A Neuroadaptive AI Chatbot for Customizing Learning Experiences. *arXiv preprint arXiv:2503.07599*. https://doi.org/10.48550/arXiv.2503.07599

Barbe, W. B., Swassing, R. H., & Milone, M. N. (1979). *Teaching through modality strengths: Concepts and practices*. Zaner-Bloser.

Baumgartner, H., & Steenkamp, J. B. E. (2001). Response styles in marketing research: A cross-national investigation. *Journal of Marketing Research, 38*(2), 143–156. https://doi.org/10.1509/jmkr.38.2.143.18840

Beckmann, J., Bertel, S., & Zander, S. (2015). Performance & emotion - A study on adaptive e-learning based on visual/verbal learning styles. In M. B. Nunes, & M. McPherson (Eds.), *Proceedings of the international conference. E-learning 2015* (pp. 27–34). Proceedings of the International Association for Development of the Information Society.

Belsey, D. A., Kuh, E., & Welsch, R. E. (1980). *Regression diagnostics: Identifying influential data and sources of collinearity*. Wiley.

Bergdahl, N., Nouri, J., & Fors, U. (2020). Disengagement, engagement and digital skills in technology-enhanced learning. *Education and Information Technologies, 25*(2), 957–983. https://doi.org/10.1007/s10639-019-09998-w

Bloom, B. S. (1956). *Taxonomy of Educational Objectives: The Classification of Educational Goals* (1st ed.). David McKay Company.

Bloom, B. S. (1984). The 2 sigma problem: The search for methods of group instruction as effective as one-to-one tutoring. *Educational Researcher, 13*(6), 4–16. https://doi.org/10.3102/0013189X013006004

Bloom, B. S., Engelhart, M. D., Furst, E. J., Hill, W. H., & Krathwohl, D. R. (1956). *Taxonomy of educational objectives: The classification of educational goals. Handbook 1: Cognitive domain*. Longmans.

BMWi – Bundesministerium für Wirtschaft und Energie. (2020). *Einsatz von Künstlicher Intelligenz in der Deutschen Wirtschaft*. BMWi. Stand der KI-Nutzung im Jahr 2019.

Le Borgne, Y.-A., Bellas, F., Cassidy, D., Vuorikari, R., Kralj, L., Obae, C., Pasichnyk, O., Bevek, P., van Deyzen, B., Laitala, A., Sharma, M., Wulgaert, R., Niewint-Gori, J., Gröpler, J., Joyce, A., Rondin, E., Gilleran, A., Janakievska, G., & Weber, M. (2023). *AI report by the European Digital Education Hub's Squad on Artificial Intelligence in Education*. Publications Office of the European Union. https://doi.org/10.2797/828281

Bortz, J., & Döring, N. (2006). *Forschungsmethoden und Evaluation: Für Human- und Sozialwissenschaftler* (4th ed.). Springer Medizin Verlag.

Du Boulay, B. (2000). Can we learn from ITSs?. In G. Gauthier, C. Frasson, & K. VanLehn (Eds.), *Intelligent Tutoring Systems: 5th International Conference. ITS 2000. lecture notes in computer science. vol 1839* (pp. 9–17). Springer Berlin Heidelberg. https://doi.org/10.1007/3-540-45108-0_3

Bower, M. (2019). Technology-mediated learning theory. *British Journal of Educational Technology, 50*(3), 1035–1048. https://doi.org/10.1111/bjet.12771

Bowerman, B. L., & O'Connell, R. T. (1990). *Linear statistical models: An applied approach* (2nd ed.). PWS-Kent.

Boyatzis, R. E., & Kolb, D. A. (1991). Assessing individuality in learning: The learning skills profile. *Educational Psychology, 11*(3–4), 279–295. https://doi.org/10.1080/0144341910110305

Bredo, E. (1997). The social construction of learning. In G. D. Phye (Ed.), *Handbook of Academic Learning* (pp. 3–45). Academic Press. https://doi.org/10.1016/B978-0-12-554255-5.X5000-5

Breusch, T. S., & Pagan, A. R. (1979). A simple test for heteroscedasticity and random coefficient variation. *Econometrica, 47*, 1287–1294.

Brinkerhoff, J. D., Klein, J. D., & Koroghlanian, C. M. (2001). Effects of overviews and computer experience on learning from hypertext. *Journal of Educational Computing Research, 25*(4), 427–440. https://doi.org/10.2190/0FE0-GATH-TBAH-XDKC

Broadbent, D. E. (1958). *Perception and communication.* Pergamon Press.

Brod, G. (2021). Toward an understanding of when prior knowledge helps or hinders learning. *npj Science of Learning, 6*(1), 24. https://doi.org/10.1038/s41539-021-00103-w

Brown, E. (2007). *The use of learning styles in adaptive hypermedia* [Doctoral dissertation, University of Nottingham]. Nottingham ePrints. https://eprints.nottingham.ac.uk/10577/1/ejb-thesis-for-ethesis-archive.pdf

Brown, T. A. (2015). *Confirmatory factor analysis for applied research.* The Guilford Press.

Brown, E., Brailsford, T., Fisher, T., Moore, A., & Ashman, H. (2006). Reappraising cognitive styles in adaptive web applications. *Proceedings of the 15th International Conference on World Wide Web*, 327–335. https://doi.org/10.1145/1135777.1135827

Bruning, R. H., Schraw, G. J., Norby, M. M., & Ronning, R. R. (2004). *Cognitive psychology and instruction* (4th ed.). Pearson Education.

Brusilovsky, P. (1996). Methods and techniques of adaptive hypermedia. *User Modelling and User-Adapted Interaction, Special Issue on Adaptive Hypertext and Hypermedia,* Springer Nature, *6*, 87–129. https://doi.org/10.1007/BF00143964

Brusilovsky, P. (1998). Methods and techniques of adaptive hypermedia. In P., Brusilovsky, A., Kobsa, & J. Vassileva, (Eds.), *Adaptive hypertext and hypermedia* (pp. 1–43). Springer Dordrecht. https://doi.org/10.1007/978-94-017-0617-9_1

Brusilovsky, P. (1999). Adaptive and intelligent technologies for web-based education. *Künstliche Intelligenz: Special Issue on Intelligent Systems and Teleteaching, 13*(4), 19–25.

Brusilovsky, P. (2001). Adaptive hypermedia. *User Modeling and User-Adapted Interaction, 11*(1), 87–110. https://doi.org/10.1023/A:1011143116306

Brusilovsky, P. (2007). Adaptive navigation support. In P. Brusilovsky, A. Kobsa, & W. Nejdl (Eds.), *The adaptive web* (pp. 263–290). Springer Berlin Heidelberg. https://doi.org/10.1007/978-3-540-72079-9

Brusilovsky, P., & Millán, E. (2007). User models for adaptive hypermedia and adaptive educational systems. In P. Brusilovsky, A. Kobsa, & W. Nejdl (Eds.), *The adaptive web* (pp. 3–53). Springer Berlin Heidelberg. https://doi.org/10.1007/978-3-540-72079-9

Brusilovsky, P., & Pesin, L. (1998). Adaptive navigation support in educational hypermedia: An evaluation of the ISIS-Tutor. *Journal of Computing and Information Technology, 6*(1), 27–38.

Brusilovsky, P. & Peylo, C. (2003). Adaptive and Intelligent Web-based Educational Systems. *International Journal of Artificial Intelligence in Education, 13*(2–4), 159–172.

Bryan, J. H., & Bryan, T. H. (1983). The social life of the learning disabled youngster. *Current Topics in Learning Disabilities, 1*, 57–85.

Bundesministerium für Bildung und Forschung. (n.d.-a). *Der DQR*. Retrieved March 4, 2024, from https://www.dqr.de/dqr/de/home/home_node.html

Bundesministerium für Bildung und Forschung. (n.d.-b). *KI B^3 – Künstliche Intelligenz in die berufliche Bildung bringen.* Retrieved March 4, 2024, from https://www.inno-vet.de/innovet/de/die-projekte/alle-projekte-von-a-bis-z/ki-b.html

Bürgermeister, A., Kampa, M., Rakoczy, K., Harks, B., Besser, M., Klieme, E., Blum, W., & Leiß, D. (2012). *Adaptiv - Schüler [Fragebogenskala: Version 1.0].* In *Conditions and Consequences of Classroom Assessment - Fragebogenerhebung (Co^2CA) [Skalenkollektion: Version 1.0].* (Data collected in 2005). Forschungsdatenzentrum Bildung am DIPF. https://doi.org/10.7477/42:46:0

Burton, J. K., Moore, D. M. M., & Magliaro, S. G. (2004). Behaviorism and instructional technology. In D. H. Jonassen (Ed.), *Handbook of research on educational communications and technology* (pp. 3–36). Lawrence Erlbaum Associates. https://doi.org/10.4324/9781410609519

Byrne, B. M. (2010). *Structural equation modeling with AMOS: Basic concepts, applications, and programming* (2nd ed.). Routledge. https://doi.org/10.4324/9780203805534

Byrnes, J. P. (1996). *Cognitive development and learning in instructional contexts.* Allyn and Bacon.

Campbell, D. T., & Stanley, J. C. (1963). *Experimental and quasi-experimental designs for research.* Houghton Mifflin Company.

Campo, M., Amandi, A., & Biset, J. C. (2021). A software architecture perspective about Moodle flexibility for supporting empirical research of teaching theories. *Education and Information Technologies, 26*(1), 817–842. https://doi.org/10.1007/s10639-020-10291-4

Caravias, V. (2018). Teachers conceptions and approaches to blended learning: A literature review. In I. Management Association (Ed.), *Online course management: Concepts, methodologies, tools, and applications* (pp. 912–934). IGI Global Scientific Publishing. https://doi.org/10.4018/978-1-5225-5472-1.ch046

Carbonell, J. R. (1970). AI in CAI: An artificial-intelligence approach to computer-assisted instruction. *IEEE Transactions on Man-Machine Systems, 11*(4), 190–202. https://doi.org/10.1109/TMMS.1970.299942

Carifio, J., & Perla, R. J. (2008). Resolving the 50-year debate around using and misusing Likert scales. *Medical Education, 42*(12), 1150–1152. https://doi.org/10.1111/j.1365-2923.2008.03172.x

Carver, C. A., Howard, R. A., & Lane, W. D. (1999). Enhancing student learning through hypermedia courseware and incorporation of student learning styles. *IEEE Transactions on Education, 42*(1), 33–38. https://doi.org/10.1109/13.746332

Cedefop. (n.d.). *European Qualifications Framework (EQF).* European Centre for the Development of Vocational Training. Retrieved July 19, 2024, from https://www.cedefop.europa.eu/en/projects/european-qualifications-framework-eqf

Cedefop. (2024, June 24). *Artificial intelligence in EU workplaces: Another great divide? First insights from Cedefop's AI skills survey.* 16th Cedefop Brussels Seminar. https://www.cedefop.europa.eu/

Cedefop. (2025). *Skills empower workers in the AI revolution: First findings from Cedefop's AI skills survey* (Policy brief). Publications Office of the European Union. https://doi.org/10.2801/6372704

Cedefop/OECD (2021). *The next steps for apprenticeship.* Luxembourg: Publications Office. Cedefop reference series; No 118. http://data.europa.eu/doi/10.2801/085907

Cedefop & Tissot, P. (2014). *Terminology of European education and training policy.* Luxembourg: Publications Office. https://doi.org/10.2801/15877

Champely, S. (2020). *pwr: Basic functions for power analysis* (Version 1.3–0) [R package]. https://CRAN.R-project.org/package=pwr

Chang, Y. H., Chen, Y. Y., Chen, N. S., Lu, Y. T., & Fang, R. J. (2016). Yet another adaptive learning management system based on Felder and Silverman's learning styles and Mashup. *Eurasia Journal of Mathematics, Science and Technology Education, 12*(5), 1273–1285. https://doi.org/10.12973/eurasia.2016.1512a

Chang, T. W., Kurcz, J., El-Bishouty, M. M., Kinshuk, & Graf, S. (2015). Adaptive and personalized learning based on students' cognitive characteristics. In Kinshuk, & Huang, R. (Eds.). *Ubiquitous learning environments and technologies* (pp. 77–97). Springer Berlin Heidelberg. https://doi.org/10.1007/978-3-662-44659-1_5

Chang, M., Popescu, E., Kinshuk, Chen, N. S., Jemni, M., Huang, R., Spector, J. M., & Sampson, D. G. (Eds.). (2019). *Foundations and Trends in Smart Learning: Proceedings of 2019 International Conference on Smart Learning Environments.* Springer Singapore. https://doi.org/10.1007/978-981-13-6908-7

Chao, P. J., Hsu, T. H., Liu, T. P., & Cheng, Y. H. (2021). Knowledge of and competence in artificial intelligence: Perspectives of Vietnamese digital-native students. *IEEE Access, 9*, 75751–75760. https://doi.org/10.1109/ACCESS.2021.3081749

Chavan, A., & Pavri, S. (2004). Open-source learning management with Moodle. *Linux Journal, 2004*(128), 2.

Chaw, L. Y., & Tang, C. M. (2024). Exploring the relationship between digital competence proficiency and student learning performance. *European Journal of Education, 59*(1), e12593. https://doi.org/10.1111/ejed.12593

Chen, K. Z., & Li, S. C. (2021). Sequential, typological, and academic dynamics of self-regulated learners: Learning analytics of an undergraduate chemistry online course. *Computers and Education: Artificial Intelligence, 2*, 100024. https://doi.org/10.1016/j.caeai.2021.100024

Chen, X., Xie, H., Zou, D., & Hwang, G. J. (2020). Application and theory gaps during the rise of artificial intelligence in education. *Computers and Education: Artificial Intelligence, 1*, 100002. https://doi.org/10.1016/j.caeai.2020.100002

Chiu, T. K., Xia, Q., Zhou, X., Chai, C. S., & Cheng, M. (2023). Systematic literature review on opportunities, challenges, and future research recommendations of artificial intelligence in education. *Computers and Education: Artificial Intelligence, 4*, 100118. https://doi.org/10.1016/j.caeai.2022.100118

Chrysafiadi, K., Virvou, M., Tsihrintzis, G. A., & Hatzilygeroudis, I. (2023). Evaluating the user's experience, adaptivity and learning outcomes of a fuzzy-based intelligent tutoring system for computer programming for academic students in Greece. *Education and Information Technologies, 28*(6), 6453–6483. https://doi.org/10.1007/s10639-022-11444-3

Cobb, P., & Bowers, J. (1999). Cognitive and situated learning perspectives in theory and practice. *Educational Researcher, 28*(2), 4–15. https://doi.org/10.3102/0013189X028002004

Coffield, F., Moseley, D. Hall, E., & Ecclestone, K., (2004a). *Learning styles and pedagogy in post-16 learning: A systematic and critical review.* Learning and Skills Research Centre. https://www.leerbeleving.nl/wp-content/uploads/2011/09/learning-styles.pdf

Coffield, F., Moseley, D., Hall, E., & Ecclestone, K. (2004b). Should we be using learning styles? What research has to say to practice. Learning and Skills Research Centre. http://www.itslifejimbutnotasweknowit.org.uk/files/LSRC_LearningStyles.pdf

Cohen, J. (1988). *Statistical power analysis for the behavioral sciences* (2nd ed.). Lawrence Erlbaum Associates.

Collins, D. (2003). Pretesting survey instruments: an overview of cognitive methods. *Quality of Life Research, 12*, 229–238. https://doi.org/10.1023/A:1023254226592

Cook, R. D., & Weisberg, S. (1982). *Residuals and influence in regression.* Chapman & Hall.

Cope, B., Kalantzis, M., & Searsmith, D. (2020). Artificial intelligence for education: Knowledge and its assessment in AI-enabled learning ecologies. *Educational Philosophy and Theory, 53*(12), 1229–1245. https://doi.org/10.1080/00131857.2020.1728732

Cortina, J. M. (1993). What is coefficient alpha? An examination of theory and applications. *Journal of Applied Psychology, 78*(1), 98–104. https://doi.org/10.1037/0021-9010.78.1.98

Creswell, J. W., & Creswell, J. D. (2018). *Research design: Qualitative, quantitative, and mixed methods approaches* (5th ed.). Sage Publications.

Cronbach, L. J. (1951). Coefficient alpha and the internal structure of tests. *Psychometrika, 16*(3), 297–334. https://doi.org/10.1007/BF02310555

Crowder, R.G., & Wagner, R.K. (1992). *The psychology of reading: An introduction* (2nd ed.) Oxford University Press.

Cui, W., Xue, Z., & Thai, K. P. (2018). Performance comparison of an AI-based adaptive learning system in China. *2018 Chinese automation congress (CAC)*, 3170–3175. IEEE. https://doi.org/10.1109/CAC.2018.8623327

Davis, B., & Sumara, D. J. (2005). Challenging images of knowing: Complexity science and educational research. *International Journal of Qualitative Studies in Education, 18*(3), 305–321. https://doi.org/10.1080/09518390500082293

De Visser, E. J., Pak, R., & Shaw, T. H. (2018). From 'automation' to 'autonomy': the importance of trust repair in human–machine interaction. *Ergonomics, 61*(10), 1409–1427. https://doi.org/10.1080/00140139.2018.1457725

Dignum, V. (2021). The role and challenges of education for responsible AI. *London Review of Education, 19*(1), 1–11. https://doi.org/10.14324/lre.19.1.01

Duncan, R. M. (1995). Piaget and Vygotsky revisited: Dialogue or assimilation?. *Developmental Review, 15*(4), 458–472. https://doi.org/10.1006/drev.1995.1019

Durbin, J., & Watson, G. S. (1951). Testing for serial correlation in least squares regression. II , *Biometrika, 38,* 159–178. https://doi.org/10.1093/biomet/38.1-2.159

Ebbinghaus, H. (1885). *Memory: A Contribution to Experimental Psychology.* Teachers College, Columbia University.

EdSurge. (2016). *Decoding Adaptive.* Pearson. https://www.pearson.com/content/dam/one-dot-com/one-dot-com/global/Files/about-pearson/innovation/Pearson-Decoding-Adaptive-v5-Web.pdf

El-Bishouty, M. M., Aldraiweesh, A., Alturki, U., Tortorella, R., Yang, J., Chang, T. W., & Graf, S. (2019). Use of Felder and Silverman learning style model for online course design. *Educational Technology Research and Development, 67*(1), 161–177. https://doi.org/10.1007/s11423-018-9634-6

El-Sabagh, H. A. (2021). Adaptive e-learning environment based on learning styles and its impact on development students' engagement. *International Journal of Educational Technology in Higher Education, 18*(1), 53. https://doi.org/10.1186/s41239-021-00289-4

English Oxford Living Dictionary. (n.d.). Artificial Intelligence. In *Oxford Reference.* Retrieved January 10, 2025, from https://www.oxfordreference.com/view/10.1093/oi/authority.20110803095426960

Essalmi, F., Ayed, L. J. B., Jemni, M., & Graf, S. (2015). Generalized metrics for the analysis of e-learning personalization strategies. *Computers in Human Behavior, 48*, 310–322. https://doi.org/10.1016/j.chb.2014.12.050

Europass. (n.d.). *Description of the eight EQF levels.* European Union. Retrieved July 19, 2024, from https://europass.europa.eu/en/description-eight-eqf-levels

Fasihuddin, H., Skinner, G., & Athauda, R. (2017). Towards adaptive open learning environments: Evaluating the precision of identifying learning styles by tracking learners' behaviours. *Education and Information Technologies, 22*, 807–825. https://doi.org/10.1007/s10639-015-9458-5

Felder, R. M. (1996). Matters of style. *ASEE Prism, 6*(4), 18–23.

Felder, R. M. (2002). Learning and teaching styles in engineering education. *Engineering Education,* 78(7), 674–681. (Original work published 1988)

Felder, R.M., & Henriques, E.R. (1995). Learning and teaching styles in foreign and second language education. *Foreign Language Annals, 28*(1), 21–31. https://doi.org/10.1111/j.1944-9720.1995.tb00767.x

Felder, R., Litzinger, T., Lee, S. H., & Wise, J. (2005, June 12–15). *A study of the reliability and validity of the Felder-Soloman index of learning styles* [Paper presentation]. 2005 Annual Conference, Portland, Oregon, United States.

Felder, R. M., & Silverman, L. K. (1988). Learning and teaching styles in engineering education. *Engineering Education, 78*(7), 674–681.

Felder, R. M., & Soloman, B. A. (1997). *Index of Learning Styles questionnaire (ILS).* [Database report]. North Carolina State University. https://learningstyles.webtools.ncsu.edu/

Felder, R. M., & Soloman, B. A. (2000). *Learning styles and strategies.* https://engr.ncsu.edu/wp-content/uploads/drive/1WPAfj3j5o5OuJMiHorJ-lv6fON1C8kCN/styles.pdf

Felder, R. M., & Spurlin, J. (2005). Applications, reliability and validity of the index of learning styles. *International Journal of Engineering Education, 21*(1), 103–112.

Feldman, J., Monteserin, A., & Amandi, A. (2015). Automatic detection of learning styles: State of the art. *Artificial Intelligence Review, 44*(2), 157–186. https://doi.org/10.1007/s10462-014-9422-6

Field, A., Miles, J., & Field, Z. (2012). *Discovering statistics using R.* SAGE Publications.

Filippidis, S. K., & Tsoukalas, I. A. (2009). On the use of adaptive instructional images based on the sequential–global dimension of the Felder–Silverman learning style theory. *Interactive Learning Environments, 17*(2), 135–150. https://doi.org/10.1080/10494820701869524

Fleming, N. D., & Mills, C. (1992). Not another inventory, rather a catalyst for reflection. *To Improve the Academy, 11*(1), 137–155. https://doi.org/10.1002/j.2334-4822.1992.tb00213.x

Fletcher, T. D. (2022). *QuantPsyc: Quantitative psychology tools* (Version 1.6) [R package]. https://CRAN.R-project.org/package=QuantPsyc

Fox, J. (2016). *Applied regression analysis and generalized linear models* (3rd ed.). SAGE Publications.

Fox, J. (2022). *polycor: Polychoric and polyserial correlations* (R package version 0.8–1). https://CRAN.R-project.org/package=polycor

Fox, J., & Weisberg, S. (2019). *An R companion to applied regression* (3rd ed.). Sage. https://socialsciences.mcmaster.ca/jfox/Books/Companion/

Gambo, Y., & Shakir, M. (2021). An artificial neural network (ann)-based learning agent for classifying learning styles in self-regulated smart learning environment. *International Journal of Emerging Technologies in Learning, 16*(18), 185–199.

García, P., Amandi, A., Schiaffino, S., & Campo, M. (2007). Evaluating Bayesian networks' precision for detecting students' learning styles. *Computers & Education, 49*(3), 794–808. https://doi.org/10.1016/j.compedu.2005.11.017

García, P., Schiaffino, S., & Amandi, A. (2008). An enhanced Bayesian model to detect students' learning styles in Web-based courses. *Journal of Computer Assisted Learning, 24*(4), 305–315. https://doi.org/10.1111/j.1365-2729.2007.00262.x

Geary, D. C. (1995). Reflections of evolution and culture in children's cognition: Implications for mathematical development and instruction. *American Psychologist, 50*(1), 24–37. https://doi.org/10.1037/0003-066X.50.1.24

Gee, J. P. (2003). What video games have to teach us about learning and literacy. *Computers in entertainment, 1*(1), 1–4. https://doi.org/10.1145/950566.950595

Gligorea, I., Cioca, M., Oancea, R., Gorski, A. T., Gorski, H., & Tudorache, P. (2023). Adaptive learning using artificial intelligence in e-learning: A literature review. *Education Sciences, 13*(12), 1216. https://doi.org/10.3390/educsci13121216

Goldhammer, F., Gniewosz, G., & Zylka, J. (2016). ICT engagement in learning environments. In S. Kuger, E. Klieme, N. Jude, & D. Kaplan (Eds.), *Methodology of educational measurement and assessment. Assessing contexts of learning: An international perspective* (pp. 331–351). Springer Cham. https://doi.org/10.1007/978-3-319-45357-6_13

Goldhammer, F., & Hartig, J. (2020). Testwertinterpretation, Testnormen und Testeichung. In H. Moosbrugger, & A. Kelava (Eds.), *Testtheorie und Fragebogenkonstruktion* (pp. 171–195) Springer Berlin Heidelberg. https://doi.org/10.1007/978-3-662-61532-4_9

Gomede, E., de Barros, R. M., & de Souza Mendes, L. (2021). Deep auto encoders to adaptive e-learning recommender system. *Computers and Education: Artificial Intelligence, 2*, 100009. https://doi.org/10.1016/j.caeai.2021.100009

Graf, S. (2007). *Adaptivity in learning management systems focussing on learning styles* [Doctoral dissertation, Technische Universität Wien]. reposiTUm. https://resolver.obvsg.at/urn:nbn:at:at-ubtuw:1-20983

Graf, S., & Kinshuk, K. (2007). Providing adaptive courses in learning management systems with respect to learning styles. In T. Bastiaens & S. Carliner (Eds.), *Proceedings of E-Learn 2007: World Conference on E-Learning in Corporate, Government, Healthcare, and Higher Education* (pp. 2576–2583). Association for the Advancement of Computing in Education (AACE). https://www.learntechlib.org/primary/p/26739/

Graf, S., Kinshuk, K., & Liu, T. C. (2008). Identifying learning styles in learning management systems by using indications from students' behaviour. *2008 eighth IEEE international conference on advanced learning technologies*. 482–486. https://doi.org/10.1109/ICALT.2008.84

Graf, S., Liu, T. C. & Kinshuk, K. (2010). Analysis of learners' navigational behaviour and their learning styles in an online course. *Journal of Computer Assisted Learning, 26*(2), 116–131. https://doi.org/10.1111/j.1365-2729.2009.00336.x

Graf, S., Viola, S. R., & Kinshuk, T. L. (2006). Representative characteristics of Felder-Silverman learning styles: An empirical model. In Kinshuk, D, G. Sampson, J. M. Spector, & P. Isaías (Eds.), *Proceedings of the international conference on cognition and exploratory learning in digital age* (pp. 235–242), International Association for Development of the Information Society. http://hdl.handle.net/20.500.12708/51416

Graf, S., Viola, S. R., Leo, T., & Kinshuk. (2007). In-depth analysis of the Felder-Silverman learning style dimensions. *Journal of Research on Technology in Education, 40*(1), 79–93. https://doi.org/10.1080/15391523.2007.10782498

Graham, L., Berman, J., & Bellert, A. (2015). *Sustainable learning*. Cambridge University Press. https://doi.org/10.1017/CBO9781107280243

Gredler, M. E. (2009). Hiding in plain sight: The stages of mastery/self-regulation in Vygotsky's cultural-historical theory. *Educational Psychologist, 44*(1), 1–19. https://doi.org/10.1080/00461520802616259

Greeno, J. G. (1998). The situativity of knowing, learning, and research. *American Psychologist, 53*(1), 5–26. https://doi.org/10.1037/0003-066X.53.1.5

Greeno, J. G., Collins, A. M., & Resnick, L. B. (1996). Cognition and learning. In D. C. Berliner, & R. C. Calfee (Eds.), *Handbook of educational psychology* (pp. 15–46). Lawrence Erlbaum Associates.

Grivokostopoulou, F., & Hatzilygeroudis, I. (2013). Teaching AI Search Algorithms in a Web-Based Educational System. In M. B. Nunes, & M. McPherson (Eds.), *Proceedings of the international conference. E-learning 2013* (pp. 83–90). International Association for Development of the Information Society. https://files.eric.ed.gov/fulltext/ED562127.pdf

Guan, C., Mou, J., & Jiang, Z. (2020). Artificial intelligence innovation in education: A twenty-year data-driven historical analysis. *International Journal of Innovation Studies, 4*(4), 134–147. https://doi.org/10.1016/j.ijis.2020.09.001

Gupta, S., Bostrom, R. P., & Huber, M. (2010). End-user training methods: what we know, need to know. *ACM SIGMIS Database: The database for advances in information systems, 41*(4), 9–39. https://doi.org/10.1145/1899639.1899641

Gutschow, K. & Lorig, B. (2022). Kodifizierte Zusatzqualifikationen – Ziele, Modelle und Verbreitung. *Berufsbildung in Wissenschaft und Praxis, 51*(3), 27–30.

Hage, N. (1996). *Lehrevaluation und studentische Veranstaltungskritik: Projekte, Instrumente und Grundlagen*. Bundesministerium für Bildung, Wissenschaft, Forschung und Technologie.

Harrell, F. E. (2023). *Hmisc: Harrell miscellaneous* (R package version 5.1–1). https://CRAN.R-project.org/package=Hmisc

Hart, S. A. (2016). Precision education initiative: Moving toward personalized education. *Mind, Brain, and Education, 10*(4), 209–211. https://doi.org/10.1111/mbe.12109

Hasan, B., & Ali, J. M. (2004). An empirical examination of a model of computer learning performance. *Journal of Computer Information Systems*, *44*(4), 27–33.

Hattie, J. (2008). *Visible learning: A synthesis of over 800 meta-analyses relating to achievement* (1st ed.). Routledge. https://doi.org/10.4324/9780203887332

Hayes, A. F. (1996). Permutation test is not distribution-free: Testing H_0: $\rho = 0$. *Psychological Methods*, *1*(2), 184–198. https://doi.org/10.1037/1082-989X.1.2.184

Hayes, A. F. (2018). *Introduction to mediation, moderation, and conditional process analysis: A regression-based approach* (2nd ed.). The Guilford Press.

Helberger, N., & Diakopoulos, N. (2023). The European AI act and how it matters for research into AI in media and journalism. *Digital Journalism*, *11*(9), 1751–1760. https://doi.org/10.1080/21670811.2022.2082505

Henrie, C. R., Halverson, L. R., & Graham, C. R. (2015). Measuring student engagement in technology-mediated learning: A review. *Computers & Education*, *90*, 36–53. https://doi.org/10.1016/j.compedu.2015.09.005

Hietajärvi, L., Salmela-Aro, K., Tuominen, H., Hakkarainen, K., & Lonka, K. (2019). Beyond screen time: Multidimensionality of socio-digital participation and relations to academic well-being in three educational phases. *Computers in Human Behavior*, *93*, 13–24. https://doi.org/10.1016/j.chb.2018.11.049

Hinojo-Lucena, F. J., Aznar-Díaz, I., Cáceres-Reche, M. P., & Romero-Rodríguez, J. M. (2019). Artificial intelligence in higher education: A bibliometric study on its impact in the scientific literature. *Education Sciences*, *9*(1), 51. https://doi.org/10.3390/educsci9010051

Hoaglin, D., & Welsch, R. (1978). The hat matrix in regression and ANOVA. *American Statistician*, *32*(1), 17–22. https://doi.org/10.1080/00031305.1978.10479237

Hoc, J. M. (2000). From human–machine interaction to human–machine cooperation. *Ergonomics*, *43*(7), 833–843. https://doi.org/10.1080/001401300409044

Holmes, W., Bialik, M. & Fadel, C. (2019). *Artificial intelligence in education: Promises and implications for teaching and learning*. Center for Curriculum Redesign. http://bit.ly/AIEDBOOK

Holstein, K., & Doroudi, S. (2021). Equity and Artificial Intelligence in Education: Will "AIEd" Amplify or Alleviate Inequities in Education?. *arXiv preprint arXiv:2104.12920*. https://doi.org/10.48550/arXiv.2104.12920

Holstein, K., McLaren, B. M., & Aleven, V. (2019). Co-designing a real-time classroom orchestration tool to support teacher-AI complementarity. *Journal of Learning Analytics*, *6*(2), 27–52. https://doi.org/10.18608/jla.2019.62.3

Honebein, P. C. (1996). Seven goals for the design of constructivist learning environments. *Constructivist Learning Environments: Case studies in Instructional Design*, *11*(12), 11–24.

Honey, P., & Mumford, A. (1992). *The Manual of Learning Styles* (3rd ed.). Peter Honey.

Hou, H. T. (2012). Exploring the behavioral patterns of learners in an educational massively multiple online role-playing game (MMORPG). *Computers & Education*, *58*(4), 1225–1233. https://doi.org/10.1016/j.compedu.2011.11.015

Howell, D. C. (2010). *Statistical methods for psychology* (7th ed.). Cengage Learning.

Huang, J., & Chen, Z. (2016). The research and design of web-based intelligent tutoring system. *International Journal of Multimedia and Ubiquitous Engineering*, *11*(6), 337–348.

Huang, C. S., Yang, S. J., Chiang, T. H., & Su, A. Y. (2016). Effects of situated mobile learning approach on learning motivation and performance of EFL students. *Journal of Educational Technology & Society, 19*(1), 263–276.

Hubackova, S., & Semradova, I. (2016). Evaluation of blended learning. *Procedia-Social and Behavioral Sciences, 217*, 551–557. https://doi.org/10.1016/j.sbspro.2016.02.044

Hussein, A. A., & Al-Chalabi, H. K. M. (2020). Pedagogical agents in an adaptive E-learning system. *Science and Research Journal, 3*, 24–30.

Hwang, G. J., Sung, H. Y., Chang, S. C., & Huang, X. C. (2020). A fuzzy expert system-based adaptive learning approach to improving students' learning performances by considering affective and cognitive factors. *Computers and Education: Artificial Intelligence, 1*, 100003. https://doi.org/10.1016/j.caeai.2020.100003

Hwang, G. J., Xie, H., Wah, B. W., & Gašević, D. (2020). Vision, challenges, roles and research issues of Artificial Intelligence in Education. *Computers and Education: Artificial Intelligence, 1*, 100001. https://doi.org/10.1016/j.caeai.2020.100001

Institut für Qualitätsentwicklung Hessen. (2013). *Individualisierung - Lehrkräfte [Fragebogenskala: Version 1.0]*. In *Hessischer Referenzrahmen Schulqualität - Fragebogenerhebung [Skalenkollektion: Version 1.0]*. (Data collected in 2011). Forschungsdatenzentrum Bildung am DIPF. https://doi.org/10.7477/44:48:1

Jagannathan, S., Ra, S., & Maclean, R. (2019). Dominant recent trends impacting on jobs and labor markets - an overview. *International Journal of Training Research, 17*, 1–11. https://doi.org/10.1080/14480220.2019.1641292

Jegatha Deborah, L., Baskaran, R., & Kannan, A. (2014). Learning styles assessment and theoretical origin in an e-learning scenario: a survey. *Artificial Intelligence Review, 42*, 801–819. https://doi.org/10.1007/s10462-012-9344-0

Johnson, R. B., Onwuegbuzie, A. J., & Turner, L. A. (2007). Toward a definition of mixed methods research. *Journal of Mixed Methods Research, 1*(2), 112–133. https://doi.org/10.1177/1558689806298224

Jonassen, D. H., & Grabowski, B. L. (1993). *Handbook of individual differences, learning, and instruction* (1st ed.). Lawrence Erlbaum Associates.

Jonassen, D. H., & Grabowski, B. L. (2012). *Handbook of individual differences, learning, and instruction* (2nd ed.). Routledge.

Joseph, L., Abraham, S., Mani, B. P., & Rajesh, N. (2022). Exploring the effectiveness of learning path recommendation based on Felder-Silverman learning style model: A learning analytics intervention approach. *Journal of Educational Computing Research, 60*(6), 1464–1489. https://doi.org/10.1177/07356331211057816

Jung, C. G. (1971). *Psychological Types*. Princeton University Press.

Kabudi, T., Pappas, I., & Olsen, D. H. (2021). AI-enabled adaptive learning systems: A systematic mapping of the literature. *Computers and Education: Artificial Intelligence, 2*, 100017. https://doi.org/10.1016/j.caeai.2021.100017

Kaiser, H. F. (1960). The application of electronic computers to factor analysis. *Educational and psychological measurement, 20*(1), 141–151. https://doi.org/10.1177/001316446002000116

Kankaraš, M., & Capecchi, S. (2024). Neither agree nor disagree: use and misuse of the neutral response category in Likert-type scales. *METRON, 83*, 111–140. https://doi.org/10.1007/s40300-024-00276-5

Karagiannis, I., & Satratzemi, M. (2018). An adaptive mechanism for Moodle based on automatic detection of learning styles. *Education and Information Technologies, 23*, 1331–1357. https://doi.org/10.1007/s10639-017-9663-5

Karakostas, A., & Demetriadis, S. (2011). Enhancing collaborative learning through dynamic forms of support: the impact of an adaptive domain-specific support strategy. *Journal of Computer Assisted Learning, 27*(3), 243–258. https://doi.org/10.1111/j.1365-2729.2010.00388.x

Kardan, S., & Conati, C. (2015). Providing adaptive support in an interactive simulation for learning: An experimental evaluation. *Proceedings of the 33rd Annual Conference on Human Factors in Computing Systems* (pp. 3671–3680). Association for Computing Machinery. https://doi.org/10.1145/2702123.2702424

Khalil, M., & Ebner, M. (2015). Learning analytics: principles and constraints. In S. Carliner, C. Fulford & N. Ostashewski (Eds.), *Proceedings of Edmedia 2015: World Conference on Educational Media and Technology* (pp. 1789–1799). Association for the Advancement of Computing in Education (AACE). https://www.learntechlib.org/primary/p/151455/

Khensous, G., Boumedjout, A., & Labed, K. (2024). Exploring the role of artificial intelligence in education. In L. Dekhici, K. Guerraiche, R. Azzemou, & J. Jlassi (Eds.), *Intelligent methods and alternative economic models for sustainability* (pp. 155–169). IGI Global Scientific Publishing. https://doi.org/10.4018/979-8-3693-1418-0.ch007

Kika, A., Leka, L., Maxhelaku, S., & Ktona, A. (2019). Using data mining techniques on Moodle data for classification of student's learning styles. *Proceedings of the 47th international academic conference* (pp. 26–33). International Institute of Social and Economic Sciences. https://doi.org/10.20472/iac.2019.047.010

Kim, J., Lee, H., & Cho, Y. H. (2022). Learning design to support student-AI collaboration: Perspectives of leading teachers for AI in education. *Education and Information Technologies, 27*(5), 6069–6104. https://doi.org/10.1007/s10639-021-10831-6

Kinshuk. (2016). *Designing adaptive and personalized learning environments* (1st ed.). Routledge.

Kintu, M. J., Zhu, C., & Kagambe, E. (2017). Blended learning effectiveness: the relationship between student characteristics, design features and outcomes. *International Journal of Educational Technology in Higher Education, 14*(1), 1–20. https://doi.org/10.1186/s41239-017-0043-4

Kirschner, P. A. (2017). Stop propagating the learning styles myth. *Computers & Education, 106*, 166–171. https://doi.org/10.1016/j.compedu.2016.12.006

Kiviniemi, M. T. (2014). Effects of a blended learning approach on student outcomes in a graduate-level public health course. *BMC Medical Education, 14*(1), 1–7. https://doi.org/10.1186/1472-6920-14-47

Klímová, B., & PraŽák, P. (2019). Mobile blended learning and evaluation of its effectiveness on students' learning achievement. In S. K. S. Cheung, LK. Lee, I. Simonova, T. Kozel, & LF. Kwok (Eds.), *Blended learning: Educational innovation for personalized learning: 12th international conference. Lecture notes in computer science* (pp. 216–224). Springer International Publishing. https://doi.org/10.1007/978-3-030-21562-0_18

Kline, P. (1999). *The handbook of psychological testing* (2nd ed.). Routledge.

Kline, R. B. (2023). *Principles and practice of structural equation modeling* (5th ed.). The Guilford Press.

Knutov, E., De Bra, P., & Pechenizkiy, M. (2009). AH 12 years later: a comprehensive survey of adaptive hypermedia methods and techniques. *New Review of Hypermedia and Multimedia, 15*(1), 5–38. https://doi.org/10.1080/13614560902801608

Kobsa, A. (1995). Supporting user interfaces for all through user modeling. *Advances in Human Factors/Ergonomics, 20*, 155–157. https://doi.org/10.1016/S0921-2647(06)80027-4

Kochmar, E., Vu, D. D., Belfer, R., Gupta, V., Serban, I. V., & Pineau, J. (2020). Automated personalized feedback improves learning gains in an intelligent tutoring system. In I. Bittencourt, M. Cukurova, K. Muldner, R. Luckin, E. Millán (Eds.), *Artificial Intelligence in Education: 21st International Conference. AIED 2020. lecture notes* in computer science (pp. 140–146). Springer Cham. https://doi.org/10.1007/978-3-030-52240-7_26

Kommers, P., Stoyanov, S., Mileva, N., & Mediano, C. M. (2008). The effect of adaptive performance support system on learning achievements of students. *International Journal of Continuing Engineering Education and Life-Long Learning, 18*(3), 351–365. https://doi.org/10.1504/IJCEELL.2008.018837

Kolb, D. A. (1984). *Experiential learning: Experience as the source of learning and development*. Prentice-Hall.

Kolb, D. A. (1985). *Learning-style inventory: Self-scoring inventory and interpretation booklet*. McBer.

Kong, S. C., Cheung, W. M. Y., & Zhang, G. (2021). Evaluation of an artificial intelligence literacy course for university students with diverse study backgrounds. *Computers and Education: Artificial Intelligence, 2*, 100026. https://doi.org/10.1016/j.caeai.2021.100026

Kruger, J., & Dunning, D. (1999). Unskilled and unaware of it: how difficulties in recognizing one's own incompetence lead to inflated self-assessments. *Journal of Personality and Social Psychology*, *77*(6), 1121. https://doi.org/10.1037//0022-3514.77.6.1121

Krumpal, I. (2013). Determinants of social desirability bias in sensitive surveys: a literature review. *Quality & Quantity*, *47*(4), 2025–2047. https://doi.org/10.1007/s11135-011-9640-9

Kuljis, J., & Liu, F. (2005, July 4–6). *A comparison of learning style theories on the suitability for elearning* [Conference presentation]. IASTED International Conference on Web Technologies, Applications, and Services, Calgary, Alberta, Canada.

Kumar, S. R., Ramesh, T., & Aswini, K. R. N. (2024). An Adaptive Optimization Algorithm for Personalized Learning Pathways in E-Learning. *International Journal of BIM and Engineering Science, 9*(2), 28–36. https://doi.org/10.54216/IJBES.090204

Kunze, L., & Frey, D. (2021). Digitale Lehre an der Hochschule: Warum Blended Learning so gut funktioniert. In D. Frey, & M. Uemminghaus (Eds.), *Innovative Lehre an der Hochschule: Konzepte, Praxisbeispiele und Lernerfahrungen aus COVID-19* (pp. 69–86). Springer Berlin Heidelberg. https://doi.org/10.1007/978-3-662-62913-0_4

Kurt, S. (2021, September 12). *Adaptive learning: What is it, what are its benefits, and how does it work?* Educational Technology. https://educationaltechnology.net/adaptive-learning-what-is-it-what-are-its-benefits-and-how-does-it-work/

Lakshmi, N., Rao, R. S., & Reddy, S. S. (2013). An overview of preprocessing on web log data for web usage analysis. *International Journal of Innovative Technology and Exploring Engineering*, *2*(4), 274–279.

Lalima & Dangwal, K. L. (2017). Blended learning: An innovative approach. *Universal Journal of Educational Research, 5(1), 129–136.* https://doi.org/10.13189/ujer.2017.050116

Lao, L., Petridou, E., Knautz, K., Rott, K. J., & Schmidt-Hertha, B. (2024). *Evaluationsbericht: Ergebnisse und Schlussfolgerungen der Evaluation der Zusatzqualifikation „KI und maschinelles Lernen" im Rahmen des Projekts „Künstliche Intelligenz in die berufliche Bildung bringen (KI B^3).* https://www.ki-fortbildung.de/downloadbereich

Law, N. W. Y. (2019, June 25–29). Human development and augmented intelligence [Conference keynote abstract]. In S. Isotani, E. Millán, A. Ogan, P. Hastings, B. McLaren & R. Luckin (Eds.), *Artificial intelligence in education. 20th international conference,* Chicago, IL, United States. Springer Nature Switzerland. https://doi.org/10.1007/978-3-030-23204-7

Lawrence, G. (1982). *People types and tiger stripes: A practical guide to learning styles* (2nd ed.). Center for Applications of Psychological Type.

Legg, S., & Hutter, M. (2007). Universal intelligence: A definition of machine intelligence. *Minds and machines, 17*(4), 391–444. https://doi.org/10.1007/s11023-007-9079-x

Lehmann, R. (2010). *Lernstile als Grundlage adaptiver Lernsysteme in der Softwareschulung.* Waxmann.

Lenzner, T., Neuert, C., & Otto, W. (2016). *Cognitive pretesting.* GESIS Survey Guidelines. GESIS – Leibniz Institute for the Social Sciences. https://doi.org/10.15465/gesis-sg_en_010

Levene, H. (1960). Robust tests for equality of variances. In I. Olkin, S. G. Ghurye, W. Hoeffding, W. G. Madow, & H. B. Mann (Eds.), *Contributions to probability and statistics: Essays in honor of Harold Hotelling* (pp. 278–292). Stanford University Press.

Li, L. Y. (2019). Effect of prior knowledge on attitudes, behavior, and learning performance in video lecture viewing. *International Journal of Human–Computer Interaction, 35*(4–5), 415–426. https://doi.org/10.1080/10447318.2018.1543086

Li, J., Xue, E., Li, C., & He, Y. (2023). Investigating latent interactions between students' affective cognition and learning performance: Meta-analysis of affective and cognitive factors. *Behavioral Sciences, 13*(7), 555. https://doi.org/10.3390/bs13070555

Licht, B. G., & Kistner, J. A. (1986). Motivational problems of learning-disabled children: Individual differences and their implications for treatment. *Psychological and Educational Perspectives on Learning Disabilities, 2,* 25–255.

Limongelli, C., Sciarrone, F., & Vaste, G. (2011). Personalized e-learning in Moodle: the Moodle_LS System. *Journal of E-Learning and Knowledge Society, 7*(1), 49–58. https://doi.org/10.20368/1971-8829/487

Lindner, A., & Romeike, R. (2019). Teachers' perspectives on artificial intelligence. In S. Pozdniakov, & V. Dagienė (Eds.), *Informatics in schools. New ideas in school informatics. 12th International conference on informatics in schools: Situation, evaluation and perspectives* (pp. 22–29). Springer Cham. https://doi.org/10.1007/978-3-030-33759-9

Ling, H. C., & Chiang, H. S. (2022). Learning performance in adaptive learning systems: a case study of web programming learning recommendations. *Frontiers in Psychology, 13,* 770637, 1–6. https://doi.org/10.3389/fpsyg.2022.770637

Lipson, J. I. (1984). *Educational technology in Voc Ed,* National Center Publications. https://eric.ed.gov/?id=ED240385

Litzinger, T. A., Lee, S. H., Wise, J. C., & Felder, R. M. (2007). A psychometric study of the index of learning styles©. *Journal of Engineering Education, 96*(4), 309–319. https://doi.org/10.1002/j.2168-9830.2007.tb00941.x

Liu, C. H., & Matthews, R. (2005). Vygotsky's philosophy: Constructivism and its criticisms examined. *International Education Journal, 6*(3), 386–399.

Livesay, G. A., Dee, K. C., Nauman, E. A., & Hites Jr, L. S. (2002, June 16–19). *Engineering student learning styles: A statistical analysis using Felder's index of learning styles* [Conference presentation]. Annual Conference of the American Society for Engineering Education, *Montreal, Quebec, Canada.*

Lucas, M., Bem-haja, P., Santos, S., Figueiredo, H., Ferreira Dias, M., & Amorim, M. (2022). Digital proficiency: Sorting real gaps from myths among higher education students. *British Journal of Educational Technology, 53*(6), 1885–1914. https://doi.org/10.1111/bjet.13220

Machado, A., & Staddon, J. (2023). Learning from a behaviorist perspective. *International Encyclopedia of Education (Fourth Edition),* 12–21. https://doi.org/10.1016/B978-0-12-818630-5.14002-3

Magnisalis, I., Demetriadis, S., & Karakostas, A. (2011). Adaptive and intelligent systems for collaborative learning support: A review of the field. *IEEE transactions on Learning Technologies, 4*(1), 5–20. https://doi.org/10.1109/TLT.2011.2

Mampadi, F., Chen, S., & Ghinea, G. (2009). The effects of prior knowledge on the use of adaptive hypermedia learning systems. In J.A., Jacko, (Ed.), *Human-computer interaction. Interacting in various application domains. 13th international conference* (pp. 156–165). Springer Berlin Heidelberg. https://doi.org/10.1007/978-3-642-02583-9_18

Manea, A. D., Stan, C., & Albulescu, I. (2023). Individualization, differentiation and interactivity-paradigms of effective learning. *Educatia 21*, (25), 306–313. https://doi.org/10.24193/ed21.2023.25.34

Martin, M. (1978). Speech recoding in silent reading. *Memory and Cognition,* 6, 108–114. https://doi.org/10.3758/BF03197435

Mason, M. (2008). What is complexity theory and what are its implications for educational change?. *Educational Philosophy and Theory, 40*(1), 35–49. https://doi.org/10.1111/j.1469-5812.2007.00413.x

Mayer, R. E. (2001). *Multimedia Learning.* Cambridge University Press.

Mayer, R. E. (2005). *The Cambridge Handbook of Multimedia Learning.* Cambridge University Press.

Mayer, R. E., & Fiorella, L. (2022). *The Cambridge handbook of multimedia learning* (3rd ed.). Cambridge University Press. https://doi.org/10.1017/9781108894333

Mayer, R. E., & Moreno, R. (2003). Nine ways to reduce cognitive load in multimedia learning. *Educational Psychologist, 38*(1), 43–52. https://doi.org/10.1207/S15326985EP3801_6

McCarthy, B. (1987). *The 4MAT system: Teaching to learning styles with right/left mode techniques.* EXCEL.

McCarthy, J., Minsky, M. L., Rochester, N., & Shannon, C. E. (2006). A proposal for the Dartmouth summer research project on artificial intelligence, August 31, 1955. *AI Magazine, 27*(4), 12–14. https://doi.org/10.1609/aimag.v27i4.1904

McDonald, J. K., Yanchar, S. C., & Osguthorpe, R. T. (2005). Learning from programmed instruction: Examining implications for modern instructional technology. *Educational Technology Research and Development*, *53*(2), 84–98. https://doi.org/10.1007/BF02504867

Menard, S. (1995). *Applied logistic regression analysis.* Sage Publications.

Merriam-Webster. (n.d.). *Artificial Intelligence.* In Merriam-Webster.com dictionary. Retrieved January 10, 2025 from https://www.merriam-webster.com/dictionary/artificial%20intelligence

Mirari, K. (2022). The Effectiveness of adaptive learning systems in personalized education. *Journal of Education Review Provision*, *2*(3), 70–76. https://doi.org/10.55885/jerp.v2i3.194

Mitchell, M. (2019). *Artificial intelligence: A guide for thinking humans.* Farrar, Straus and Giroux.

Mitchell, T. J., Chen, S. Y., & Macredie, R. D. (2005). Hypermedia learning and prior knowledge: domain expertise vs. system expertise. *Journal of Computer Assisted Learning*, *21*(1), 53–64. https://doi.org/10.1111/j.1365-2729.2005.00113.x

Mobasher, B. (2007). Data mining for web personalization. In P. Brusilovsky, A. Kobsa, & W. Nejdl (Eds.), *The adaptive web: Methods and strategies of web personalization* (pp. 90–135). Springer Berlin Heidelberg. https://doi.org/10.1007/978-3-540-72079-9_3

Moore, J. (1999). The basic principles of behaviorism. In B.A. Thyer (Ed.), *The philosophical legacy of behaviorism. Studies in cognitive systems* (pp. 41–68). Springer Dordrecht. https://doi.org/10.1007/978-94-015-9247-5_2

Morrison, K. (2008). Educational philosophy and the challenge of complexity theory. *Educational Philosophy and Theory*, *40*(1), 19–34. https://doi.org/10.1111/j.1469-5812.2007.00394.x

Morze, N., Varchenko-Trotsenko, L., Terletska, T., & Smyrnova-Trybulska, E. (2021). Implementation of adaptive learning at higher education institutions by means of Moodle LMS. *Journal of Physics: Conference Series*, *1840*(1), 1–13. https://doi.org/10.1088/1742-6596/1840/1/012062

Myers, R. (1990). *Classical and modern regression with applications* (2nd ed.). PWS-Kent.

Myers, I. B., & Myers, P. B. (1980). *Gifts Differing: Understanding Personality Type.* Davies-Black Publishing.

Myers, I. B., & Myers, P. B. (1995). *Gifts Differing: Understanding Personality Type* (2nd. ed.). Davies-Black Publishing.

Nafea, S. M., Siewe, F., & He, Y. (2019). On recommendation of learning objects using Felder-Silverman learning style model. *IEEE Access*, *7*, 163034–163048. https://doi.org/10.1109/ACCESS.2019.2935417

Nakic, J., Granic, A., & Glavinic, V. (2015). Anatomy of student models in adaptive learning systems: A systematic literature review of individual differences from 2001 to 2013. *Journal of Educational Computing Research*, *51*(4), 459–489. https://doi.org/10.2190/EC.51.4.e

Naser, S. S. A. (2008). Developing visualization tool for teaching AI searching algorithms. *Information Technology Journal*, *7*(2), 350–355. https://doi.org/10.3923/itj.2008.350.355

Nguyen, V. A. (2017). The impact of online learning activities on student learning outcome in blended learning course. *Journal of Information & Knowledge Management, 16*(04), 1750040. https://doi.org/10.1142/S021964921750040X

Nistor, N., Lerche, T., & Lehmann, R. (2008). Die lernprozessorientierte Adaptivität der Lernumgebungen. *Zeitschrift für E-Learning: Lernkultur und Bildungstechnologie, 3*(3), 7–17.

Norman, G. (2010). Likert scales, levels of measurement, and the "laws" of statistics. *Advances in Health Sciences Education, 15*(5), 625–632. https://doi.org/10.1007/s10459-010-9222-y

Nunnally, J. C. (1978). *Psychometric theory.* McGraw-Hill.

OECD. (2019). *OECD Skills Outlook 2019: Thriving in a Digital World.* OECD Publishing. https://www.oecd.org/content/dam/oecd/en/publications/reports/2019/05/oecd-skills-outlook-2019_c8896fe0/df80bc12-en.pdf

Ooms, J. (2024). *writexl: Export data frames to Excel 'xlsx' format* (Version 1.5.1) [R package]. CRAN. https://CRAN.R-project.org/package=writexl

Ortigosa, A., Paredes, P., & Rodriguez, P. (2008). An adaptive hierarchical questionnaire based on the index of learning styles. *Proceedings of the Workshop on Authoring of Adaptive and Adaptable Hypermedia.* 45–53.

Ouyang, F., & Jiao, P. (2021). Artificial intelligence in education: The three paradigms. *Computers and Education: Artificial Intelligence, 2*, 100020. https://doi.org/10.1016/j.caeai.2021.100020

Özyurt, Ö., & Özyurt, H. (2015). Learning style based individualized adaptive e-learning environments: Content analysis of the articles published from 2005 to 2014. *Computers in Human Behavior, 52*, 349–358. https://doi.org/10.1016/j.chb.2015.06.020

Pagani, L., Argentin, G., Gui, M., & Stanca, L. (2016). The impact of digital skills on educational outcomes: evidence from performance tests. *Educational studies, 42*(2), 137–162. https://doi.org/10.1080/03055698.2016.1148588

Paivio, A. (1971). *Imagery and verbal processes.* Holt, Rinehart and Winston.

Paivio, A. (1986). *Mental representations: A dual-coding approach.* Oxford University Press.

Paivio, A. (2006). *Mind and its evolution: A dual coding theoretical interpretation.* Lawrence Erlbaum Associates.

Papadimitriou, A., & Gyftodimos, G. (2017). The role of learner characteristics in the adaptive educational hypermedia systems: the case of the MATHEMA. *International Journal of Modern Education and Computer Science, 9*(10), 55–68. https://doi.org/10.5815/ijmecs.2017.10.07

Pashler, H., McDaniel, M., Rohrer, D., & Bjork, R. (2009). Learning styles: Concepts and evidence. *Psychological Science in the Public Interest, 9*(3), 105–119. https://doi.org/10.1111/j.1539-6053.2009.01038.x

Pask, G. (1976). Conversational techniques in the study and practice of education. *British Journal of Educational Psychology, 46*, 12–25. https://doi.org/10.1111/j.2044-8279.1976.tb02981.x

Pask, G. (1982). SAKI: Twenty-five years of adaptive training into the microprocessor era. *International Journal of Man-Machine Studies, 17*(1), 69–74. https://doi.org/10.1016/S0020-7373(82)80009-6

Paramythis, A., & Loidl-Reisinger, S. (2004). Adaptive learning environments and e-learning standards. *Electronic Journal on E-Learning, 2*(1), 181–194.

Pavlov, I. P. (1960). *Condition reflexes: An investigation of the physiological activity of the cerebral cortex*. Dover Publications.

Pearson, K. (1896). VII. Mathematical contributions to the theory of evolution.—III. Regression, heredity, and panmixia. *Philosophical Transactions of the Royal Society of London. Series A, Containing Papers of a Mathematical or Physical Character, 187*, 253–318. https://doi.org/10.1098/rsta.1896.0007

Pellegrino, J. W., & Lyon, D. R. (1979). The components of a componential analysis, *Intelligence, 3*, 169–186.

Pelletier, K., McCormack, M., Muscanell, N., Reeves, J., Robert, J., & Arbino, N. (2024). *EDUCAUSE Horizon Report: Teaching and Learning Edition*. EDUCAUSE. https://www.educause.edu/

Peng, H., Ma, S., & Spector, J. M. (2019). Personalized adaptive learning: an emerging pedagogical approach enabled by a smart learning environment. *Smart Learning Environments, 6*(1), 1–14. https://doi.org/10.1186/s40561-019-0089-y

Petridou, E., & Lao, L. (2024). Identifying challenges and best practices for implementing AI additional qualifications in vocational and continuing education: a mixed methods analysis. *International Journal of Lifelong Education, 43*(4), 1–16. https://doi.org/10.1080/02601370.2024.2351076

Phani Krishna, K. V., Mani Kumar, M., & Aruna Sri, P. S. G. (2018). Student information system and performance retrieval through dashboard. *International Journal of Engineering and Technology, 7*(2.7), 682–685. https://doi.org/10.14419/ijet.v7i2.7.10922

Piaget, J. (1970). Piaget's theory. In P. Mussen (Ed.), *Carmichael's manual of child psychology* (pp. 703–732). Wiley.

Platsidou, M., & Metallidou, P. (2008). Validity and Reliability Issues of Two Learning Style Inventories in a Greek Sample: Kolb's Learning Style Inventory and Felder & Soloman's Index of Learning Styles. *International Journal of Teaching and Learning in Higher Education, 20*(3), 324–335.

Poling, A., Carr, J. E., & LeBlanc, L. A. (2002). Operant conditioning. *Encyclopedia of Psychotherapy*, 271–287. https://doi.org/10.1016/B0-12-343010-0/00154-9

Popescu, E. (2008). *Dynamic adaptive hypermedia systems for e-learning* [Doctoral dissertation, Université de Technologie de Compiègne]. HAL Archives. https://theses.hal.science/tel-00343460v1

Popescu, E. (2010). Adaptation provisioning with respect to learning styles in a Web-based educational system: an experimental study. *Journal of Computer Assisted Learning, 26*(4), 243–257. https://doi.org/10.1111/j.1365-2729.2010.00364.x

Pritchard, A. (2013). *Ways of learning: Learning theories and learning styles in the classroom* (3rd ed.). Routledge. https://doi.org/10.4324/9781315852089

Punde, P. A., Jadhav, M. E., & Manza, R. R. (2017). A study of eye tracking technology and its applications. *2017 1st International Conference on Intelligent Systems and Information Management* (pp. 86–90). IEEE. https://doi.org/10.1109/ICISIM.2017.8122153

Puntambekar, S., & Hübscher, R. (2005). Tools for scaffolding students in a complex learning environment: What have we gained and what have we missed?. *Educational Psychologist, 40*(1), 1–12. https://doi.org/10.1207/s15326985ep4001_1

Raj, N. S., & Renumol, V. G. (2022). A systematic literature review on adaptive content recommenders in personalized learning environments from 2015 to 2020. *Journal of Computers in Education, 9*(1), 113–148. https://doi.org/10.1007/s40692-021-00199-4

R Core Team. (2023). *R: A language and environment for statistical computing*. R Foundation for Statistical Computing. https://www.R-project.org/

Rehman, I., Mahabadi, N., Sanvictores, T., & Rehman, C. I. (2017). *Classical conditioning*. StatPearls Publishing.

Reid, J. (1995). *Managing learner support* (1st ed.). Routledge.

Revelle, W. (2024). *psych: Procedures for psychological, psychometric, and personality research* (R package version 2.4.6). Northwestern University. https://CRAN.R-project.org/package=psych

Riedl, M. O. (2019). Human-centered artificial intelligence and machine learning. *Human Behavior and Emerging Technologies, 1*(1), 33–36. https://doi.org/10.1002/hbe2.117

Rienties, B., & Toetenel, L. (2016). The impact of learning design on student behaviour, satisfaction and performance: A cross-institutional comparison across 151 modules. *Computers in Human Behavior, 60*, 333–341. https://doi.org/10.1016/j.chb.2016.02.074

Ristić, I., Marija, R. R., Tijana, S. T., Vilmoš, T., & Momčilo, B. (2023). The effects and effectiveness of an adaptive e-learning system on the learning process and performance of students. *International Journal of Cognitive Research in Science, Engineering and Education, 11*(1), 77–92. https://doi.org/10.23947/2334-8496-2023-11-1-77-92

Romanelli, F., Bird, E., & Ryan, M. (2009). Learning styles: a review of theory, application, and best practices. *American Journal of Pharmaceutical Education, 73*(1).

Röpke, R., Zaric, N., & Schroeder, U. (2018). Lernstil-basierte Evaluation von Nutzungsverhalten der Lernplattform eines Blended Learning Kurses der RWTH Aachen, *Gesellschaft für Informatik*, 207–218.

Ross, P. (1987). Intelligent tutoring systems. *Journal of Computer Assisted learning, 3*(4), 194–203. https://doi.org/10.1111/j.1365-2729.1987.tb00331.x

Rosseel, Y. (2012). *lavaan: An R package for structural equation modeling. Journal of Statistical Software, 48*(2), 1–36. https://doi.org/10.18637/jss.v048.i02

Rott, K. J., Lao, L., Petridou, E. & Schmidt-Hertha, B. (2022). Needs and requirements for an additional AI qualification during dual vocational training: Results from studies of apprentices and teachers. *Computers and Education: Artificial Intelligence, 3*, 100102. https://doi.org/10.1016/j.caeai.2022.100102

Russell, T. L. (1997). Technology wars: winners and losers-the no significant difference phenomenon. *Educom Review, 32*, 44–47.

Schiaffino, S., Garcia, P., & Amandi, A. (2008). eTeacher: Providing personalized assistance to e-learning students. *Computers & Education, 51*(4), 1744–1754. https://doi.org/10.1016/j.compedu.2008.05.008

Schiefele, U., & Schreyer, I. (1994). Intrinsische Lernmotivation und Lernen. Ein Überblick zu Ergebnissen der Forschung. *Zeitschrift für Pädagogische Psychologie/German Journal of Educational Psychology, 8*(1), 1–13.

Schimanke, F., Mertens, R., & Vornberger, O. (2014). Spaced repetition learning games on mobile devices: Foundations and perspectives. *Interactive Technology and Smart Education, 11*(3), 201–222. https://doi.org/10.1108/ITSE-07-2014-0017

Schmid, U., Goertz, L., & Behrens, J. (2016). *Monitor Digitale Bildung: Berufliche Ausbildung im digitalen Zeitalter*. Bertelsmann Stiftung.

Schmidt, B. (2004). *Virtuelle Lernarrangements für Studienanfänger: didaktische Gestaltung und Evaluation des "Online-Lehrbuchs" Jugendforschung und der begleitenden virtuellen Seminare*. Herbert Utz Verlag.

Schuh, K. L. (2003). Knowledge construction in the learner-centered classroom. *Journal of Educational Psychology, 95*(2), 426–442. https://doi.org/10.1037/0022-0663.95.2.426

Schunk, D. H. (1991). Self-efficacy and academic motivation. *Educational Psychologist, 26*(3–4), 207–231. https://doi.org/10.1080/00461520.1991.9653133

Schunk, D. H. (2001). Social cognitive theory and self-regulated learning. In B. J. Zimmerman & D. H. Schunk (Eds.), *Self-regulated learning and academic achievement: Theoretical perspectives* (2nd ed., pp. 125–151). Routledge.

Schunk, D. H. (2012). *Learning theories: An educational perspective* (6th ed.). Allyn and Bacon.

Schunk, D. H., & Pajares, F. (2002). The development of academic self-efficacy. *Development of Achievement Motivation,* 15–31. https://doi.org/10.1016/B978-012750053-9/50003-6

Schwinger, M., Kärchner, H., & Gehle, M. (2020). *Modularer Fragebogen zur Evaluation von digitalen Lehr-Lern-Szenarien (Studierende).* Innovationsforum Wirksamkeitsanalyse, Projekt digital gestütztes Lehren und Lernen in Hessen. Philipps-Universität Marburg.

Selwyn, N. (2019). *Should robots replace teachers? AI and the future of education.* John Wiley & Sons.

Semeniako, Y., Mardarova, I., Lystopad, O., Rybak, O., Samoilenko, V., & Hrechanovska, O. (2024). Strengthening students' proficiency in digital technologies and the SMART society. *Revista Romaneasca pentru Educatie Multidimensionala, 16*(1), 608–622. https://doi.org/10.18662/rrem/16.1/840

Shapiro, S. S., & Wilk, M. B. (1965). An analysis of variance test for normality (complete samples). *Biometrika,* 52(3/4), 591–611. https://doi.org/10.1093/biomet/52.3-4.591

Shrestha, S., & Pokharel, M. (2021). Educational data mining in Moodle data. *International Journal of Informatics and Communication Technology (IJ-ICT), 10*(1), 9–18. https://doi.org/10.11591/ijict.v10i1.pp9-18

Siemens, G. (2012). Learning analytics: Envisioning a research discipline and a domain of practice. LAK 2012: P*roceedings of the 2nd international conference on learning analytics and knowledge* (pp. 4–8). Association for Computing Machinery. https://doi.org/10.1145/2330601.2330605

Skinner, B. F. (1937). Two types of conditioned reflex: A reply to Konorski and Miller. *The Journal of General Psychology, 16*(1), 272–279. https://doi.org/10.1080/00221309.1937.9917951

Skinner, B. F. (1953). *Science and human behavior*. Free Press.

Skinner, B. F. (1958). Teaching machines: From the experimental study of learning come devices which arrange optimal conditions for self-instruction. *Science, 128*(3330), 969–977. https://doi.org/10.1126/science.128.3330.969

Skinner, B. F. (1978). *Was ist Behaviorismus?.* Rowohlt.

Soflano, M., Connolly, T. M., & Hainey, T. (2015). Learning style analysis in adaptive GBL application to teach SQL. *Computers & Education, 86*, 105–119. https://doi.org/10.1016/j.compedu.2015.02.009

Song, C., Shin, S. Y., & Shin, K. S. (2024). Implementing the dynamic feedback-driven learning optimization framework: a machine learning approach to personalize educational pathways. *Applied Sciences, 14*(2), 916. https://doi.org/10.3390/app14020916

Staddon, J. E., & Cerutti, D. T. (2003). Operant conditioning. *Annual Review of Psychology, 54*(1), 115–144. https://doi.org/10.1146/annurev.psych.54.101601.145124

Stadelmann, T., Keuzenkamp, J., Grabner, H., & Würsch, C. (2021). The AI-atlas: didactics for teaching AI and machine learning on-site, online, and hybrid. *Education Sciences, 11*(7), 318. https://doi.org/10.3390/educsci11070318

Stamenković, S., Jovanović, N., Vasović, B., Cvjetković, M., & Jovanović, Z. (2023). Software tools for learning artificial intelligence algorithms. *Artificial Intelligence Review, 56*(9), 10297–10326. https://doi.org/10.1007/s10462-023-10436-0

Steib, C. J. & Stoffers, K. (2022). Blended Learning in der beruflichen Weiterbildung. *ZBW Zeitschrift für Berufs- und Wirtschaftspädagogik, 118*(2), 296–334. https://doi.org/10.25162/zbw-2022-0012

Stevens, J. P. (2002). *Applied multivariate statistics for the social sciences* (4th ed.). Lawrence Erlbaum Associates.

Straka, G. A., & Macke, G. (2003). Handlungskompetenz und Handlungsorientierung als Bildungsauftrag der Berufsschule – Ziel und Weg des Lernens in der Berufsschule? *Berufsbildung in Wissenschaft und Praxis, 4*, 43–47.

Suartama, I., Setyosari, P., Sulthoni, S., & Ulfa, S. (2020). Development of ubiquitous learning environment based on Moodle learning management system. *International Association of Online Engineering, 14*(14), 182–204.

Sullivan, G. M., & Artino Jr, A. R. (2013). Analyzing and interpreting data from Likert-type scales. *Journal of Graduate Medical Education, 5*(4), 541–542. https://doi.org/10.4300/JGME-5-4-18

Sweller, J., Ayres, P., & Kalyuga, S. (2011). *Cognitive Load Theory.* Springer New York. https://doi.org/10.1007/978-1-4419-8126-4

Szogs, M.; Oettinghaus, L.; Krüger, M.; Große, A.; Korneck, F. (2021). *Adaptive Erleichterung [Ratingmanualskala: Version 1.0].* In *Ratingmanual zur Einschätzung der Unterrichtsqualität im Physikunterricht* [Ratingmanual: Version 1.0]. Erstanwendung 2018. Frankfurt am Main: Forschungsdatenzentrum Bildung am DIPF. https://doi.org/10.7477/614:326:1

Taylor, D. L., Yeung, M., & Bashet, A. Z. (2021). Personalized and adaptive learning. In J. Ryoo, & K. Winkelmann (Eds.), *Innovative Learning Environments in STEM Higher Education* (pp. 17–34). Springer Cham. https://doi.org/10.1007/978-3-030-58948-6_2

Thyagharajan, K. K., & Nayak, R. (2007). Adaptive content creation for personalized e-learning using web services. *Journal of Applied Sciences Research, 3*(9), 828–836.

Torchiano, M. (2020). *effsize: Efficient effect size computation* (Version 0.8.1) [R package]. https://doi.org/10.5281/zenodo.1480624, https://CRAN.R-project.org/package=effsize

Tramm, T., & Naeve-Stoß, N. (2020). Curricula für die berufliche Bildung–Lernfeldstruktur zwischen Situations-und Fächerorientierung. In R. Arnold, A. Lipsmeier, & M. Rohs (Eds.) *Handbuch Berufsbildung,* (pp. 309–324). Springer VS. https://doi.org/10.1007/978-3-658-19312-6_26

Truong, H. M. (2016). Integrating learning styles and adaptive e-learning system: Current developments, problems and opportunities. *Computers in Human Behavior, 55*, 1185–1193. https://doi.org/10.1016/j.chb.2015.02.014

Tseng, J. C., Chu, H. C., Hwang, G. J., & Tsai, C. C. (2008). Development of an adaptive learning system with two sources of personalization information. *Computers & Education, 51*(2), 776–786. https://doi.org/10.1016/j.compedu.2007.08.002

Tu, C. H., & McIsaac, M. (2002). The relationship of social presence and interaction in online classes. *The American Journal of Distance Education*, 16(3), 131–150. https://doi.org/10.1207/S15389286AJDE1603_2

Tuckman, B. W., & Harper, B. E. (2012). *Conducting educational research.* Rowman & Littlefield Publishers.

Tudge, J., & Scrimsher, S. (2003). Lev Vygotsky on education: A cultural-historical, interpersonal, and individual approach to development. In B. Zimmerman & D. Schunk (Eds.), *Educational psychology: A century of contributions* (1st ed., pp. 207–228). Lawrence Erlbaum Associates.

Turing, A.M. (1950). Computing machinery and intelligence. *Mind*, *59*, 433–460. https://doi.org/10.1093/mind/LIX.236.433

Twomey, P. (2018). *The future of work and education for the digital age: Building on the Hamburg statement and the G20 roadmap for digitalization – Towards a G20 framework for artificial intelligence in the workplace.* Consejo Argentino Para Las Relaciones Internacionales. https://t20argentina.org/wp-content/uploads/2018/06/TF1-1-11-Policy-Briefs_T20ARG_Towards-a-G20-Framework-For-Artificial-Intelligence-in-the-Workplace.pdf

Tzur, S., Katz, A., & Davidovich, N. (2021). Learning supported by technology: Effectiveness with educational software. *European Journal of Educational Research*, *10*(3), 1137–1156. https://doi.org/10.12973/eu-jer.10.3.1139

Ueno, M., & Miyazawa, Y. (2018). IRT-based adaptive hints to scaffold learning in programming. *IEEE Transactions on Learning Technologies*, *11*(4), 415–428. https://doi.org/10.1109/TLT.2017.2741960

UNESCO (2019, April 2023). *How can artificial intelligence enhance education?.* https://en.unesco.org/news/howcan-artificial-intelligence-enhance-education

Van der Lingen, E., Åmo, B. W., & Pettersen, I. B. (2020). The relationship between entrepreneurial experience and preferred learning styles. *Education + Training*, *62*(7/8), 863–876. https://doi.org/10.1108/ET-11-2019-0263

Van Someren, M., Barnard, Y. F., & Sandberg, J. (1994). *The think aloud method: a practical approach to modelling cognitive.* Academic Press.

Van Zwanenberg, N., Wilkinson, L. J., & Anderson, A. (2000). Felder and Silverman's Index of Learning Styles and Honey and Mumford's Learning Styles Questionnaire: how do they compare and do they predict academic performance?. *Educational Psychology*, *20*(3), 365–380. https://doi.org/10.1080/713663743

Vincent-Lancrin, S., & Van der Vlies, R. (2020). *Trustworthy artificial intelligence (AI) in education: Promises and challenges. OECD education working papers No. 218*, OECD Publishing. https://doi.org/10.1787/a6c90fa9-en

Viola, S. R., Graf, S., & Leo, T. (2006). Analysis of Felder-Silverman index of learning styles by a data-driven statistical approach. *Eighth IEEE International Symposium on Multimedia* (pp. 959–964). IEEE. https://doi.org/10.1109/ISM.2006.30

Visentin, D. C., Cleary, M., & Hunt, G. E. (2020). The earnestness of being important: Reporting non-significant statistical results. *Journal of Advanced Nursing*, *76*(4), 917–919. https://doi.org/10.1111/jan.14283

Vygotsky, L. S. (1978). *Mind in society: The development of higher psychological processes.* Harvard University Press. https://doi.org/10.2307/j.ctvjf9vz4

Vygotsky, L. (1987). *The collected works of L. S. Vygotsky, Volume 1: Problems of general psychology,* (R. W. Rieber & A. S. Carton, Eds). Plenum Press.

Wambua, R. M., Gakuu, C., Kidombo, H., & Ndege, S. (2021). Learner support system and academic performance of distance learning students in selected Kenyan public universities. *Teacher Education through Flexible Learning in Africa, 1*(1). https://doi.org/10.35293/tetfle.v1i1.69

Wang, T., & Cheng, E. C. (2022). Towards a tripartite research agenda: A scoping review of artificial intelligence in education research. In E. C. K. Cheng, R. B. Koul, T. Wang, & X. Yu (Eds.), *Artificial Intelligence in Education: Emerging Technologies, Models and Applications* (pp. 3–24). Springer Singapore. https://doi.org/10.1007/978-981-16-7527-0_1

Wang, S., Christensen, C., Cui, W., Tong, R., Yarnall, L., Shear, L., & Feng, M. (2020). When adaptive learning is effective learning: comparison of an adaptive learning system to teacher-led instruction. *Interactive Learning Environments, 31*(2), 793–803. https://doi.org/10.1080/10494820.2020.1808794

Wang, H. C., Li, T. Y., & Chang, C. Y. (2006). A web-based tutoring system with styles-matching strategy for spatial geometric transformation. *Interacting with Computers, 18*(3), 331–355. https://doi.org/10.1016/j.intcom.2005.11.002

Watson, J. B. (1913). Psychology as the behaviorist views it. *Psychological Review, 20*(2), 158–177. https://doi.org/10.1037/h0074428

Watson, J. B., & Rayner, R. (1920). Conditioned emotional reactions. *Journal of Experimental Psychology, 3*(1), 1–14. https://doi.org/10.1037/h0069608

Wekerle, C., Daumiller, M., & Kollar, I. (2022). Using digital technology to promote higher education learning: The importance of different learning activities and their relations to learning outcomes. *Journal of Research on Technology in Education, 54*(1), 1–17. https://doi.org/10.1080/15391523.2020.1799455

Wickham, H. (2016). *ggplot2: Elegant graphics for data analysis.* Springer Cham. https://doi.org/10.1007/978-3-319-24277-4

Wickham, H., François, R., Henry, L., Müller, K., & Vaughan, D. (2023). *dplyr: A grammar of data manipulation* (R package version 1.1.4). https://CRAN.R-project.org/package=dplyr

Wickham, H., Vaughan, D., & Girlich, M. (2023). *tidyr: Tidy messy data* (Version 1.3.0) [R package]. https://CRAN.R-project.org/package=tidyr

Wiener, N. (1960). Some moral and technical consequences of automation: As machines learn they may develop unforeseen strategies at rates that baffle their programmers. *Science, 131*(3410), 1355–1358. https://doi.org/10.1126/science.131.3410.1355

Wild, S., & Schulze Heuling, L. (2020). How do the digital competences of students in vocational schools differ from those of students in cooperative higher education institutions in Germany?. *Empirical Research in Vocational Education and Training, 12*(5), 1–18. https://doi.org/10.1186/s40461-020-00091-y

Willging, P. A., & Johnson, S. D. (2009). Factors that influence students' decision to dropout of online courses. *Journal of Asynchronous Learning Networks, 13*(3), 115–127.

Willis, G. B., (1999). *Cognitive interviewing: A "how to" guide* [Conference presentation]. Meeting of the American Statistical Association. https://www.hkr.se/contentassets/9ed7b1b3997e4bf4baa8d4eceed5cd87/gordonwillis.pdf/

Wood, D., Bruner, J. S., & Ross, G. (1976). The role of tutoring in problem solving. *Child Psychology & Psychiatry & Allied Disciplines, 17*(2), 89–100. https://doi.org/10.1111/j.1469-7610.1976.tb00381.x

Woolf, B. (1991). AI in Education. In S. C. Shapiro (Ed.), *Encyclopedia of Artificial Intelligence* (2nd ed., pp. 1–18). John Wiley & Sons. https://web.cs.umass.edu/publication/docs/1991/UM-CS-1991-037.pdf

Wright, B. M. (2017). Blended learning: Student perception of face-to-face and online EFL lessons. *Indonesian Journal of Applied Linguistics*, *7*(1), 64–71. https://doi.org/10.17509/ijal.v7i1.6859

Wu, T., He, S., Liu, J., Sun, S., Liu, K., Han, Q. L., & Tang, Y. (2023). A brief overview of ChatGPT: The history, status quo, and potential future development. *IEEE/CAA Journal of Automatica Sinica*, *10*(5), 1122–1136. https://doi.org/10.1109/JAS.2023.123618

Yang, S. J. (2021). Guest editorial: Precision education - A new challenge for AI in education. *Educational Technology & Society*, *24*(1), 105–108.

Yang, S. J., Ogata, H., Matsui, T., & Chen, N. S. (2021). Human-centered artificial intelligence in education: Seeing the invisible through the visible. *Computers and Education: Artificial Intelligence*, *2*, 100008. https://doi.org/10.1016/j.caeai.2021.100008

Yilmaz-Soylu, M., & Akkoyunlu, B. (2009). The effect of learning styles on achievement in different learning environments. *Turkish Online Journal of Educational Technology-TOJET*, *8*(4), 43–50.

Zawacki-Richter, O., Marín, V. I., Bond, M., & Gouverneur, F. (2019). Systematic review of research on artificial intelligence applications in higher education–where are the educators?. *International Journal of Educational Technology in Higher Education*, *16*(1), 1–27. https://doi.org/10.1186/s41239-019-0171-0

Zeileis, A., & Hothorn, T. (2002). Diagnostic checking in regression relationships. *R News*, *2*(3), 7–10. https://CRAN.R-project.org/doc/Rnews/

Zhang, K., & Aslan, A. B. (2021). AI technologies for education: Recent research & future directions. *Computers and Education: Artificial Intelligence*, *2*, 100025. https://doi.org/10.1016/j.caeai.2021.100025

Zhang, L., Basham, J. D., & Yang, S. (2020). Understanding the implementation of personalized learning: A research synthesis. *Educational Research Review*, *31*, 100339. https://doi.org/10.1016/j.edurev.2020.100339

Zhang, J. H., Zou, L. C., Miao, J. J., Zhang, Y. X., Hwang, G. J., & Zhu, Y. (2019). An individualized intervention approach to improving university students' learning performance and interactive behaviors in a blended learning environment. *Interactive Learning Environments*, *28*(2), 231–245. https://doi.org/10.1080/10494820.2019.1636078

Zhou, M., & Brown, D. (Eds.) (2015). *Educational learning theories* (2nd ed.). Education Open Textbooks. https://oer.galileo.usg.edu/education-textbooks/1

Zhou, C., Kuang, D., Liu, J., Yang, H., Zhang, Z., Mackworth, A., & Poole, D. (2020). AISpace2: an interactive visualization tool for learning and teaching artificial intelligence. *Proceedings of the AAAI Conference on Artificial Intelligence*, *34*(09), 13436–13443. https://doi.org/10.1609/aaai.v34i09.7068

Zimmerman, B. J., & Schunk, D. H. (Eds.). (2001). *Self-regulated learning and academic achievement: Theoretical perspectives*. Routledge.

Zywno, M. (2003, June 22–25). *A contribution to validation of score meaning for Felder Soloman's index of learning styles* [Paper presentation]. 2003 Annual Conference, Nashville, Tennessee, United States. https://doi.org/10.18260/1-2--12424

MIX
Papier aus verantwortungsvollen Quellen
Paper from responsible sources
FSC® C105338

If you have any concerns about our products,
you can contact us on
ProductSafety@springernature.com

In case Publisher is established outside the EU,
the EU authorized representative is:
Springer Nature Customer Service Center GmbH
Europaplatz 3, 69115 Heidelberg, Germany

Printed by Libri Plureos GmbH
in Hamburg, Germany